D1624284

A WORLD ABLAZE

A World Ablaze

THE RISE OF MARTIN LUTHER
AND THE BIRTH OF THE REFORMATION

Craig Harline

OXFORD
UNIVERSITY PRESS

OXFORD
UNIVERSITY PRESS

Oxford University Press is a department of the University of Oxford. It furthers
the University's objective of excellence in research, scholarship, and education
by publishing worldwide. Oxford is a registered trade mark of Oxford University
Press in the UK and certain other countries.

Published in the United States of America by Oxford University Press
198 Madison Avenue, New York, NY 10016, United States of America.

CIP data is on file at the Library of Congress
ISBN 978-0-19-027518-1

9 8 7 6 5 4 3 2 1

Printed by Edwards Brothers Malloy, United States of America

Lo, this is the fire with which they complain that all the world is now ablaze!

Dr. Martin Luther to Pope Leo X, May 1518,

regarding his 95 theses

Contents

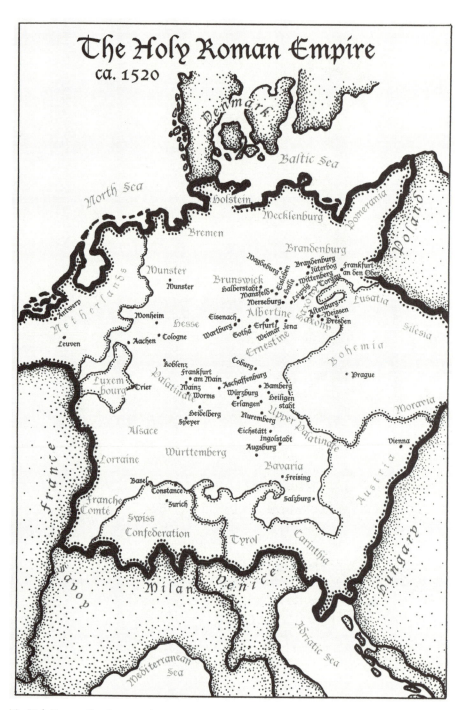

The Holy Roman Empire around 1520.

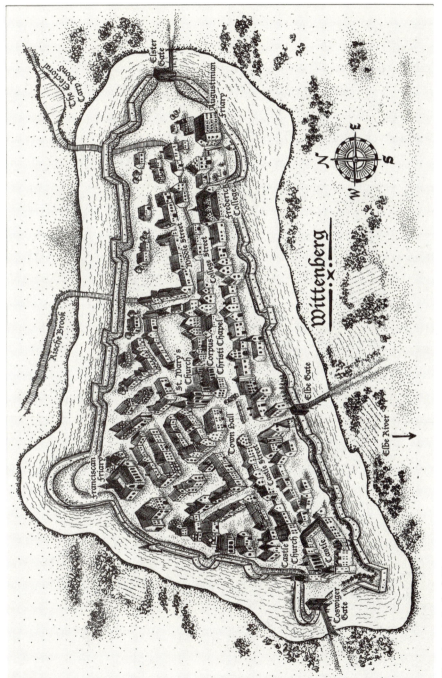

Wittenberg in Luther's Time.

A WORLD ABLAZE

A Word Before

OF MAKING MANY BOOKS THERE is no end, said Ecclesiastes in chapter 12, and he probably should have added, *especially if they're about Martin Luther.* This is even more true whenever a big Luther anniversary comes along, like the one so enormously upon us in 2017: 500 whole years since the 95 upsetting theses.

But even in ordinary years, a fellow as prolific, and cheeky, and quotable—as earth-rattling—as Luther, who is blamed or praised for changing just about everything in the Entire Western World, is going to have his story told more often than most, and in more ways than most too, because no story is ever told the same way twice, not even a famous one like his. As Luther said himself, even the everlasting gospel, the most famous story of all, was told in all sorts of ways—bluntly, spun out, this way, that—so why wouldn't the story of his thoroughly corruptible flesh be too?

My own peculiar telling of his story, meant especially for readers who know the name Luther but aren't exactly sure why, features not just my own sort of spinning, and shading, and coloring, but also just his first few trembly years of fame—i.e., from around the time in late 1517 when the obscure Brother Martin first put together his upsetting theses, until early 1522 when as a European-wide celebrity he came out of hiding and started putting his ideas to serious work. It also features a stubborn attempt to set the story relentlessly in his own world and to see through its eyes, not ours, so that we have a fighting chance to grasp the otherness and drama and absolute improbability of the whole astonishing thing. Which means it finally features (just to warn anybody hoping for monumental) Brother Martin, the flesh-and-blood sometimes-cranky friar-professor, instead of Luther, the giant bronze icon who changed the Entire Etc.

What Luther did (and didn't do) during these four-plus years would certainly have giant bronze-worthy consequences that lived on long after he was dust, but this book isn't about those (which are still being argued over). It's about the events of these few years alone, to stress how unlikely and fragile and bewildering they were, and thus to experience them as much as possible in the same nerve-wracking and uncertain way that he did, instead of with an eye roving toward the future, as if the outcome was never in doubt. That's why, for example, I call him mostly "Brother Martin" or "Dr. Martin"—not because I'm necessarily on his side, or am his special friend, but because people around him called him that (along with "Father Martin"). Strangers called him "Luther," and so did his enemies, who also called him much worse: when the story shifts to their perspectives, I call him "Luther" too. But calling him only that would make him distant, when the point is to get up close.

Sure, there are a few exceptions to this Luther-worldly telling, to help move things along. Thus, even though numbers of Bible verses aren't given (because there weren't any numbered verses yet), the story is in mostly modern English (with Bible citations from the New Revised Standard Version), "proposition" and "article" take the more modern form "thesis," distances are in miles and feet, dates are (eventually) in months and days, and places and names are in whatever form seemed best-suited, or most familiar, to English-readers, instead of always in the original or in English—and so Köln is Cologne, Friedrich is Frederick, François is Francis, and Karel V is Charles V, but Johann, Johannes, Jan, and Hans are all as is, instead of John, while less famous Karels are as is too. And Martin, of course, is always just Martin.

Curtain Up

A HEBREW-READING KNIGHT

Near Jena, in Thuringia. March 4, 1522. Shrove Tuesday, When Nothing is Ever as it Seems.

The young travelers were hungry and thirsty—yes of course for knowledge, which was why they'd set out on this long journey in the first place, but at the moment they'd have gladly settled for a little food and drink instead. They were also wet and tired from being slapped around by a storm, and so a good fire and bed sounded just fine too. The problem was, it was Shrove Tuesday, and so when they finally entered Jena and started asking about rooms, all they heard at every single inn was that there were none.

Just as the two travelers, barely 19 years old, headed back out the gate toward a nearby village, to see what they could find there, a respectable-looking man who for some wondrous reason was also out in the godforsaken weather pointed them instead toward the much-closer Black Bear Inn, just outside Jena's walls. And blesséd day, the host there certainly did have a room.

No swarming crowds here, saw the young men as they clumped over the threshold. Only a solitary fellow in the stove-room, at a table, reading a book in the dim candlelight. He looked up, said a friendly hello, and waved them over, but the muddy and wet pair politely declined and plopped down on a bench near the door. When the fellow kept up his friendliness and drank to their health, though, well they just couldn't refuse any longer. They went drippily inside and sat with him, and ordered some wine, so they could drink his health back, and they no doubt took off their boots and hung their soaked clothing near the stove to get dry.

3

Seated up close like this, the travelers could now see the red hood and doublet and hose and long sword that told them this fellow was a knight. The knight asked where they were from but didn't wait for an answer, since he'd already guessed from their accents that they were Swiss. Yes, from St. Gall, they nodded. Ah, coming from that distant southerly direction, and at their tender age, then they must, guessed the knight, be students, headed to the University of Wittenberg. Well, they would find there two of their countrymen: the brothers (and professors) Hieronymus and Augustine Schurff. This delighted the students, because they were carrying letters of introduction to both men!

If the knight knew all this, then maybe he knew as well what the students wanted most of all to know, wanted even desperately to know: was Dr. Martin Luther back in town? Because they were traveling all this way not just to study Holy Scripture but to study it with him, and they'd heard he'd been gone from Wittenberg for almost a year now.

And the knight did know. No, Luther wasn't in Wittenberg at this moment. But Philip Melanchthon was there, and they could take Greek from him and Hebrew from others, both of which they really ought to learn, by the way, if they were serious about studying the Bible. "Praised be God!" exclaimed the students, because they wanted to study with Master Philip too. Still, it was especially Luther they'd hoped for, since they had been planning their whole lives to become priests, and they'd heard he was now teaching against the Mass and the priesthood: they had to know more about that.

"Where have you studied so far?" asked the knight.

"At Basel," said the students.

"Is Erasmus there?" asked the curious knight, about the famous man of letters. "What is he up to?"

"Nobody really knows, because he keeps to himself." By now the students were wondering how this knight could possibly know about such unknightly subjects as the Schurffs and Erasmus and Greek and Hebrew, and were amazed that he kept throwing Latin words into his sentences. What sort of a knight was this?

"Boys, what do they think about this Luther in Switzerland?" the knight continued.

"Sir, there are many different opinions. Some can't praise him enough and they thank God for him, but others say he's a scandalous heretic. Especially the pastors!"

"Ah yes," replied the unsurprised knight, "Those pastors!"

That broke whatever ice was left, because now the second student reached familiarly and even impolitely across the table to see what the knight was reading: the Psalms—in Hebrew. "I'd have my little finger cut off if I could learn that language," said the student.

"Oh you can, if you stick with it, as I'm doing. I do a little every day," said the knight.

While they were talking, the host entered to set the dining table in the next room, as it was good and dark outside now and time to eat. He'd overheard the students asking about Martin Luther, and so while walking by them he said, "If you'd been here two days ago you would have had your wish. He sat at your very table, in that very place," he pointed. Hearing that, the students cursed the muddy roads that had slowed them down, but they still liked the idea of being at the very house and table where the famous Luther had been.

The host went back out, a little smile on his face, then hush-hushedly waved the first student over and said, "Since you're so eager to see Martin Luther, I'll tell you that that's him, sitting next to you."

"You're just saying that," said the disbelieving student, "because you know how much I want to see him."

"It's the truth, but don't let on that you know."

The student went back into the stove-room and during a lull whispered to his friend what the host had told him about the knight, but the friend didn't believe it either: "You must have heard wrong," he said. The host must have said "Hutten," as in Ulrich von Hutten, the famous literary knight, because this fellow looked a lot more like a knight than he did a priest.

Two traveling merchants also looking for shelter now entered the room as well, to dry off, followed soon by the host who said that dinner was ready, and that they should all move to the dining table. The students hung back and shyly asked the host whether he would be kind enough to give them just a small portion to eat, right where they were sitting, as they were low on money, but the host assured them he wouldn't charge them much. The mysterious knight, overhearing, went even further: "Come on over, I'll look after the bill," he said.

The knight kept up his friendly chatter during the meal, nattering on about how the German princes and nobles and town-delegates now assembled in Nuremberg were more worried about jousting and sleigh rides and vanities and whoring than they were about actually solving problems. And he hoped that the next generation of Germans would actually pay attention to gospel truth, since

Luther at the Black Bear Inn.

unlike their parents they hadn't yet been poisoned by popish errors, which were a devil of a thing to root out. One of the merchants broke in to say that he didn't understand much about the whole recent storm around the pope "but this I do say: either this Luther is an angel from heaven, or a devil from hell." During all this talk, the knight stayed so cheery that none of his companions would have ever guessed that just a day or two before at a tavern in Erfurt he'd gotten into a big vein-popping argument over these very same subjects.

When the dinner ended, the merchants went to check on their horses, and the host edged closer to the students to say, "Don't worry about the cost. Martin paid for you." They looked at the still-seated knight again: so he really was Luther? The students thanked him for his kindness, and said they had taken him for Ulrich von Hutten. The knight turned to the host: "These Swiss think I am Ulrich von Hutten!" That's ridiculous, said the host: "You are Martin Luther!" Which made the knight really laugh: "They think I'm Hutten. You say I'm Luther. Pretty soon I'll be Marcolf!" the famous bawdy peasant in a popular old story. Now the students were really confused. Finally the knight offered them all a tall glass of beer and proposed that "for their evening Grace" they should drink together. But when the students went to take a glass, he pulled it back and said he'd forgotten: they weren't used to "our outlandish" Thuringian beer. So they all drank one more glass of wine instead.

Quenched, the knight stood up, threw a cloak over his shoulder, shook their hands, and said, "When you get to Wittenberg, give my greeting to Dr. Schurff!" The students said they'd be glad to, but there was one problem: "What's your name, so we can say who greets him?" The knight thought and said, "Just say, 'He who should come salutes you.'" Then he went upstairs to bed, leaving the students as mystified as before.

What the knight in the red hood didn't tell the students was that he wasn't a knight at all but an outlaw, traveling in disguise for his own safety: anyone who spotted him and had the nerve to grab him could earn a nice reward from the emperor.

And what the knight also didn't tell them was that he was on his way to Wittenberg too, just like they were, because he had work to finish there.

Or more precisely, to start.

1

Theses, Theses Everywhere

Wittenberg, the Friary of the Hermits of St. Augustine. Late August, 1517, When Summer Semester is Winding Down.

Mortared bulwarkly into an old southeastern stretch of the wall that had surrounded Wittenberg for more than 200 years were two sturdy towers, about 150 feet apart. Just a few years before, the two towers had also been mortared into the brand-new home of the Hermits of St. Augustine, as had the stretch of old wall that ran between the towers, because that way the ever-thrifty hermits needed to put up just three-plus walls for their new rectangular building instead of the usual four, plus they got two sturdy towers in the bargain.

Sure, the hermits lopped off most of one of the towers, because they wanted just its mighty foundation, but they left the southwest tower mostly as it was, because they wanted its extra room.

Just like the new building it was now joined to, by three narrow passageways, this tower had three (remodeled) levels: a *cloaca* or cesspit on the first, a small sleeping room for crammed-in visiting-student hermits on the second, and a little heated study on the third—the only heated room in the whole building, because even a self-denying hermit didn't mind a little heat when he was studying, especially in a town where the frosts could last into June. The hermits could have called the whole thing the "study tower" or "visitor tower," but at least one of them seemed to like calling it the "*cloaca* tower" instead, as if the ground level were the really crucial part of the whole thing.

Oh, that hermit, like the others, was in the actual *cloaca* plenty, but he was in the third-level study even more, and not just for the heat, but especially to carry out the lofty purpose of that lofty room, which was of course to study.

To tell the truth, the 30 or so hermits who lived in the new building weren't really hermits at all, seeing as how not a single one of them actually lived alone. They weren't even what most ancient bona fide hermits had long ago turned into, which was monks: men who, like hermits, left the world to find God but who, unlike hermits, did so while living together. No, these so-called hermits had chosen yet another option in the full-time male religious life: that of friars—from French *frère*, and Latin *frater*, or brother.

Yes, friars came together seven times a day to sing the Hours of the Divine Office, just like monks, and they wore matching habits, just like monks, and they shaved the hair on the top of their head into a big fleshy unattractive circle (the tonsure), just like monks, and they looked for God together, just like monks. But what made friars different from monks was that instead of sealing themselves away in a monastery they went out into the smack-dab middle of the world—caring for the poor and sick, and preaching, and educating. Educating. That's what the friar on the topmost level of the tower was busy preparing for right now. And at the topmost educational level of his world too—the university.

Brother Martin Luder in the tower was also Doctor Martin Luder, not just a friar in the order of the nonhermit Hermits of St. Augustine but a professor of theology at the local university. Sometimes he looked every bit the actual hermit, sitting in his study for hours on end, but that had more to do with being a professor than a hermit: even though professors had to be social creatures part of the time, going out in front of students the way they did, they also needed big chunks of hermitlike time alone to think, and write, and prepare to go out in front of all those students.

What made this day different from others was Brother Martin's certainty that some people were going to be furious with what he was preparing. Even though that made him a little nervous, it wouldn't stop him, because he had sworn to profess the true gospel, and so he would, as usual, profess it.

SCHOOLBOY

It must have still seemed like a dream sometimes, being up here in the tower at all.

It was all God's doing, he was sure of that. Because as a boy in hilly Mansfeld young Martin never could have imagined being a friar, or studying theology, or especially being a professor.

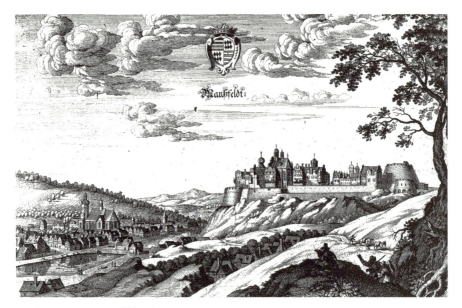

Matthäus Merian, *Mansfeld*.

Oh, he could have imagined going to school, and maybe even going to university, since his mother, Margarethe Lindemann, understood better than most that school was a way for a copper-smelter's son like hers to move a few respectable links up the social chain. And young Martin did well enough at school to stay in it, and out of the family smelter, going from Mansfeld's grammar school to its Latin school, and then at 14 and 15 to even better Latin schools in Magdeburg and Eisenach, which was an absolutely sure sign that somebody besides his mother thought he had what it took to be among the very few people of his world—less than one in 100—who went on to university, where classes were in much more sophisticated Latin than the let's-get-acquainted sort he'd learned in Mansfeld.

That somebody was right, because young Martin survived the floggings and humiliations and drudgery that were the hallmarks of schools for the young, and in April 1501 he headed 60 miles south of Mansfeld to the University of Erfurt, fifth oldest (1392) and third biggest (500 students) of the 16 or so universities in the entire Holy Roman Empire.

Martin's father, Hans Luder, was soon wide awake to the possibilities of higher education too, and now gladly paid out even more for tuition, books, paper, ink, quills, scholar's robe, linens, firewood, board, room, and so on, than ever before, because what a boon to the family business it would be if his son should study law! And what a boost to family fortunes if he should somehow get a foothold in local politics, or become a councilor to the Count of Mansfeld or even to the count's overlord, the Duke of Saxony himself, as Margarethe's cousin Johann Lindemann now was!

And so Martin suffered the usual hazing of new university students that almost always seemed to involve soot and feces and "prophetic water" (urine) and fake donkey ears, all supposedly meant to awaken him to his new status but probably more to allow older students a little revenge for their own suffering years before. He endured the monklike regime of his dormitory at Erfurt, called "Heaven's Gate"—up at 4 a.m., class at 6 a.m., two meals a day, no girls allowed inside, and chanting through all 150 Psalms every 15 days. And more than anything, Martin studied the grammar, rhetoric, and logic that all new students studied, and that were dished out in the methods used since universities were invented four centuries before: lectures, repetitions, and disputations.

Up to three times a day, he hustled over to dimly lit lecture halls where a Master read and commented on some authoritative text while students scribbled and dozed. Every day and night he attended dimly lit repetitions where he reviewed what he'd heard in lectures. And every Friday he attended a dimly lit practice disputation where a Master set out some disputable assertions (called propositions or articles, then much later "theses"), a few advanced students defended those assertions, a few other advanced students attacked them, and younger students like Martin watched wide-eyed.

Surely Martin attended as well the crowning spectacle of higher education, the very occasional public disputation, held during important ceremonies like

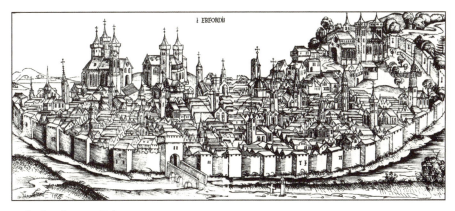

Michael Wolgemut, *Erfurt 1493.*

graduation, or even as separate extraordinary events, because what better way to celebrate something big than with a few hours of fine-sliced arguing in front of the whole school, and visitors too? Disputations weren't just fun and games and long stretches of dullness, mind you. All the posturing and exaggerating and attacking were also supposed to produce some clarity and even truth, but usually it was all more about winning than truth-seeking—more like a tournament in fact, with (usually) figurative snorts and blows and thrusts and parries instead of the actual sort.

Martin did well enough in his basic studies at Erfurt that at the soonest possible moment, in September 1502, he became part of an even smaller elite in his world: one of the three in ten university students who actually earned a Bachelor of Arts degree (meaning the three basic Arts of grammar, rhetoric, and logic). Although he finished a modest 30th in a class of 57, it was enough to make him want to continue his studies, and to earn what only one in ten university students ever earned: a Master of Arts degree. This meant studying the remaining four Arts (music, arithmetic, geometry, and astronomy), plus Aristotle's *Metaphysics*, Aristotle's *Ethics*, Aristotle's *Politics*, Aristotle's *Natural Philosophy* (later called Science), in fact Aristotle's Just About Everything, and doing a lot more disputing than ever before. Martin may not have loved the attacking part of disputing, because when wounded his angry side came furiously out, but disputing surely helped him hone his talent for reducing huge messes of words and thoughts to a pithy if sometimes racy few, which talent might have had much to do with why he finished second in his class this time, out of 17. When he received his MA in January 1505, it meant he was qualified to lecture on all seven Arts, to run disputations, and, if he wanted, to study for another Master's degree in one of the three advanced subjects available at universities: theology, law, and medicine.

Martin did indeed want to study even more, or at least his father wanted him to, as long as the subject was law. And so Martin dutifully made the 15-mile trip from Erfurt to Gotha, where he could buy a huge edition of the standard law book, the *Corpus Juris*. He started class with it in May 1505, and like other new students began memorizing the titles of laws.

But one long day in July, Martin took his books back to the shop in Gotha for a refund, and told everybody he was quitting law, because he wanted instead to be a *Mönch*—the word German-speakers used to mean either "monk" or "friar."

BROTHER MARTIN

What in the world had happened?

Maybe a few weeks of law were enough to convince Martin that he hated the subject. Or maybe he was trying to escape a marriage father Hans had arranged for him. But it was mostly, said Martin, because God gave him no choice.

By that, he could have meant how seriously he'd started to worry about the state of his soul. He'd always been sensitive, and had worried about his soul before, including two years before when he'd accidentally stabbed himself in the leg with the student dagger he always carried, then almost bled to death in a field. But the sudden death of a couple of law professors and students around January 1505 scared Martin so badly that, he said, he almost died himself. Sudden death could make anybody worry, of course, even in a world where sudden death happened all the time—in fact maybe especially in such a world, because it was impossible to pretend it couldn't happen to you. Still, these particular deaths were worse than usual. One of them even made him worry about his body as well as his soul, because, as some later hinted, he might have actually caused that death, in a duel. Years later he even supposedly said himself, "Because of God's extraordinary decision I was made a friar, so that they could not capture me. Otherwise, I very easily would have been captured." That was wonderfully vague, but it wasn't far-fetched that civic authorities in Erfurt were indeed after him, just as they were after other students who fought duels, including one who had recently killed the protégé of a French cardinal. University authorities, however, wouldn't have wanted the bad publicity of such a thing, and could have well been happy to just let Martin disappear into a monastery. But again, the whole story was vague. If it was true, then even if the death was accidental or in self-defense, it would have been easy for Martin to feel that the only way to pay for the deed, the only way to avoid further investigation, the only way to save his soul, was to devote himself full-time to God.

But Martin could have had another terrifying event in mind too, when he said God gave him no choice. In the summer of 1505, Martin was summoned home to Mansfeld, very possibly to hear the news about the arranged marriage. That alone might have stunned Martin, but what terrified him happened on the walk back to Erfurt, when one of Thuringia's heaven-splitting thunderstorms suddenly broke out, frightening him so badly that he frantically cried out, "Help me St. Anne, I will become a *Mönch*." Now, vowing to become a monk or friar was common enough for extrasensitive souls fretting over their salvation, since it was fairly common knowledge that if you died wearing a monk's or friar's cowl, you could hope for special treatment at the Last Judgment. But having the vow forced upon him this dramatically could have easily made Martin feel that God was behind it all, and had even arranged the thunderstorm expressly for him, to make it absolutely clear that his particular soul would require something a lot more drastic than the ordinary burgher's life that he, and especially his father, had envisioned for him. At first Martin regretted how rashly he'd made that vow. But knowing that not honoring it might lead to even more wrath from God, he sold his law books and decided to follow through: he was going to enter the religious life.

Whatever was behind the decision, his business-minded father was livid and immediately disowned Martin. It was fine to be pious, but something else altogether to throw away all of Hans's hopes and hard-earned money. Only many months later, after two of his other sons died of the plague and a rumor went around that Martin had too, did Hans grudgingly go along. He must have felt like God wasn't giving him any choice either.

Erfurt's 25 churches and 11 monasteries and friaries and 28 parishes made it one of the churchiest towns in northern Christendom, and gave Martin plenty of places to choose from to start his new life. On July 16, 1505, he announced his decision at a farewell dinner with friends: he would enter the local Hermits of St. Augustine, an order of friars founded in 1244 by Pope Innocent IV himself—the only religious order ever founded by a pope. The next day a couple of friends walked with him to the gate, where he asked to be admitted.

It was no surprise that Martin chose a place known for its strict living, because if entering a religious house improved your chances at salvation, then entering a strict religious house had to improve them even more. These were after all the *Observant* Hermits of St. Augustine, who implied with that frontal adjective that they actually followed the order's rules—unlike their more relaxed brothers, the *Conventual* Hermits, from whom they'd split away.

But it wasn't just the strictness that appealed to Martin, because he could have gotten even more of that with the local Carthusian monks. No, it was the Augustinians' mighty tradition of learning too. Martin wanted to keep on studying after all, but just not law. The Augustinians had ties to all sorts of universities and pushed their members to study theology, which Martin sensed might help with all the fretting he was doing over his salvation. Yes, he could have also gotten university-level theology with the Dominicans or Franciscans, who were also friars, but he later said that the first were too proud and the second too casual. The Augustinians were just right.

It was also possible, of course, that the Augustinians were the only ones who would take his possibly tainted soul in, or who believed that he had motives besides just wanting to escape trouble. "The entire Order took care of me," he said, in the same quotation mentioned earlier about escaping capture. Whatever the case, the friars were satisfied by his story, which he told during the day or two he spent in the guest room, and they let him start the usual short probation.

Martin threw himself into his new life, positively eager to obey its hundreds of rules and thus make himself acceptable to the order and especially to God. Being the most strictly obedient friar in a strict religious house had to just about guarantee your salvation, he thought. And at first it seemed to work: as he passed his short probation of a few months, then his long probation of a year, his fretting calmed down a little. But almost as soon as he took in late 1506 the final vows that made him a full-fledged black-robed Augustinian friar, the fretting, or *Anfechtungen* (which meant something more than "attacks" or "temptations"), came back, worse than ever, with the Devil seeming to whisper constantly in his ear that someone as undeniably sinful as he was could never possibly be saved.

No matter what Brother Martin did, his sense of sin wouldn't leave him. He tried to keep every single rule, and when he broke a rule he more than made up for it with severely penitent deeds, but all the coarse clothing he wore and floors he scrubbed and latrines he cleaned and flesh he chastised and begging he did, not to mention all the blanketless sleeping in winter and three-day fasts and all-night vigils and sometimes six-hour confessions, still weren't enough to make him feel like he'd ever be rid of his sins, and thus be righteous, or justified, before a perfect and righteous and therefore surely demanding God. Even when he did something right on the outside, there was still something wrong with him inside, usually a lot of pride at having done the thing right. No wonder that when as a newly ordained priest he said his very first mass in May 1507, in the Erfurt friary church in front of family and friends, he stumbled and bumbled and wanted to run at the thought of his imperfect self handling the body and blood of Christ.

SCHOOLMEN

Surely Martin hoped that finally starting to study theology in 1507, at the University of Erfurt, might help calm him down.

When he'd first entered the friary, he read backward and forward his new little Latin Bible with the red cover, until he knew where everything was on just about every page. But studying theology at the university was less about studying the Bible than about studying assorted commentaries on it, by theologians he (and others) would soon not-so-kindly call scholastics, or "schoolmen." Since about 1100, these schoolmen had labored mightily to build up a nice, tidy system of rational Christian theology with the help of those masters of rationality, the philosophers of ancient Greece and Rome, especially Aristotle. But the more Brother Martin studied scholastic theology, the less he liked it. Most scholastics seemed to prefer ancient pagan philosophers to the ancient church fathers that Brother Martin and other "churchmen" liked better. And the new rational theology was turning out to be less tidy than everybody had hoped anyway. In fact, it had divided into rival teeth-baring Aristotle-inspired schools, starting with the two most important: (1) *realists,* who said that reason could help us discover everlasting truth, and (2) *nominalists,* who said that we use reason to create truth we then simply give names to (*nomen* means name), and that God's truth in the Bible was superior to reason anyway. These two main schools branched predictably into subschools and, even more predictably, into subschools of subschools, but one of the things all schoolmen could agree on, especially the nominalist theologians who mostly taught Brother Martin, was the answer to the question that most plagued him: How in the world (and the eternities) could you be saved? And their answer was this: just do what lies within you, and trust God to do the rest.

Oh, the scholastics knew that nobody had enough good lying around inside to save himself. No, everybody was saved, or justified, by God's grace, just like the church had always taught. But the scholastics were also sure, like Aristotle, that you did have enough good inside to *improve* yourself, or as a Christian might put it, to do enough good works to get you to a sort of halfway station between sin and grace, which allowed you to receive a sort of preliminary grace. When you got that, *then* your will could cooperate with God's so that you could receive, especially through the sacraments of the church, the full grace of God, which justified you, or made you righteous, and thus saved you.

This was justification by grace, through doing every blesséd thing you possibly could.

It was all meant to give comfort and hope to chronically imperfect humans, but it was icy-cold comfort to Brother Martin, who felt like "the most wretched man on earth." How could he know whether he was doing everything that lay inside him, and thus pleasing God? He could always think of something he could do better, or some other sin he needed to confess. After all, even the scholastics admitted you could never know for sure whether you'd done enough. And so when the friars sang Psalm 22 in choir, "My God, my God, why have you forsaken me?" Brother Martin really *meant* it. He suffered from what the professional religious called the "bath of hell," or overscrupulousness, a sort of occupational hazard for people whose full-time job was to look inside and find sin. To Brother Martin, it was like fishing in a barrel, and so he exasperated his confessors more than most. They tried telling him that the big pile of sins he was always confessing were fake sins, and that next time he should come with some real sins that actually needed forgiving. Still, he found it hard to believe that any sin was small. After all, God was perfect, and the Bible commanded him to be perfect, and the constitution of the Observant Augustinians said that someday he would actually be able to obey every single requirement perfectly. Maybe he still just wasn't trying hard enough.

His torments were so great, and "so much like hell, that no tongue could adequately express them, no pen could describe them, and one who had not himself experienced them could not believe them." And no one seemed able to help him: all he heard was to do his best and ask Christ for help, but why in the world would a sinless Christ help somebody who was so obviously sinful?

Brother Martin kept on studying, though, because he was still sure that he would find answers in theology—just not in the sort of theology he'd learned so far. From about 1509 on, in fact, he was more and more sure that there was a serious problem not just with his soul but with the current theology of salvation, and the problem's main name was that "chatterbox" Aristotle.

Aristotle wasn't totally worthless. For logic, and natural philosophy, and other this-worldly topics he was just fine, thought Brother Martin. He'd even taught Aristotle's *Ethics* one year to Arts students, although he liked that work less and less every year. And he even found plenty to like in nominalist theology. But what Brother Martin didn't like was how the pagan Aristotle had wormed his way so thoroughly into the Christian theology of salvation, resulting in such wrongheaded ideas as that humans were free to choose good or evil, or that the rational system of reward and punishment so popular in this world somehow applied to heaven too, or especially that humans had enough good lying within them to develop good habits and then actually become good, even without any help from the Holy Ghost! That didn't fit Brother Martin's experience at all.

There had to be better answers.

DOCTOR MARTINUS

Searching for answers obviously wasn't just some intellectual exercise for Brother Martin, but the ultimate definition of a matter of life and death . . . and salvation.

Surely that helped explain why he kept studying so hard, not only earning the Bachelor of the Bible degree in March 1509 and the Bachelor of the *Sentences* (the most important textbook on the Bible) in autumn 1509, but also getting even more attention from Johann von Staupitz, vicar-general (or superior) of all German Observant Augustinians and a professor of theology at the new University of Wittenberg. In 1511, Dr. Staupitz transferred Brother Martin from Erfurt to Wittenberg, where he wanted him not only to finish his Master of Theology but become a Doctor of Theology as well. On a memorable day in May 1512, under a pear tree in the courtyard of the new friary, Staupitz told him the news. The doctorate wouldn't involve any further study, he explained, just a huge 50-gulden fee that Prince Frederick of Saxony, founder and patron of the university, had already agreed to pay.

Oh, and it would also involve taking Staupitz's place as a professor of theology: he was just too busy to do the job right.

Brother Martin furiously resisted. His health was already ruined from disciplining his body for so long, he said, plus his young age (he was only 28) meant he would have to put up with the jealousy of other friars, and besides he wasn't necessarily eager to make his ideas "public" in class, as a professor had to do. Why couldn't he just keep being a regular preacher inside the small comfort-giving

Lucas Cranach, *Luther as Augustinian Friar.*

walls of the friary, and keep searching in private for answers about salvation? But Staupitz insisted: he knew Brother Martin's talents, and also that a favorite old way to deal with a chronic soul-fretter was to keep him so busy he wouldn't have time to fret. Brother Martin, remembering his vow of obedience, finally gave in, but it felt like another thing God had forced him to do.

And so Brother Martin took his Master of Theology degree on October 9, 1512, in Wittenberg, then on October 18 and 19, at the church in Prince Frederick's new castle (which church doubled as the university church), he put on the hat and other symbols that made him Doctor Martinus. Joining hands with the dean of the theology faculty, Andreas Karlstadt, Dr. Martin swore to obey the Roman church, and to teach no idle and foreign things but only the gospel truth. And of course the ceremony included the usual hours-long disputation, after which students carried the newly minted doctor through the streets while the bells of the city church rang wildly.

The next year Dr. Martin started teaching, one book of the Bible at a time, in the order of his choice—first the Psalms for almost two years, from 1513 to 1515, then Romans in 1515–16, Galatians in 1516–17, and Hebrews from spring 1517. But like any professor worth the salt (or venison, or boar, or wood) he was sometimes literally paid in, he kept on learning and studying, now up in the *cloaca* tower, looking for better answers to the question of how his miserable soul could ever be saved. Salvation wasn't the only subject he studied, of course, but it was always the foundation of everything else.

While still a student, he'd begun learning the tradition of salvation taught in monasteries, long before there were such things as universities or scholastics, and the most popular spokesman for which was St. Bernard of Clairvaux (d. 1153). This tradition didn't rely on the logical language of Aristotle but the mysterious language of Paul—words like "grace" and "mercy" and "faith"—and it read the Bible to find God, not to build a nice tidy system of theology. Brother Martin knew Paul, of course, since he read the Bible through twice a year, but in his mind and soul Paul's message about grace and mercy were always overwhelmed by the Bible's many other passages about the righteous, perfect, and stern God. Thanks to Bernard, and Staupitz, and an older brother in the order, Brother Martin started to believe Paul: no wonder he felt lost and unable to please God, he realized—nobody could! It was even *necessary* to feel lost and unworthy, so that when God's grace came you understood to your bones that it was He who did *all* the saving, not you. You had no say in your own salvation. All you could do was get yourself sufficiently humble to recognize your sinful state, and see how badly you needed God's grace.

This was justification by grace, through humility.

It helped soothe Brother Martin for a while, certainly more than "do all that lies inside" ever did, and it found its way into his first lectures on the Psalms. Show your humility to God and be saved, was the message he saw there. But he soon grew unsatisfied with this answer too.

In 1515 Brother Martin began also to study the tradition of salvation taught by the church fathers, especially Augustine (d. 430), who'd been furious with his rival Pelagius (d. 420) for saying that humans certainly did have it inside them to do good, and that they earned God's grace by acting on that goodness and keeping all of God's commandments. Hadn't Pelagius read Paul? fumed Augustine. You couldn't do *any* good work or keep any commandment on your own, but had to be *first* filled with grace, which God gave you entirely at His initiative and not because of any virtue or good works on your part. When you received this "operative grace" from God, *then* you could do what would indeed justify and sanctify and regenerate you. But because God was the instigator and motivator, it was still really all God's doing. Augustine's view won out, and Pelagius was declared a heretic. But lo and behold, the scholastics had revived Pelagius, thought Brother Martin. Sure, they admired Augustine on just about every subject in the world, but they ignored or waved away his writings on grace, saying he'd just been exaggerating, to make a point, the way anybody did in a disputation. Naturally they didn't want to be accused of Pelagianism, so they said that God ultimately saved you, but then came up with things like having to earn preliminary grace, which to Brother Martin was just dressed-up Pelagianism—just another way to say you could save yourself.

From 1515 on, Brother Martin studied as well the tradition of salvation taught by the spiritual writers (later called mystics), who wanted to unify their souls with God not only in some distant heavenly future but right here and now. And the way to do that, they said, wasn't through humility or anything else but simple *Gelassenheit*—being resigned and completely passive before God and letting Him fill you with His grace. It was the most perfect theology he'd ever seen, said Brother Martin, outside the Bible and Augustine. He liked one anonymous spiritual work so much that he had part of it printed in spring 1516, as the *Theologia Deutsch,* or German Theology—his very first publication. No, not even humility was the way to salvation, he decided, because getting humility could itself become a good work, and raise the same old nagging question: How much humility was enough? The key was total passivity.

And finally from certain men of letters in the faculty of Arts, who called themselves *literati* (lettered ones) or *poetae* (poets) or *graeculi* (little Greeks), because of their interest in ancient Latin and Greek (all of them were later called humanists), Brother Martin learned the new tradition of reading the Bible in its original languages, to get as close to the source as possible. In 1516, for instance, when Erasmus's new Greek New Testament appeared, he saw that the Greek word *metanoia*, always rendered into the Latin Bible as *poenitentia* and always taken to mean "doing penance"—as in the church's sacrament of penance—actually meant "coming to your senses." Penance wasn't about a lot of penitential good deeds but a whole change of heart!

All these ideas started coming together into his new theology of salvation as he lectured on Romans, beginning in 1515, and then Galatians and Hebrews too, and even as he wrote to friends. It didn't appear all at once but in pieces, amid all sorts of other subjects he was studying and teaching as well.

By the time he was done lecturing on Romans in 1516, Brother Martin was sure there wasn't a thing you could do to help save yourself: you still had to try to keep the law, or commandments, but the point of the law was to make you realize you couldn't keep it on your own, and this turn to God. He was also sure that, just like the spiritual writers said, all you could do in that turning was assent to God's grace and let yourself be filled with it. And unlike Augustine, he was lastly sure that the point of grace was not to now help you do all sorts of good deeds that would save you. No, he was convinced from his own reading of Paul that your nature never changed at all, even *after* you were justified by God's grace: you were still a sinner, but your sinful state wasn't any longer "imputed," or held against you. Instead it was like Old Testament Boaz putting his cloak on Ruth: she was still Ruth but was now covered by grace. Certainly this new, covered person did good works, especially toward her neighbor, but she did them quite naturally, because God was with her, rather than because she was trying to save herself. "For we are not, as Aristotle believes, made righteous by the doing of just deeds," Brother Martin wrote in October 1516. Instead, *after* being made righteous by God's grace, "we do just deeds."

This new answer made Brother Martin a lot more hopeful about his and everyone else's chances at salvation than the old answer had, and it went along with his new hopeful view of God too, which came mostly from Staupitz. Brother Martin had always seen God as righteous and perfect and therefore stern and harsh. That was why he'd always hated the phrase "the righteousness of God," as in Romans 1: just like the scholastics and Aristotle's *Ethics,* he'd assumed that God's

Johann von Staupitz.

righteousness meant that God would give you what you deserved, and for most people that just couldn't be good news. But Staupitz taught Brother Martin that he had things backwards: he had to start by thinking of God as a loving father who *wanted* to give him His mercy and grace, and whose righteousness was as much about mercy as about justice. In fact, God's sense of justice meant that He would surely be merciful to someone as inherently disadvantaged as the sinfully human Martin Luther. In other words, God gladly gave you *more* than you deserved, or earned, contrary to what Aristotle and the scholastics said. Well, that opened the gates of paradise for Brother Martin. "The one who is righteous will live by faith," also in Romans 1, didn't mean you became righteous by your good deeds and then got faith, but that God made you righteous through your faith—which meant trusting God's Word, believing, and assenting.

This was justification by grace, through faith alone.

And this was his big insight, the foundation of everything else in his theology. Sure, you also needed grace in the scholastic and monastic views of justification, but you got it through good works or humility. Brother Martin was saying, based on his reading of Paul, and the spiritual writers, that grace came *only* through passive faith.

Near the end of his life, he wrote that this idea had come to him in a flash, even though he couldn't say exactly when it came. More likely it came gradually, especially over those months and years when he was lecturing on Romans and Galatians and Hebrews, because even after the new idea started emerging, he was still sometimes saying things that made students think they needed good works, or humility, to save themselves: "faith alone" was a hard idea to believe, even for him. He wrote to a brother friar in April 1516, but he might as well have been writing to himself, "Why was it necessary for [Christ] to die if we can obtain a good conscience by our words and afflictions? Accordingly you will find peace only in Him and only when you despair of yourself and your own works."

The idea sank in more and more, and it was liberating and fresh for Brother Martin. But it wasn't a totally new idea or even an un-Catholic idea. He went out of his way himself to show that it was very old, going all the way back to Paul, or even to the Old Testament prophet Habbakuk, who first wrote "the one who is righteous will live by faith." Others before Dr. Martin had said similar things, like the Augustinian Gregory of Rimini (d. 1358), and some of his contemporaries were saying them too, like the Italian Gasparo Contarini in 1511, or the Frenchman Jacques Lefèvre d'Étaples, who concluded in 1512 that works had nothing to do with salvation. And of course Staupitz taught Brother Martin so memorably about faith alone that he admitted, "If it had not been for Dr. Staupitz, I would have sunk into hell." There was even more precedent than Dr. Martin knew: the second Council of Orange in 529 said much the same thing about grace that he was now saying, but because no theologians ever cited that council it was forgotten. The Blessed Simon Fidati of Cascia (d. 1348) was so close to Brother Martin in his view of justification that he was later called his forerunner, and the scholastic (no less) Thomas Bradwardine (d. 1349) even used the formula "by faith alone."

The potential problem for Brother Martin, though, was that at the moment, justification by faith alone, especially his particular version of it, wasn't even close to a majority view in the church. It could even get you into trouble, as it did Contarini and d'Étaples. That was why Prince Frederick's secretary, George Spalatin, asked Brother Martin in early 1517 to publish something showing that he wasn't actually against good works, the way some theologians were now saying he was. In the spring he therefore put out his first original booklet, *The Seven Penitential Psalms,* to explain himself more, but not at all to apologize. It didn't get much attention or cause him any trouble, luckily. But he was sure that this new thing he was writing in the tower was guaranteed to itch the wool-covered backs of many theologians, and cause a fuss.

THE BIG DISPUTATION

From up here in the tower he could look out to the south and see the moat below, then some fields beyond the moat, and the Elbe River beyond that. Summer had come late this year, but crops were growing now, and unfortunately so was an epidemic that made your head ache and gave you a fever and ruined your appetite, and Brother Martin didn't want to catch that, since he was thin enough. But most on his mind at the moment were his next lecture on Hebrews—and especially the theses he was writing for what he was calling his *Disputation Against Scholastic Theology.*

Writing out a bunch of theses for a disputation was the best way a professor of theology could imagine to try out any ideas he might have on a subject that was bothering him—or in other words, on a subject that hadn't yet been settled by the church. And the big public sort of disputation, as well as members of the university, was the best way most any professor could imagine to get his ideas out to as many people as possible. Of course, using a disputation to attack scholastic theology was positively dripping with irony, since the scholastics had basically invented the disputation. And using a disputation to get at theological truth was offensive to some monkish theologians, since St. Bernard had said that posturing and exaggerating and attacking were fine for practicing rhetoric and logic but completely "inappropriate . . . in the study of Christian doctrine." But Dr. Martin was a friar, not a monk, and friars worked at universities, and they'd adapted just fine to its ways; besides, not only had Aristotle and Cicero argued with their foes, but Jesus and Paul and Augustine had too. And if arguing was good enough for them, well, who could argue against it?

This time Brother Martin wasn't just going to peck at scholastic theologians, a little in the neck here or leg there, as he'd done before. Instead he was going to go after their whole curséd body, because he blamed them for the whole stinking mess that the theology of salvation was now in. He'd gone after them privately since 1509, writing derogatory notes in the margins of his books, and in September 1516 he'd gone after them a little in public through one of his students, Bartholomäus Bernhardi, who for his graduation disputation wrote up a few theses straight out of Augustine's writings and Brother Martin's lectures, which even offended a few of Brother Martin's old professors in Erfurt. But now Dr. Martin wanted to strike the fatal blow himself, with the theses he was writing right now, for the disputation to be held during the graduation of another student of his, named Franz Günther.

There was no magic number of theses for a disputation: you just kept writing them in a somewhat logical sequence until you'd set down everything you wanted to discuss. Bernhardi had drawn up only three theses for his disputation, Karlstadt had drawn up 151 for one of his, the Italian Pico della Mirandola had once composed 900, and Dr. Martin would one day have 404 directed against him. For this disputation, Dr. Martin came up with 99.

What mattered wasn't the number of theses, which most people usually ended up forgetting, but how you wrote them. A thesis wasn't supposed to assert absolute truth or even what the author believed, but to draw out problems with a subject by provoking and exaggerating. Still, the way the author put theses together gave you a hint of what he really thought about a subject—especially if he'd been making his thoughts as clear as Brother Martin had lately on the subject of salvation.

He started fittingly with Augustine, right in thesis 1, which said it was ridiculous to claim that Augustine had just been kidding about grace: saying he exaggerated when speaking against the heretic Pelagius "is to say that Augustine tells lies almost everywhere." The next theses had a lot of Augustine in them too: "without the grace of God the will produces an act that is perverse and evil," and also the key to the whole matter, "The best and infallible preparation for grace and the sole disposition toward grace is the eternal election and predestination of God." There was no way to prepare for salvation. Only God could prepare you, and grant it to you, and save you.

Other theses went after Aristotle: "We do not become righteous by doing righteous deeds but, having been made righteous, we do righteous deeds," and "Virtually the entire *Ethics* of Aristotle is the worst enemy of grace." As for those who say "that no one can become a theologian without Aristotle"? Dr. Martin responded, "no one can become a theologian unless he becomes one without Aristotle," because "Aristotle is to theology as darkness is to light."

Still other theses went after Aristotle's more recent scholastic champions, especially William of Ockham (d. 1347) and Gabriel Biel (d. 1495). "And this is false, that doing all that one is able to do can remove the obstacles to grace." In fact it was "impossible to fulfill the law in any way without the grace of God," because "every deed of the law without the grace of God appears good outwardly, but inwardly it is sin." Why? Because when you did "good deeds" without first receiving grace, you did them to improve your standing with God, making them selfish, and thus useless: when good works "are brought forward as ground for justification, they are no longer good." But when you were filled with the grace that saved, you naturally turned outward and did good deeds to others.

Finally came a disclaimer that showed just how nervous Dr. Martin was about his 99 daring theses: "In these statements we wanted to say and believe that we have said nothing that is not in agreement with the Catholic Church and the teachers of the church."

Whenever he finished composing the theses, he walked back through the narrow passageway of his tower and either handed them to another friar (his secretary) for neat copying, or if they were neat enough he or the secretary took them to the university printer, Johann Rhau-Grunenberg, whose shop stood near the friary. He wasn't exactly the most sophisticated or tidy printer—Wittenberg wasn't a big enough town to attract such a fellow—but he was always willing.

Copies of theses for disputations were one of the most common things university printers put out, and should have been the easiest too, since they were on a single page and since professors usually needed just a few dozen copies, to pass around. When Rhau was finished, Brother Martin went to inspect and fetch the copies—and saw to his dismay that the 99 theses had become 100: Rhau had skipped a number. (Other editions would reduce them to 97.) Brother Martin took them anyway, giving one (or even his original handwritten version) to the university beadle to do what was usually done with theses meant for public disputation: post them on the door of the castle church at the other end of town, since that church was the university church too, and the church's door was where university news and announcements were therefore always posted. Brother Martin might have even made the 13-minute walk down the partly cobblestoned street and put the copy on the door himself, with a nail or some glue, amid all the other announcements and theses already there, surely arranging his to make sure it would be seen. He or the beadle probably put another copy of the theses on the door of the city church, and certainly Dr. Martin sent out copies to friends and colleagues elsewhere, including his old friend Christoph Scheurl all the way in Nuremberg, and not just for them to toss into their crowded and cobwebbed files but because Dr. Martin was hoping to entice some of them to come to remote Wittenberg and dispute, or watch: maybe the little town wasn't enough to attract them, but surely the prospect of a fiery disputation over a subject as big as this was! Every theologian cared about salvation, and the subject badly needed reformation. He didn't use that word "reformation" much, unlike many others who'd tossed it around so easily over the last century, and he certainly never used it when talking about the entire church: the church was God's and only God could reform it. But the university curriculum and the way theology was being taught were most decidedly the work of humans and could therefore most certainly be improved by them.

The big 99-theses disputation he'd been longing for took place as scheduled on September 4, 1517, during the graduation ceremony at the castle church. If the disputants treated every single thesis (they didn't always), then it surely would have taken more hours than some in the audience preferred. And surely sparks flew at times during the exchanges, but just as surely heads nodded off too: nobody recorded the details—exactly who disputed, or what specific proofs were offered for the theses, or even how many people attended. But most disappointingly of all, none of the friends or colleagues whom Brother Martin had invited to participate even showed up. And any sparks that flew didn't start any sort of fire. The whole thing just fizzled out.

Oh, his old professors in Erfurt got upset again about the theses. He tried making up with them and offered to come and dispute the theses there too, any time they pleased, to show his good will. But he didn't hear back, which made him anxious. He liked those professors, and some of the ideas they'd taught him, and hadn't meant anything personal with his theses. And so when he couldn't bear the silence any more, Dr. Martin wrote them again, months later, with no luck, and when he was in Erfurt on business for his order he even tried visiting one of those professors. But the man had his servant say he wasn't home.

That was painful for Brother Martin, but even more painful was that this was about the only reaction he got at all to his earth-shattering theses. The thing he'd worked so hard on, the thing he was sure would take the world by storm and clarify the doctrine he cared so much about and so badly wanted to see improved in the church—the doctrine of how anyone could possibly be saved—turned out to be strictly, well, academic.

2

A Most Vehement Papist

Wittenberg, Outside the Elster Gate. Early Autumn, 1517, When the Wind is Fresh.

I f he were an apprentice carpenter, painter, or shoemaker of Wittenberg, then he would surely be making the 23-mile trip on foot, even though it would take him most of the day to get there and another day to get back, because he'd heard that the precious thing he was going to get would cost somebody of his lowly station a whole half gulden. That was more than 1 percent of what he earned in a year, so there was no way he was going to fork out even more to rent a horse or a seat on a cart just so he could get back home that same night, because that horse or seat was sure to cost him even more than going on foot and lodging at some flea-infested weak-beered inn would.

Of course, if he were a full-fledged journeyman or even master carpenter, painter, or shoemaker, then he might still make the trip on foot, because the whole gulden that somebody of his station was supposed to pay for the precious thing was probably more than 1 percent of his income too. But then again, he might decide that renting a horse or seat to get back home fast was well worth the price, because here in 1517 time was of course money, and staying the night at some flea-infested weak-beered inn would cost him two whole days of income instead of just one, plus the cost of the inn and weak beer besides.

And if he were one of the very rare merchants in town who earned more than 500 gulden a year, then he could certainly make the trip on his very own horse or wagon, plus stay the night anyway if he wanted, and at a fine place too, even though the precious thing he was going to get would cost him a whole six gulden. But come to think of it he was even more likely to just pay somebody to go buy the precious thing for him.

And if the pilgrim from Wittenberg were a woman, then she would have to pay whatever her husband or father was required to pay for the precious thing, but if he wasn't alive then she would have to negotiate the price when she got there, and she almost certainly wouldn't be traveling alone but with other people who were going her way too.

Any Wittenberger making the journey would have spent plenty to do so—in gulden, time, trouble, or all three—which told you just how precious this thing they were going to get, called an indulgence, really was. All indulgences were precious, of course, but this one was especially so: the Wittenberger had heard that buying one for yourself would forgive all of your sins right now and also keep you out of purgatory after you died, and that buying one for your dearly departed mother or father or child would get them out of purgatory that very day.

Any Wittenberger could actually have gotten an indulgence or two or even 17,000 without ever leaving Wittenberg at all, at the church in Prince Frederick's fine castle at the west edge of town. There you could venerate one or two or all 17,000 relics in the prince's stupendous collection, which meant confessing, praying in front of the relic, touching it or at least touching something that had touched it (like water that was run over the relic then sold in a little vial), and of course making an offering. But almost all of the precious indulgences available at the castle church were plain-old-ordinary precious indulgences, good for reducing your time in purgatory by just 100 days or so. Sure, if you venerated every single relic there then you could pile up 1.7 million days, but almost no Wittenberger had that kind of time or money. Plus even though 1.7 million days was a long, long time, it still wasn't forever. How could you know whether your particular set of sins didn't need another 1.7 million days beyond the first 1.7 million?

But this new extra-precious indulgence promised to keep you out of purgatory for good, because it was a *full* indulgence or, as the preachers called it, a plenary indulgence, good for every single sin you or your dearly departed had ever committed. You could get one of these at the castle church in Wittenberg too, but only on All Saints (November 1) and a few other days, and waiting around that long could be dangerous to your soul, with death as sudden as it often was. Plus the plenary indulgence at the castle church didn't seem to promise quite as much as this new extra-precious one did. But the problem with the new indulgence, if you were a Wittenberger, was that it wouldn't be coming to town anytime soon: Prince Frederick had forbidden it from every square inch of Saxony, since it so blatantly competed with the indulgences in his own castle church. No, if you lived in Wittenberg and wanted to lay hold of the unusual graces offered by this extra-special indulgence, then you had to go across one of Saxony's many convoluted borders to do so. And the closest town to do that was at Jüterbog, a solid day's journey away on foot.

A pilgrim from Wittenberg would have seen the tall twin towers of the St. Nicholas church, where the indulgence was being offered, even before walking through Jüterbog's imposing gate. Once through the gate, you kept walking straight ahead, past two other churches, all the way to the far side of town, and there on your left was St. Nicholas's. It wasn't as fine as Prince Frederick's castle church, which had been recently and quickly built and therefore had a nice uniform look, while St. Nicholas's had been built over a couple of centuries and was all mixed up—rough brown and gray stones at the front, smooth reddish-brown brick at the back, with some stones flung between the brick here and there as well. But it was lovely anyway, especially inside, with 30 altars, and walls covered with murals of saints and prophets, and ceiling ribs painted in red and beige and dark gray, and a main altarpiece dating from 1425 that unfolded almost miraculously into 24 panels from sacred history, and one of the finest and tallest carved stone tabernacles (for the blesséd sacrament) in all German lands, and a big wooden sculpture of Jesus resting his weary thorn-crowned head in his hand. It was a most suitable place indeed to get the special new indulgence, which was being offered by the pope himself.

The pope's special indulgence-preacher, who was still carrying the new indulgence from place to place, had stopped several months before in St. Nicholas's, with his entourage, and climbed into the pulpit midway up the nave to exhort the audience to take advantage of what he had brought.

"Why don't you have fears about your sins?" the preacher had reportedly said. "Why don't you confess now to the vicars of our Most Holy Pope?" who were there with him for that very purpose. "You priest, you nobleman, you merchant, you wife, you maiden, you married people, you youth, you old man," you aren't ashamed to visit a tavern, or to dance, but you can't come forward and admit your sins? Didn't they all know that their lives hung by "a thin thread" and that they could perish at any moment? "For the day it is well, but ill tomorrow. Today alive and tomorrow dead." Luckily for them, there was available . . . for a limited time . . . this extraordinary indulgence, which he waved before them, and which could bring them "complete forgiveness of all sins." All they had to do was be contrite and confess and make an offering, which offering would go toward building the new St. Peter's in Rome. It was a small price to pay for guaranteed salvation. Think of the example of Lawrence, who gave away his whole inheritance and "let his body be burned" in order to be free of his sins. "So why are you standing there? Run for the salvation of your souls" and get this indulgence! And run for the salvation of your dearly departed too, who could also be saved by it. Didn't they hear the voices of their "wailing dead parents and others," crying out from their pain and saying, "From this you could redeem us with a small alms and yet you do not want to do so. You let us lie in flames." Now was the time "to hear the voice of God" and do something about it.

These many months later, the words practically still echoed in the church for the visiting Wittenberger, who in the meantime had heard still other words supposedly preached there too, some of which made you wonder whether there hadn't been a little stretching in the retelling, that's how remarkable they were— like that this particular indulgence was so extraordinary it could forgive even the worst sin you could imagine, like violating the Mother of God herself! And that if St. Peter himself were there in person at this moment, why even he couldn't offer any greater grace than this indulgence could! And that the pope's coat of arms on the flag that the preacher's entourage held up high was as powerful as the cross of Christ itself! And that this indulgence was even good for future sins not yet committed! And of course the preacher was said to have used that favorite line of the indulgence-preachers of the last 40 years or so: as soon as the coin in the box rings, the soul from purgatory springs.

Whatever any Wittenberger might have heard about the powers of the special new indulgence, it had been enough to move him or her to go to the trouble of going all this way to Jüterbog, even months after the indulgence-bearing preacher was gone. Because that preacher had thought ahead, leaving behind not just a big wooden offerbox for latecomers to drop their alms into, but also printed copies of the one-page indulgence letter that could be filled in when the bearer did the required confession—either right there in St. Nicholas's, or when the pilgrim got back home.

And so the pilgrim from Wittenberg made an offering, and got the precious indulgence, and maybe stayed a scratchy night in Jüterbog. Arriving back in Wittenberg, through the Elster Gate again, he or she could have made the required confession straightaway at the little mud-and-timber dirt-floored church of the Augustinian friary that stood just inside the gate, or maybe they preferred the city church of St. Mary's a couple of hundred yards farther, because there were rumors that the friars might not exactly love this new indulgence.

Certainly in one of those churches, or while just walking along the street, the Wittenberger would have run into Brother Martin Luther (as he now signed his name), who was already weary of hearing about this new extra-special indulgence that various parishioners had flashed at him whenever he wanted to talk about their penance.

KINDNESSES

Dr. Martin couldn't study up in his tower all day, because he had too many other things to do.

Some days he was too busy to go through the skinny passageway into the tower study at all, and even on days when he did go through he was constantly being called away—every few hours to sing the Hours of the Divine Office in the little friary church, at 10 and 5 to eat in the friary's refectory, at noon every Monday and Friday to give his latest lecture on Hebrews, on certain Fridays to run disputations, every few weeks to inspect one of the 11 friaries he was responsible for as Staupitz's district vicar, every once in a while to check on the friary's fish pond he watched over, every night at 8 to go to his cell down the hall and sleep (until

Wittenberg in 1546; the Augustinian Friary is to the far right.

4), and of course every day to say Mass or preach or hear confession or all three, because Dr. Martin wasn't just a professor to that elite group known as students, or a brother to his fellow 30 friars, but a shepherd to hundreds of ordinary souls.

In a little place like Wittenberg, smaller even than Eisleben where he was born, or Mansfeld where he was raised, and way smaller than Magdeburg and Eisenach and Erfurt where he'd gone to school, Brother Martin could easily have come to recognize almost every one of those souls by now, even the women he avoided looking at and hearing confession from. Three hundred fifty years after being settled by Flemish migrants used to relentlessly flat land, and who therefore called the sandy white hill they saw "white mountain" (*witten berg*), the town on the Elbe River still had only 2,100 people in not even 400 houses, and just three long streets plus various short ones. The wall and moat surrounding the town made serious growth unlikely, and so did its location at the northern edge of Saxony, which to many southern Germans seemed like the end of civilization. To be sure, a few people paid to praise the place in print called it "the gem of Thuringia" (the part of Saxony where it was located), but most others, and not just the city's enemies, called it a stinking, poor, miserable, filthy, unhealthy, half-frozen, joyless, mucky sand dune.

In moments of frustration, even Brother Martin might mutter things like that about his adopted home, like when he couldn't get a book he wanted, or when its streets were muckier than usual since the recently laid cobblestones ran down the centers of those streets only, or when the place smelled like a pigsty thanks not just to the sewage and what the butchers threw out but also to the pigs of the monks of St. Anthony, which wore bells on their ears and were allowed to roam around so locals could piously feed them and save the monks some money. But if Brother Martin stopped to remember that most towns everywhere stank, and that around 90 percent of German towns actually had fewer than 2,000 people, and that no town in Frederick's Saxony had more than 10,000, and that the prince was doing all he could to spruce Wittenberg up, and that God had a funny habit of doing his best work in the lowliest and most unexpected places, then the town might not seem so bad. The main thing was, in a place this small he was sure to bump into some parishioner who'd gone over to Jüterbog, or maybe Zerbst, to get an indulgence. Not everybody who came to confess had one, of course; in fact, people were getting a lot fewer of them than those in charge of the indulgence had hoped. But Brother Martin didn't care about the figures: whether 100 or just two Wittenbergers had gotten one, it was still too many for him.

When he'd first bumped into indulgences among parishioners some years before, he hadn't necessarily been against them, as long as they were used the way they were supposed to, which was as one small part of the sacrament of penance. That sacrament, said scholastic theologians, had three parts: (1) being contrite about your sin, (2) confessing your sin to a priest who then gave you absolution, or forgiveness, which took away your guilt, and (3) paying for your sin by doing "satisfaction" for it—from Latin *satis facere*, "to do enough," as in, enough to please God. You "did enough" by carrying out the punishment your confessor assigned to you, which usually meant saying so many prayers, giving so many alms, fasting so many days, going on a pilgrimage, and so on. The problem was that circumstances sometimes made it impossible for you to do your assigned punishment, or sometimes you just died first. Since every sin had to be paid for eventually, here or in the eternities, what in this world could you do? *That* was where indulgences came in.

Indulgences, or "kindnesses," had been available since around 1100. Each one was a signed-and-sealed letter stating that the assigned punishment you weren't able to carry out was forgiven, or "commuted" to something more bearable—say, making a pious offering toward a new church, or monastery, or bridge. Sure, if you died without an indulgence, you could still do your unfinished punishments in purgatory, mercifully created by God for that very purpose. But as any confessor or preacher could tell you, punishment in purgatory hurt a hell of a lot more than on earth, and took a hell of a lot longer too, as in a thousand times more, since one day on earth equaled a thousand in purgatory. That was what made an indulgence so attractive, especially the plenary version. An ordinary indulgence took time off your stay in purgatory, but a plenary indulgence let you skip the place altogether.

Either sort of indulgence was possible because the saints of the church had done far more good works than they needed for their own salvation—and the pope, as Christ's vicar, had the authority to pass out those surplus works, called the "treasury of merits," to whoever needed help covering their own unfinished satisfactions. All you had to do to get an indulgence was show the usual contrition and make the usual confession, and usually make an offering too. When the pope declared in 1476 that indulgences were now available for dead loved ones too, they became even more popular than they already were.

As a confessor with an often-heavy conscience himself, living in a world terrified of sudden death and purgatory, Dr. Martin could see how an indulgence might help a few truly penitent souls. But as he learned when parishioners first started waving indulgences in his face, indulgences weren't usually being used, or understood, the way they were supposed to be. Instead, indulgence-preachers were claiming— or at least strongly suggesting—things about indulgences that they really had no business claiming, or suggesting.

Like that indulgences could forgive sins instead of just unfinished punishments.

And that it was better to avoid punishment for your sins than to suffer it.

And that forgiveness was some sort of straightforward bargain with God: your sins for your cash.

Antichrist (with Indulgences).

And because indulgences had by now become such a popular fundraiser for all sorts of building projects (including at the University of Wittenberg), indulgence-preachers didn't seem the least bit interested in correcting any of their exaggerations either, or the misperceptions people had, because those exaggerations and misperceptions were exactly what had helped make indulgences so popular.

GENTLE KICKS

Dr. Martin had to admit that in his early days as a shepherd he hadn't known all that much about indulgences, mostly because he thought them so trite and usually just ignored them. But when he realized how popular they were among his flock, and how they so easily led people into thinking that their salvation was now a sure thing, he started paying a little attention.

Back in 1514, in a classroom lecture on Psalm 69, he lamented how many people were trying to "ease the way to heaven, by means of indulgences," making maybe a single sigh of sorrow over their sins. People should instead be making deposits to the treasury of merits, he said, with their own penitential deeds and their genuine regret (showing he was still thinking that you could help earn your way to heaven).

Then in his 1516 lectures on Romans he criticized indulgence-preachers for encouraging people to escape punishment for sins just by making an offering, which might result in a few nicely remodeled churches or monasteries but also mislead believers into thinking they were saved. And that same summer, in a sermon in the city church, he criticized his flock for buying indulgences that would help pay for parish fairs when they should have been making offerings to the poor instead.

His sermons over the past year had paid even more attention to indulgences, starting with another sermon at the city church on All Saints Eve (October 31), 1516. All Saints Day was one of the moments when people came from near and far to get the indulgences available in Prince Frederick's castle church—so many people that eight confessors were needed for a whole week just to hear all the confessions—and Brother Martin wanted to make sure they understood things rightly.

He preached on them again in that same castle church the next January 16 and 17, the anniversary of the church's construction and thus another big day for indulgences. He surely put a damper on the festivities and a frown on Prince Frederick's face when he reminded one and all that an indulgence without true contrition was worthless, that too much faith in indulgences actually hurt your penance, that indulgences didn't fulfill *all* satisfaction but just some of it, and of course that skipping satisfaction wasn't necessarily good for your soul, because punishment helped you see how much you needed God, in whom you really ought to put your trust instead of in some indulgence. Daring to say all that right outloud in the prince's indulgence-filled church, especially when the income from those indulgences had helped to build the University of Wittenberg and still kept it running, showed just how irritated Brother Martin was getting.

Then he preached on indulgences at the city church again in February, telling the audience that suffering was part of being Christian, so they should just accept their punishments instead of buying indulgences. And he preached the same thing even harder at Lent, because that was the very moment in 1517 when the preacher of the pope's new indulgence was making his pitch in Jüterbog, and violating all the rules about how indulgences were supposed to be taught and understood.

Still, for all of Brother Martin's irritation, he never completely condemned indulgences altogether. He even admitted that indulgences probably were possible because of Christ's surplus merits, and that the pope did indeed have power to dole out those merits, and that indulgences could help souls in purgatory. No, he just wanted people to see that they needed to be penitent *before* they got an indulgence or it wouldn't do any good, and that indulgences forgave only punishment, not sin, and that preachers should do a better job explaining all that.

It was the epically bad preaching of the indulgence-preacher who'd come through Jüterbog, a Dominican friar named Johann Tetzel, that finally pushed Brother Martin in the summer of 1517 to study the subject of indulgences more seriously than he ever had before. And the more he studied, the more convinced he became that something was wrong with not just how Friar Tetzel was preaching indulgences, but with the theology that was supposedly holding them up too. In other words, even if Friar Tetzel had preached perfectly rightly and followed the absolutely purest practices, something would still be smelling fishy about the whole indulgence business.

And the more people he ran into coming back from Jüterbog, the more Brother Martin wanted to do even more than just preach and nag.

RISKY BUSINESS

One thing Dr. Martin surely learned from his study was that just as he hadn't been the first to discover justification by faith, so he wasn't the first to say some unflattering things about indulgences.

In Paris, Peter Abelard had already criticized them by 1120; in England, John Wycliffe (d. 1384) said that the pope had no jurisdiction over purgatory and Geoffrey Chaucer (d. 1400) poked fun at indulgence-preachers; in Bohemia, Jan Hus (d. 1415) said that real penance didn't need indulgences; in German lands, Johann Rucherat von Wesel (d. 1481) called indulgences a pious fraud, Gottschalk Hollen of Brother Martin's own Augustinian order said in 1452 that "Repentance is better than indulgences," and Dietrich Morung of Würzburg in 1476 ridiculed the new papal bull that said indulgences worked in purgatory too—all before Brother Martin was even born.

More recently, all sorts of men of letters criticized them as well, starting with the best-selling Erasmus, which surprised no one, but even the famously orthodox theologians at the University of Paris were soon joining in. German princes and towns sometimes raged furiously against indulgences, though not exactly for theological reasons—more usually it was because big chunks of the offerings for a particular indulgence had left the place where they'd been collected. But if the offerings went to local projects, like the University of Wittenberg or one of Prince Frederick's bridges, then rulers liked indulgences just fine. Assorted German clergymen criticized indulgences after 1500 for purely religious reasons, including Johann Staupitz, whose sermons on the subject in 1516 sounded very much like those Brother Martin would soon give himself, which wasn't surprising, since the men saw each other more than usual around that time. In fact, Staupitz seemed more than anyone to be pushing Brother Martin to do something serious against this new indulgence—as in more than just giving a few sermons. He needed to do something at the university too, where it really counted.

Just about all learned people expected any sort of unsettled theological matter in the church to be worked out by theology professors at universities, especially through disputations. That was exactly what Brother Martin had tried to do with his 99 theses on justification, which was indeed an unsettled subject, and it was what he and Staupitz had in mind now with indulgences, another such subject. The problem was, indulgences weren't just any old unsettled subject. They were instead an exceedingly touchy one, because of who was in charge of them: the pope himself. If you talked about indulgences in any sort of critical way, as you were bound to do in a disputation, you couldn't help looking like you weren't only criticizing indulgences but the pope himself too. Sure, all sorts of learned people, probably even including some popes, knew there were problems with indulgences. But if the

Hieronymus Schurff.

problems you cared about on the subject happened not to be the same as those the pope cared about, then even if your theology was thoroughly sound and well-intended and based on recognized authorities, it would look like you were saying the pope was wrong. And that wouldn't exactly be good news for your professorial career.

No wonder that when Brother Martin first mentioned to his friend Hieronymus Schurff, on a wagon ride, that he wanted to do something serious about indulgences, his friend just about fell out: "Don't write against the pope! It won't be tolerated!" Brother Martin could have insisted he wasn't writing or disputing against the pope, just against indulgences, but Master Schurff understood things rightly: writing against indulgences automatically meant writing against the pope. Staupitz knew that too, but he still thought something public needed to be done and that Brother Martin was the person to do it. Not only was he a university professor who could at least claim a theoretical right to treat unsettled subjects (Staupitz no longer could), but he was smart enough to know how to say touchy things and, for all his fretting, brave enough to say them.

And make no mistake about it, a little bravery was absolutely necessary here. Many past critics of indulgences had gotten in big trouble for their criticism. Brother Hollen was punished, Dr. Morung was excommunicated and thrown into prison for ten years, Wycliffe and Hus were condemned as heretics, Abelard and Erasmus were strongly suspected of heresy, and Johann Rucherat von Wesel, the most famous professor at the University of Erfurt at the time, was thrown into prison for life in Cologne.

A little bravery or at least foolhardiness was especially needed to speak out against this new special indulgence, because the pope wasn't just *ultimately* behind this one, like he was for all indulgences, but personally and *directly* behind it. Usually he granted some bishop or prince the right to raise funds from an indulgence for some project and then had nothing else to do with it. But he was directly in charge of all plenary indulgences, and the offerings for this new particular one were going straight to him, to build his new St. Peter's cathedral in Rome.

Brother Martin also had to be a little brave when he found out who was responsible for running the indulgence in German lands: none other than the highest ranking German churchman of all, Archbishop Albrecht of Mainz. At first, Brother Martin just assumed that the new indulgence was being preached wrongly by little 52-year-old Friar Tetzel, who should have known better: after all, Tetzel had studied theology and now taught at the Dominicans' school in Leipzig. But his long years of pitching indulgences (since 1504) had obviously made him willing to ignore rightminded theology and to play on people's misperceptions, decided Brother Martin. Yes, that had to be it. Then in the summer of 1517, Brother Martin got his hands on a copy of Albrecht's instructions for the preachers of the new indulgence and he saw that Friar Tetzel hadn't been going off script at all. Worse yet, the instructions came right out of the papal bull (or decree) authorizing the indulgence.

Dr. Martin could hardly believe it, didn't want to believe it, but there it was in fresh black ink: the indulgence officially granted complete forgiveness of sins and total escape from purgatory, complete forgiveness of sins for loved ones in purgatory, and, for another quarter gulden, absolution from whatsoever horrible crime you might commit in your life—once at a time of your choosing, and once at the hour of death. All you had to do was sincerely confess, and offer some prayers, and of course make an offering that would go to the badly needed building of St. Peter's.

Even after reading the instructions, and the bull, Brother Martin still wanted to believe they were forgeries put together by Tetzel. But whether Tetzel or the archbishop or, alas, even the pope was behind this new indulgence, Brother Martin—encouraged by Staupitz and another Augustinian friend, Wenceslas Link—agreed at last to do something serious.

Which of course meant another retreat into his tower, to write some theses for a disputation.

EVEN MORE THESES

During the rest of the summer of 1517 Brother Martin didn't say much about indulgences, probably because he was busy studying the subject, and especially because he was busy preparing for his *Disputation Against Scholastic Theology*, of September 4, which he thought a much more important subject than indulgences but which of course turned out to be so disappointing.

In August, though, during a dinner at the friary with Staupitz and George Spalatin and a couple of other friends (and to which he asked Spalatin to please bring a bottle of the castle's fine wine), and at other meetings with Staupitz near Eisleben and Grimma during 1517, the conversations inevitably got around to indulgences and how to attack them.

Out of those conversations there emerged first "A Treatise on Indulgences Published by Doctor Martin of the Order of St. Augustine in Wittenberg." It wasn't actually published, and Dr. Martin probably didn't actually write it, but only edit it, because its main points sounded more like Staupitz than they did Dr. Martin. Indulgences, the treatise concluded, had become about greed. Yes, the pope held in his hands the surplus works and merits of Christ, and he was free to distribute those, but it wasn't clear whether he could keep souls out of purgatory—and if he could, then it was cruel to do so only for money. Also, the pope could only release souls from punishments that he'd imposed himself, not those imposed by God in sacred (or canon) law. And most of all, the pope couldn't forgive souls *already* in purgatory but could only pray for them. Thus, indulgences could be useful and shouldn't necessarily be halted, but the church needed to beware of greed, and teach believers to "incessantly seek God's healing grace" instead of indulgences.

Most of these ideas from the treatise found their way into Dr. Martin's newest set of theses. He went into his tower to write them in September or October of 1517, still smarting from the thud of the *Disputation Against Scholastic Theology*. Maybe that thud was why he made these new theses a little sharper than the last— maybe the last hadn't gotten the attention they deserved because they hadn't been prickly enough. He wanted to have them ready by All Saints Eve, October 31, because not only would indulgences be overflowing at the castle church the next day, as usual, but All Saints Eve was an important day to announce up-coming disputations for the semester.

By the time he was done, he had 95 theses ready for what he was calling the *Disputation on the Power and Efficacy of Indulgences*. Just like in the "Treatise on Indulgences," he wanted to focus on indulgences themselves rather than on the pope's role in them, but in the end he couldn't avoid mentioning the pope in at least 44 of the theses, and plenty had a real sting to them.

Still, he at least tried to be careful, right from thesis 1, when he asserted, "When our Lord and Master Jesus Christ said 'Repent' he willed the entire life of believ-ers to be one of repentance." Not even the most orthodox theologian would have objected to that, he thought. Or to theses 27 and 28, which condemned the ditty "as soon as the coin in the box rings," or to 75, which called it "madness" to claim that an indulgence could absolve a man who'd violated the Mother of God. All orthodox theologians also would have agreed with his assumption in thesis 29 that purgatory actually existed, and the claim in 35 that an indulgence required real penance. Most orthodox theologians would even have agreed with thesis 34, that indulgences applied only to satisfaction, and not to sin or guilt—it was basic old theology. And the first part of thesis 44 sounded like grace-loving Brother Martin had even gone over to the side of Aristotle for a moment: "Love grows by works of love, man thereby becomes better. Man does not, however, become better by means of indulgences."

His carefulness toward the pope was also clear in theses that made Dr. Martin sound like the "most vehement papist" he claimed to be, as these seemed to defend the pope forward and backward, and left and right too. The pope never intended that buying indulgences should count as a work of mercy,

¶ Amore et studio elucidande veritatis, hec subscripta disputabuntur Wittenburge Presidente R. P. Martino Luther Eremitano Augustiniano Artiū et S. Theologie Magistro, eiusdemq ibidem lectore Ordinario. Quare petit vt qui non possunt verbis presentes nobiscum disceptare / agant id literis absentes.
In Nomine dñi nostri Ihesu Christi, Amen.

1517.

Martin Luther's 95 Theses. This edition appears to include only 87, but note that after 26 the numbering mistakenly goes back to 17—for a total of 97 theses. Note also that the first thesis 24 is transposed to 42.

said thesis 42; the pope didn't want money but only fervent prayer (48); if the pope knew what indulgence-preachers were claiming, then he'd rather burn St. Peter's to the ground than rebuild it (50); the pope was even ready to sell St. Peter's so he could pay back anyone who'd been swindled by indulgence-preachers (51); and to say that St. Peter himself couldn't grant greater graces than this indulgence was blasphemy against both Peter and the pope (77).

But maybe those careful sorts of theses were simply meant to take the sting out of the many that criticized the practice and theology of indulgences, and thus the person responsible for them too. Some of these were only indirectly critical, like the apparently tame thesis 1, that made the seemingly innocent call to a life of penance—but Brother Martin meant something much different by "penance" than most current theologians did: it wasn't about trying to save yourself with good deeds but trusting your heart to God's grace. And the theses that said the pope wanted prayers more than money and would rather burn down St. Peter's than have preachers preach wrongly were indirectly critical too—as if to say that at least a *good* pope would want and do such things. But even more theses were directly critical, like thesis 5, which said that the pope could only forgive punishments in purgatory he'd imposed himself and not those imposed by God in sacred law, because as theses 8 through 13 and 25 and 26 suggested, the pope had no jurisdiction over purgatory—a suggestion going completely against the usual idea, founded on Matthew 16, that the pope's "keys" gave him power to bind and to loose both on earth and in heaven (and presumably purgatory too). Also sharp was thesis 31, which said that the way indulgences were practiced made it hard for anyone to be truly penitent, and if you weren't truly penitent then an indulgence was useless. Thesis 32 skewered the claim of the new St. Peter's indulgence that anyone who bought it could be sure of salvation—in fact, such a person was more likely to be damned. Numbers 36 and 37 said that a truly penitent Christian didn't even need an indulgence; 43 and 45 cheekily asserted that giving to the poor or lending to the needy was better than getting an indulgence; 49 claimed that even papal indulgences were useful only if people didn't rely on them; 56 through 60 doubted the whole notion of the treasury of merits, while 62 concluded that the treasury was in fact "the most holy gospel of the glory and grace of God," not some basket of surplus good deeds.

But the most daring of all the theses came near the end, in 82 through 90, which were also the most cleverly structured. How in the world, asked 82, were responsible priests supposed to defend the pope's honor, which so richly deserved to be defended, when laypeople asked them such thorny questions as: Why didn't the pope just empty purgatory out of love instead of for money? Why were masses for the dead in purgatory still being paid for and said if those same souls had already been redeemed with indulgences? Why not just liquidate the endowments for those masses and give the money to the poor? If St. Peter's needed building so badly, then why didn't the pope just build it from his own presumably overflowing coffers? And why, if the pope was really worried about souls instead of money, did he declare null and void all other plenary indulgences people had acquired in the past, which basically compelled anybody wanting a plenary indulgence to buy this new one?

Maybe those questions really did come from laypeople, but maybe they were Brother Martin's own and he put them in other people's mouths here to protect himself, the way any good thesis-writer did. Critics of the 95 theses would soon say he really believed them all, and wasn't just tossing out ideas for discussion anymore. After all, the preface said that he was writing "in the name of the Lord Jesus Christ" (which he never said in any other disputation), and he started theses 42 through 51 with the phrase "Christians should be taught," as if he really did believe they should be taught these things.

Even if the stinging questions came from Brother Martin himself, in the end (in thesis 91) he tried to sound conciliatory: if "indulgences were preached according to the spirit and intention of the pope, all these doubts would be readily resolved. Indeed, they would not exist," it said. The pope's intentions were good, and indulgences, used properly, were perfectly acceptable.

And so almost all of the 95 theses were, as theses were supposed to be, provocative . . . but they were hardly all fiery cannonballs. They weren't even as theologically daring as his earlier 99 theses, or as some of his recent lectures on Romans, Galatians, and Hebrews. No, he mostly just wanted to clarify a (too) popular church practice. But again, just talking about indulgences in a university setting was risky, politically and ecclesiastically. In fact, these 95 theses on the trite subject of indulgences had the potential to raise more eyebrows than his 99 on scholastic theology ever had.

EVEN MORE CARE

Just as Brother Martin tried to be careful in how he put the theses together, so he had to be careful in what he now did with them.

As usual, he very probably ran them down to the shop of Johann Rhau-Grunenberg and had some copies printed to send around to friends. On All Saints Eve, he might also as usual have handed a copy to the university beadle, to post it as usual on the door of the castle church, to announce that a new disputation was coming up; or he might of course have even walked a copy down and put it up on the door himself, and the door of the city church too. But because he himself never mentioned posting the 95 theses anywhere, and no one else mentioned it either for another 25 years, people would later start arguing about whether he ever actually posted them at all.

Lucas Cranach, *The Castle Church in Wittenberg.*

He certainly might have: Dr. Martin never mentioned posting any other theses either, including the earlier 99, because posting theses was such a plain old ordinary thing to do, especially on All Saints Eve, when all sorts of them were probably hanging on the door of the castle church. He did later say that All Saints Eve was the day he first "trounced" upon indulgences, which could have meant "posting," but not necessarily: he thought the day was more important to mention than the act, because the posting itself was so routine. It was also possible that he posted the theses only several weeks later, because it was common not to publicize (and thus post) theses until those scholars invited to participate in the disputation had replied that they would, and a few weeks would have been enough to learn that information.

But it was also possible that Brother Martin didn't post the 95 theses, because they were on such a ticklish subject—and the best clue of this was that no actual disputation was *ever* held on them. He knew most scholars didn't want to touch indulgences, and he even complained about that very thing months later. He also knew that disputations on sensitive subjects could be cancelled: Prince Frederick had cancelled a disputation in May 1517 that Andreas Karlstadt had also prepared against scholastic theology (apparently Karlstadt invited too many people), and Dr. Johann Eck of the University of Ingolstadt had a disputation on the subject of usury cancelled in 1514 by the university chancellor—Eck therefore just sent his theses around. Dr. Martin might have done the same for his 95, rather than post them. He said later that he'd just wanted to have a discussion on the subject among friends, and theses sent by messenger would have allowed any initial discussion, at least, to take place by very un-public mail.

But in the end, it didn't really matter much whether Dr. Martin nailed or glued his new theses to the castle-church door. What mattered was whether anyone who mattered in the world would notice or care about them. Of course he hoped they would, and to make sure of it he did one thing for sure on that All Saints Eve in 1517: he sent the theses and a covering letter (1) to the bishop of Brandenburg (who had ecclesiastical authority over Wittenberg), (2) to a couple of other bishops with jurisdictions in Saxony, and (3) to Archbishop Albrecht himself, who was not only in charge of the indulgence in German lands but was also the ecclesiastical superior over the bishop of Brandenburg—and thus ultimately was an ecclesiastical superior over Dr. Martin too. Dr. Martin might have singled out these bishops as his first audience in the hope that they would approve his holding a disputation on the usually taboo subject of indulgences, but mostly he chose them because he wanted them to be more careful in how they handled and taught the things.

By November 11, he still hadn't heard back from any of the bishops, so he sent some copies as well to his Augustinian friend Johann Lang, to see what he thought. Before that he might have sent copies to still other friends, because on November 5 George Spalatin was asking why he hadn't gotten his copy of the theses yet.

But after that, all Brother Martin could do was wait.

3
To Heaven in a Bathing Cap

Aschaffenburg, the Archbishop's Palace. Very Late November, 1517, When Stone Buildings are Cold.

Set on slightly rising ground next to the River Main, the archbishop's palace was as impressive as it was forever meant to be, especially compared to all the little mud-and-timber dwellings of just about everybody else in the world.

But it wasn't even Albrecht's favorite: in his archbishopric of Mainz, he liked the palace in Mainz itself even more. And across all of his domains, he liked most of all the Moritzburg, in Halle, which lay in his other archbishopric, of Magdeburg. Begun in 1484 and built between architectural styles, the Moritzburg was a mix of massive old German fortress and tasteful new Italian-looking residence. And best of all to Albrecht, its chapel was bursting with so many precious relics that he was soon going to have to find an even bigger home for them, thank God. But even such a magnificent place as the Moritzburg was hard to love in frigid weather, which was one reason why the archbishop preferred the palace at Aschaffenburg, 250 miles south, this time of year.

If the old saying was true that "where the bishop is, there is the Church," then the church in Albrecht's domains moved around all the time. The puzzle of where among his far-flung residences he currently was helped explain why the letter from Friar Martin Luther of Wittenberg, sent on October 31 from that city, didn't reach Albrecht until almost the end of November. The friar almost certainly sent it to the Moritzburg, betting that the archbishop was in Halle, but Albrecht and his court were not, and so the letter was forwarded north to yet another of the archbishop's residences at Calbe an der Saale, but he had already left that place too. Luckily some of his men were still in Calbe, and one

Aschaffenburg.

of them finally opened the letter on November 17, then forwarded it ahead to Aschaffenburg, where Albrecht actually was.

The archbishop had no problem reading the Latin letters he got every day, because he'd attended university and showed some real inclination toward learning—precisely why the friar of Wittenberg had at first placed so much hope in Albrecht, despite the archbishop's mere 27 years. If Albrecht's portrait-painter was to be believed, he was usually seated for letter-reading in a high-backed chair at one end of a big table, with benches for secretaries and advisers on either side. Looking past his longish nose and curved large lips, he peered at this latest letter and its accompanying documents with his wide-set brown eyes (the lazy eye peering, as usual, less reliably than the other), even though his councilors had surely already advised him on what they all said.

The letter started off with the usual bootlicking, acknowledging Albrecht as the greatest and "most gracious" churchman in Germany, while the friar himself was among the "dregs of humanity," a mere "speck of dust." In fact the friar's very smallness and baseness were why he had restrained himself so long from writing "to the height of your Sublimity." But his duty of fidelity to "your most Reverend Fatherhood in Christ" finally moved him, and so he hoped the archbishop might be so kind as to have a dignified look at his modest letter.

The friar then got to his real and much less humble point, which was that a new and misleading indulgence was being preached in the archbishop's lands, and in the archbishop's name, but surely without the archbishop's knowledge—and surely the archbishop would want to do something about it. The friar admitted that he hadn't actually heard in person what the preacher of the troubling indulgence was claiming, but he knew very well what parishioners were saying he'd claimed, like that it could forgive sins and guarantee your salvation, which of course it never could. The archbishop no doubt knew Peter's saying, that even the righteous would barely be saved, and Amos's and Zechariah's words that those who were saved would be "plucked from the burning" only at the last minute—and if saints and prophets were barely going to be saved, then it was ridiculous to claim that merely dropping a coin in a box would somehow do the trick for ordinary mortals. Indulgences, as the archbishop also surely knew, forgave satisfaction only, not sin, and it was up to the archbishop to see that people understood that, and to stop this preacher and this indulgence, and the instructions that had come with them (also in the archbishop's name). Because if the archbishop didn't stop this business, well, who knew but that somebody (maybe even the friar himself) might "perchance arise" and refute the indulgence in public, "to the shame of your Most Illustrious Sublimity." And surely the reputation-conscious archbishop didn't want that. "Yet I fear that it will come to pass, unless there is some speedy remedy."

With that, the friar begged the archbishop to accept his "faithful" message, offered "out of a faithful heart altogether devoted to you, Most Reverend Father, since I too am a part of your flock." Signed, Brother Martin Luther.

PS, he added, please find enclosed a copy of some recent theses on indulgences.

TROUBLE IN CATHEDRAL CITY

The last thing the archbishop needed was some "audacious monk" complaining about the St. Peter's indulgence, especially since the offerings from it so far hadn't quite piled up as high as the archbishop had hoped. What Albrecht really needed was for the indulgence to bring in a lot more offerings, and fast.

The great secret that the friar from Wittenberg didn't know was that the St. Peter's indulgence was also Archbishop Albrecht's indulgence. Yes, half the proceeds would go toward building the new St. Peter's, just like the indulgence said. But what it didn't say was that the other half would go toward paying off the archbishop's extraordinary debts.

No archbishop was ordinary, of course, not even in his debts, but Albrecht was less ordinary than most, starting with his birth in the highly noble Hohenzollern family of Brandenburg, and continuing with his extraordinary dose of ambition.

His older brother Joachim had, as expected, inherited their father's title as Margrave of Brandenburg, which title also automatically made Joachim one of the very tiny elite of seven electors in the empire, who chose a new emperor whenever the last one died. Second-son Albrecht, born in 1490, would have to find his greatness somewhere else. And he found it in the church, rising fast to various desirable offices: canon (a prestigious sort of clergyman) in the cathedral of Mainz in 1508, priest in 1512, archbishop of Magdeburg in 1513, and "administrator" of the nearby bishopric of Halberstadt that same year—a clever way to let Albrecht control that bishopric, as well as Magdeburg, without violating the rule that said you couldn't hold more than one bishopric at a time. But Albrecht was never a fellow to be bound by rules. He broke one already when he became a canon at the unlawful age of 18, and another when he became bishop at only 23, both of which he was able to break because of his family's expanding influence and especially its truly magnificent credit line: thanks to that, he could pay to Rome not only the fees required for each office but also the fines that were imposed for being too young.

As big as those fees and fines had been, they were very small beer compared to what Albrecht had had to lay out in 1514, just a year later, when the latest archbishop of Mainz died and that office fell open too. Albrecht just had to have it, and who could blame him really? The archbishop of Mainz wasn't just primate (first bishop) of the 50-plus bishops in the entire Holy Roman Empire, but also secular prince over the territory of Mainz, ecclesiastical prince over the archbishopric of Mainz (which was much bigger than the territory), archchancellor of the empire, and—the honey in the cake—one of the seven electors of the emperor, just like his brother Joachim. If Albrecht could get his many-ringed fingers on Mainz, it would give the Hohenzollerns two of the seven votes in the electoral college. But there was

Albrecht Dürer, *Albrecht von Brandenburg.*

a big problem: Albrecht wanted not only to become archbishop of Mainz, but to still be archbishop of Magdeburg and administrator of Halberstadt too.

Holding two (or three) bishoprics was even more problematic than being too young to be a bishop. Plenty of important people were against Albert's plan for both these reasons. He was barely out of grammar school, said some, while others moaned, "What isn't for sale in Rome?" Prince Frederick of Saxony, Brandenburg's neighbor and main rival, was against Albrecht's ambitions in Mainz too, but not because Albrecht was too young or would be holding multiple bishoprics: Frederick's own brother Ernest had become archbishop of Magdeburg when he was only 12, and administrator of Halberstadt too, just like Albrecht. And Frederick had pushed Ernest to also add the archbishopric of Mainz when it fell open in 1500, just as Albrecht wanted to do in 1514. No, Frederick was against Albrecht's move because he didn't want the Hohenzollerns of Brandenburg getting any bigger than they already were, or bigger than Frederick's own family, the Wettins of Saxony. There were less than a dozen great families in the empire, and these were two of them, and Frederick wanted to make sure that the Wettins stayed ahead of their nearby rivals. In fact, Frederick was still fuming that when his brother Ernest died in 1513 the Wettins had lost the bishoprics of Magdeburg and Halberstadt to Albrecht. Frederick was still plenty powerful, since he was now the senior of all seven electors, but he didn't like the idea of Hohenzollerns having two votes to his one. And the pope was against Albrecht's plan too, not so much because it violated the pope's sensibilities about bishops holding multiple offices but because he didn't like any churchman getting as powerful as Albrecht would then be.

Still, Albrecht had plenty going for him in Mainz, especially among those who actually chose the archbishop, which in this case happened to be none other than his fellow canons of the cathedral. Unlike in France or England or Spain, where kings usually appointed bishops, in the empire the chapter of the cathedral in question did the choosing. Sure, Albrecht had his flaws, like being impatient and easily influenced, and avoiding conflict to a fault, and having no real charisma and maybe more than a little greed. But he liked learning, was a big patron of the arts, and as a canon in Mainz's cathedral he had done the unimaginable and actually lived in town and fulfilled his duties (for a time) instead of paying someone else to do so, and in his short time as archbishop of Magdeburg (and administrator of Halberstadt) he had dutifully traveled around his diocese(s) to attend his flock. He was also pious in his own wealthy way, commissioning some exquisite liturgical robes and books of devotion, supporting certain reforms of the church, and constantly enlarging his gigantic collection of relics by having all sorts of agents keeping their eyes open for new possibilities, partly to beat Frederick of Saxony to them. But what Albrecht had going for him above all else was that truly magnificent family credit line.

The archbishopric of Mainz had already fallen vacant twice before, since 1504, and was still in debt from having had to twice pay to Rome the office's 14,000-gulden fee. What the electing canons of Mainz were therefore now looking for most in a candidate was someone who could pay the fee himself, and who could also maybe offer a little resistance to Frederick Wettin next door. When Albrecht eagerly assured them that he could most certainly do both, they had their man—even though he was still too young, even though he wanted to stay on as archbishop of Magdeburg and administrator of Halberstadt, and even though the usual 14,000-gulden fee was just the beginning. The pope, still not happy about the plan, insisted that Albrecht pay a fine of another 14,000 for taking on this third bishopric, and for still being too young for the office.

How in the world was even the mighty and much-promising Albrecht going to come up with almost 30,000 gulden, especially after he'd just paid his fees for the archbishopric of Magdeburg the year before? Through his good friends the Fuggers, of course, bankers to the great and powerful in much of Europe. They would not only loan Albrecht the money for the fee and the fine, but along with one of the pope's creative councilors also devise a brilliant way for Albrecht to actually pay it all back: through a special new St. Peter's indulgence. Half of the proceeds from it would go to the Fuggers for the loan, and half would go to the pope to help build St. Peter's. Since an indulgence was still the most popular way to raise money for any big project, the real surprise would have been if nobody had thought of it, especially the Fuggers, who had handled the financial side of almost all papal indulgences in German lands since 1495.

Now Albrecht wasn't thrilled about the plan either, because he saw how bad it looked. Even worldly-wise big-brother Joachim was shocked at the idea of the indulgence, perhaps mostly by the fact that Rome wanted half of the proceeds instead of the usual 30 percent. True, a big indulgence for St. Peter's preached in German lands between 1486 and 1504 had given 67 percent of the proceeds to Rome, but that was an exception. It also bothered Joachim that this new indulgence didn't require Albrecht to pay anything from his own numerous pockets—all he had to do was allow it to be preached in his territories.

Still, Albrecht soon went along with the scheme, and the pope proclaimed the new St. Peter's indulgence in a bull of March 31, 1515, saying that it would be available in Albrecht's archbishoprics of Mainz and Magdeburg for eight years. The always-cautious but well-experienced Fuggers estimated, conservatively, that this would bring in 52,287 ducats, or about 70,000 gulden. Half of that would be plenty to pay back Albrecht's loans, plus interest, plus the salaries and expenses of those who would preach the indulgence—and of course to pay the usual 3 percent commission to the Fuggers.

The bull didn't reach Albrecht for almost 18 months, though, apparently because just about everybody was still unenthusiastic about it, including Maximilian, the Holy Roman Emperor, who had to approve any foreign indulgence like this before it could be offered in the empire. Just like Prince Frederick Wettin of Saxony, Maximilian didn't love the growing influence of the Hohenzollerns of Brandenburg either, since their power was now even rivaling that of Maximilian's own great family, the Habsburgs of Austria. And so the emperor, who wouldn't mind at all if Albrecht couldn't repay his loans, held back his permission—and the bull—for more than a year. He finally went along only after wheedling out of Albrecht a cut of 1,000 gulden a year from the proceeds, and also reducing the number of years the indulgence could be preached from eight to three or four, which could sorely reduce the total amount brought in.

Still, Albrecht went ahead, and finally officially received the bull for the St. Peter's indulgence in late 1516, more than a year and a half after it had been issued. He got right to work, appointing himself as commissioner of the indulgence, several others as subcommissioners (including Johann Tetzel), and ordering thousands of copies of the indulgence letter to be printed. Here was one group enthusiastic about the indulgence all right: printers. Like just about all one-page products, indulgence-letters were fast and cheap to make, but even more attractive was that they were usually ordered in such large quantities (once up to 130,000 copies) that assorted shops were needed to print them all, spreading the printing wealth, so to speak. Plus all the shops had to do was hand the printed copies over for cash to a single churchman instead of distribute them in every direction to all sorts of irregular-paying booksellers. Some of the greatest printers in German lands worked on the St. Peter's indulgence (and, profit-conscious as always, most would soon print Dr. Martin's writings against the same indulgence as well).

In fact, printers as a whole might have made more from the St. Peter's indulgence than anybody else, including Albrecht and the pope. Yes, Dr. Martin soon believed that Tetzel and his fellow subcommissioners were raking in huge amounts of gulden, but Albrecht knew very well that wasn't the case. It was already a bad sign that he'd had to persuade and pay higher fees than usual for Dominicans to preach the indulgence, because the usual preachers of indulgences, the Franciscans, didn't like the looks of this new one. But even worse was that Germans seemed to be suffering from indulgence-fatigue, especially when it came to indulgences that went to nonlocal purposes. The big St. Peter's campaign of 1486 to 1504 had brought in 400,000 enthusiastic gulden, but people who'd gotten one then were slow to buy this new one, either because they already had one, or because they were unhappy that the new one said that all past plenary indulgences were now worthless.

The donation figures showed the new unenthusiasm. In 1517 and 1518, the Dominican subcommissioner Heinrich Breidenbach distributed around 180 indulgences in the middling town of Duderstadt (pop. 2,850) and brought in about 100 gulden in offerings, suggesting that about six of every 100 people got one, and that most of them weren't rich. And that was one of the subcommissioner's best harvests. In bigger and more prosperous Mühlhausen (pop. 10,000), only 48 gulden came in. Heiligenstadt (pop. 2,400) brought in 16 gulden, Northeim (pop. 3,000) only 13, and so on. Maybe Friar Breidenbach wasn't as persuasive as Friar Tetzel. Or maybe Tetzel wasn't selling as brilliantly as Dr. Martin supposed. Or maybe, again, Germans were just tired of things from Rome. The big town of Speyer gave 3,000 gulden for papal indulgences in 1502, but only 200 in 1517. Big Frankfurt gave 2,078 in 1488, but only 304 in 1517. The smaller amounts in many smaller towns, like Heiligenstadt, could have added up, but apparently they did not. If Breidenbach's disappointing figures were extended to, say, a total of 100 towns preached to, and each town big and small brought in on average 50 gulden for 1517, then 5,000 for the year wouldn't have been too bad; but an average of only 30 per town, for 3,000 gulden, would have been very bad. With the indulgence cut from eight years to three or four, and Prince Frederick banning it from his large lands, and various disgruntled towns deciding (quite against the rules) to skim off a share of the offerings for local projects, and the emperor getting his cut of 1,000 gulden a year, and of course the pope getting his 50 percent of everything, and the Fuggers their 3 percent, well, there wasn't enough left for Albrecht to even get close to his extraordinary debt of 30,000 gulden. And that of course was just his debt to Rome: given his extraordinariness, he probably had other debts as well.

Wait, how could Albrecht forget? He had to pay the expenses and salaries of his subcommissioners too, especially those of the very pricey Johann Tetzel, who was so far submitting expenses at the extravagant rate of 300 gulden a month, on top of his extravagant salary of 80 gulden a month. Even the canons in the fine cathedral of St. Mary's in Erfurt got only 133 a year! Of course it was hard to find a good indulgence-preacher nowadays, especially for this one, but Albrecht was beginning to doubt whether Friar Tetzel was worth all that, and he crankily reminded him that this very month the pope "had obligated him to economy."

No wonder Albrecht wasn't at all pleased to get such an insolent letter against indulgences from an audacious friar named Martin Luther.

FIRST RESPONDERS

Albrecht was no theologian, but he could smell anyway the heresy that was wafting off Luther's letter and theses. In the archbishop's mind, the pope had allowed the indulgence, and that alone made it right and the friar wrong.

Still, the always-cautious Albrecht didn't want to take action himself against this Luther and have every last German Augustinian furious with him. Instead, he sent the friar's letter and theses on to the pope, to let him decide what to do. On December 1, 1517, Albrecht also asked the expert advice of theologians at his University of Mainz. But the theologians there weren't any more eager to touch this subject than anyone else was and they didn't respond right away. Albrecht therefore wrote them again on December 10, to remind them just how urgent the matter was. They finally answered a week later, timidly saying that they really shouldn't be commenting on this subject since indulgences were the pope's business, not theirs, and the pope was the person the archbishop should really be asking. The only other thing they would say was that the University of Wittenberg knew very well that holding disputations on indulgences just wasn't done, and that the theses and the treatise from the friar did appear to "limit and restrict the power of the pope."

None of that was of much help, since it told Albrecht nothing he hadn't already known, or done. His councilors at Aschaffenburg suggested something stronger: they wanted Tetzel himself to sternly warn Luther against interfering any further with the St. Peter's indulgence, and they wanted the archbishop to bring legal action against Luther, in the archbishop's court in Magdeburg. But since Albrecht had already sent the matter to the pope, he didn't want to start any lawsuit yet. Instead, he hoped that "His Holiness would grasp the situation so as to meet the error at once" and especially "not lay the responsibility on us." Albrecht just didn't want to be seen cleaning up this mess.

And so the archbishop didn't even bother responding to the friar's audacious letter. While Albrecht waited to hear from Rome about Luther's documents, and Brother Martin waited (in vain) to hear from Albrecht, hardly another word was mentioned about those 95 theses in German lands in almost all of November 1517 and early December too.

But then the responses finally started coming in, starting with two of the bishops Brother Martin had written.

One of them, the bishop of Brandenburg, Brother Martin's own bishop, said that he certainly should not hold a disputation. The theses obviously attacked the authority of the pope and would only get him (and his bishop) into trouble. The other responding bishop, of Merseburg, was a lot more sympathetic, even saying that he would have gotten rid of indulgences in his jurisdiction a long time before if his superior hadn't been Archbishop Albrecht. He wanted to see the theses posted everywhere, just to warn everyone about the troublesome Tetzel.

Brother Martin was no doubt happy about that last response. But he was thoroughly stunned by another and totally unexpected response: the enthusiasm (and sometimes alarm) that came from hundreds of other people who had somehow managed to get their hands and eyes on a copy of the theses. How had it happened, when he'd sent out only a few? The multiplying apparently started with Ulrich von Dinstedt, a canon in the castle church of Wittenberg, who saw a copy (maybe on the church's door?) and liked it so much he sent it to Christoph Scheurl in Nuremberg, who sent around a handwritten copy to his Latin-speaking friends, then apparently arranged for some to be printed and sent even further. Since there were no laws against a printer in one place reprinting something produced by a printer in another place, the theses soon spread to Leipzig and Basel too, and from there went to still other places around the empire.

What in the world was going on? How had a bunch of theses for a university disputation suddenly become this popular? Copies of theses were printed all the time in university towns, but again usually only a dozen or so at a time, paid for by the author. They were never big moneymakers for anybody. But Dr. Martin's friends, and now assorted printers, saw something in these particular theses that made them think they might sell in serious quantities for serious amounts of money. Surely this was partly because plenty of educated people didn't love the new St. Peter's indulgence, and partly because it was still novel to criticize indulgences (and thus the pope) in print, but it was especially because resentment against Rome had grown so big in German lands during the last decade or so that printers were sure the learned would snatch this latest piece of criticism right up. In fact the Latin version of the theses was so quickly popular that a few always-cautious and profit-driven printers decided by early January 1518 to put out a German version too, for the vastly bigger German-reading and German-hearing audience, which almost nobody had ever imagined would ever happen with *any* set of academic theses. Soon, even the famous Albrecht Dürer wrote from Nuremberg to tell Dr. Martin how much he loved the German theses, and to say he was sending along a woodcut in thanks.

The interest in the new theses was "unheard of," the still-stunned Dr. Martin wrote to a friend. And it mostly disturbed him, or at least the German translation did. He'd intended the theses for some Latin-reading friends only, as ordinary laypeople would be sure to get the wrong idea: they didn't know the customs of disputation, such as that theses were "obscure and enigmatic" and not necessarily absolute assertions of truth, or that exaggerating was the bread and butter of disputing. If he'd known the theses were going to spread in German, he said, then he would have written them much differently. To make up for it, he wanted to prepare something more positive about indulgences, in German, "for I have no doubt that people are deceived not by indulgences but by the use made of them." He still didn't want to give even the slightest impression that he was against indulgences altogether. And he especially didn't want to give the slightest impression that he was against the pope himself.

But however alarmed or apologetic he might have been, Brother Martin was going to be blamed for this spread of the new theses anyway. His beloved 99 theses on scholastic theology and justification by faith might have fizzled out, but these 95 on the trite subject of indulgences were now sparking something that was spreading far beyond Wittenberg.

FIRST CONDEMNERS

The very first person to speak publicly against the audacious new theses was, not surprisingly, Johann Tetzel himself, in late November.

C. G. Böhme, *Johann Tetzel*, 1519.

Tetzel wasn't just a preacher of indulgences but the official Inquisitor of Heretical Depravity for Saxony, and thus had in theory the legal authority necessary to pursue some sort of lawsuit against Luther, which the papal bull authorizing the St. Peter's indulgence required against anyone who spoke unfavorably about it. And that legal authority made Tetzel's new boast thoroughly chilling: "in three weeks I will throw the heretic into the fire and he will go to heaven in a bathing cap," the usual headwear of heretics burned at the stake.

Tetzel got right to work gathering the evidence that would help him make good on that boast. On December 12, he persuaded the judges and town council of Halle to testify that he had never said any such thing as that the new indulgence could forgive even violating the Mother of God, as many people and the 95 theses claimed. Two days later, he persuaded 35 clergymen there to swear the same thing. Soon after that, he also decided to organize an academic disputation against Luther's audacious theses—not only to denounce them, but to use what was said at the disputation as evidence in any trial: in January 1518 he even enrolled at Brandenburg's new University of Frankfurt an der Oder, the rival of Saxony's new University of Wittenberg, so that he could join in the disputation himself. Tetzel wouldn't actually invite Luther to the disputation, or dispute directly his 95 theses, but would instead defend 106 countertheses put together by Tetzel's fellow Dominican Konrad Wimpina, of the theology faculty there at Frankfurt. Unlike Tetzel, Wimpina wouldn't have disagreed with Luther on everything. He'd even written a tract called *On the Errors of the Philosophers* that showed how some of Aristotle's ideas contradicted church dogma. But Wimpina was completely against Luther's views of indulgences, and he knew that the founder and patron of the University of Frankfurt an der Oder—the elector Joachim, brother of Archbishop Albrecht—was as well, and Wimpina didn't want to displease him.

Tetzel's disputation took place on January 20, 1518, in front of not only interested students and faculty of Frankfurt but also possibly 300 German Dominicans in town for their annual meeting. It all went quite as expected, with the 106 countertheses wholeheartedly defending the church's current practices around indulgences and painstakingly refuting all of Luther's claims: he was wrong about many things, they declared, but especially about limiting the authority of the pope, and in hinting that maybe there wasn't really a purgatory, and in suggesting that a practice allowed by the pope wasn't by definition good theology. In fact, all Luther was doing was spouting heresies that had already been condemned a hundred times in the past. At the end of the event, Tetzel was completely predictably declared the victor, the 300 Dominicans cheered (if they were there), and even if they weren't there they were soon preaching against the 95 theses anyway, all over the empire, in line with their order's mission as the hounds of the Lord to chase out heresy wherever they found it. Now Luther's name was being spread by his enemies too.

It wasn't long before Tetzel's fellow German Dominicans apparently leveled a formal charge of heresy against Luther, in Rome, to go along with the earlier complaint from Archbishop Albrecht. Luther wasn't just being preached against, in other words, but was suddenly in the sort of legal danger that Friar Tetzel had threatened just a couple of months before, the kind that ended with the offender wearing a bathing cap and tied up to a stake, in front of a big crowd, while butchers all around fried up pork sausages made just for the occasion.

Martin Luther had started a little fire of his own with his theses, but certain people were hoping that he would soon be standing in one himself.

At about the same time as the disputation in Frankfurt, another German theologian—finally not a Dominican—started going after Dr. Martin too. His name was Johann von Eck, professor at the University of Ingolstadt in faraway Bavaria, and a much more serious and tenacious opponent than Friar Tetzel ever was. In fact, Eck would cling onto Luther like a Baltic-sea barnacle for the rest of his life.

Until early 1518, the two professors had at least been friendly, after being introduced to each other through mail by their mutual friend, the always-sociable Christoph Scheurl. Surely two men with so much in common ought to get to know each other, thought Scheurl. Both Dr. Eck and Dr. Martin were trained as scholastic theologians, both liked the new taste for letters and ancient languages, both were experts in scripture, both were in their early 30s, both became doctors young (Eck at 24, Luther 28), both were hard-working but funny and even self-mocking, both liked strong beer (Eck helped make Bavarian beer even stronger), both were skilled debaters, both would write bestsellers, and both were passionate and stubborn. And so Eck sent a letter to Dr. Martin, along with the classic professorly gift of a set of theses from his latest disputation, while Dr. Martin responded happily, and told George Spalatin that Eck was even better than Erasmus!

But they were different in some ways too, and not just on the surface: Eck preached over people's heads ("how few come, and fewer stay, and the fewest get fruit from it," he complained) while Dr. Martin spoke plainly; and Eck was tall while Dr. Martin was very average; but most basically, Eck was always ready to defend current orthodoxy and practice, while Dr. Martin certainly was not.

In late December 1517 or early January 1518, Eck got a copy of the 95 theses from Scheurl, who was sure that Eck would be fascinated. Eck might have gotten a copy as well from his deeply worried chancellor at the University of Ingolstadt, who also happened to be the bishop of Eichstätt, and who badly wanted to know Eck's opinion. Eck certainly was fascinated by the theses, but not in the way Scheurl had expected. Instead Eck said he would give his life to be able to dispute them, would even walk ten miles out of his way to do so. He condemned 18 of the theses to the chancellor, then soon condemned 16 more.

Eck got even more aggressive in February or March 1518, when he decided to have a few copies of his 34 condemnations printed, so he could send them around to learned friends, in the usual professorly way. He titled his work the *Obelisks,* or daggers, after the symbol a scholar drew in the margin of a book to mark a false or heretical statement. And he proceeded to stab one thesis after the next, showing in sometimes very technical detail why they were so wrong. He even stabbed the first for saying that penance had to be a daily way of life: that was clearly wrong, because a person could be saved without going to confession or taking the Eucharist every day. He stabbed the 5th and 20th and 34th for saying that the pope could only forgive punishments in purgatory that he'd imposed himself, and not those imposed by God—as if the punishments of the pope or even of the local priest had nothing to do with God! Eck stabbed the 36th for saying that a person who had truly repented really didn't need an indulgence: wrong too, because even a penitent dying person still had to fulfill his punishment and without an indulgence he'd have to do that in purgatory. He stabbed theses 43 and 45 for saying that a person who bought an indulgence instead of helping a neighbor did wickedly: wrong once again, at least usually, because that was true only when the neighbor was in extreme need. And he stabbed many more that criticized church practices allowed by the pope.

Here was always the real problem with theses against indulgences, for Eck and many others too. Church practice, or custom, or tradition had a sort of theological authority all by itself, because that practice, custom, or tradition was usually at least allowed by the pope and maybe even encouraged by him. The famous collection of church (or canon) law called the *Decretals* and first put together by Gratian in the twelfth century said that very thing: in the church, custom was second only to divine law and the law of reason. Yet Luther's 95 theses were saying that one of the church's most popular customs for bestowing grace was questionable, and thus so was the pope who allowed it.

Oh, all sorts of other forces were already mixed into the arguing going on over the 95 theses too: the old rivalry between Augustinians and Dominicans nudged the members of each order to favor their respective champions; the rivalry between Hohenzollerns of Brandenburg and Wettins of Saxony, which spilled over into rivalry between their two universities, did the same thing; the ever-growing anger of Germans toward the pope made a lot of Germans open to entertaining just about any criticism of him; and all sorts of economic and social troubles inclined many Germans to rally behind whatever or whoever seemed to offer some sort of hope. All these forces, but especially the last two, would help turn what might have been a purely academic tiff over indulgences into something unimaginably bigger.

Still, the theological arguing mattered all by itself too, and Luther's barbs flung toward the pope were themselves a big theological offense. Even his friends saw that. That was why Hieronymus Schurff almost fell out of the wagon when Dr. Martin said he wanted to write against indulgences. And why Prince Frederick, who had the 95 theses read aloud by Spalatin while they rode along, responded by saying nothing about indulgences but instead, "You will see that the pope won't like this."

If Brother Martin's friends were saying that, then his enemies were going to say it even louder, the way Johann Tetzel already had and Johann Eck now was. Eck was sure, he concluded in his *Obelisks*, that Luther's theses proved he was an "insurgent and a despiser of the pope," and a repeater of heresies that had been condemned decades and centuries before—especially the heresy that had come

out of nearby Bohemia 100 years before, which had said that the pope wasn't supreme in the church. Eck was also offended that Luther had put out his theses
among ordinary people (even if Luther hadn't actually done it himself): sure,
indulgences needed some reforming, agreed Eck, but that discussion should
happen among theologians alone, just as Eck was now doing by virtuous example
with his very limited and controlled distribution of the *Obelisks.* In fact, putting
out controversial things among laypeople was another sign of Luther's disrespect
for the pope's authority over the church.

   When Dr. Martin saw the *Obelisks,* he was deeply wounded. And not so much
because they disagreed with him as because he'd supposed that he and Eck were
friends. When Eck heard that, he could only say, "Does Luther really believe that
I could be his friend when he fights against the unity of the church?" Because
that was what was at stake when you criticized the pope, whether you did it directly or not.

It was only fitting that the third person to condemn the 95 theses should be
the Most Reverend Pope Leo X himself, who was finally responding to the
December plea for help from Archbishop Albrecht, even if he wasn't going to
reply directly to Albrecht himself.

   To Leo, the trouble over indulgences sounded at first like just another squabble
between rival religious orders, in this case Dominicans and Augustinians, which
happened all the time. Or at the worst it was probably just another professor
being accused of heresy, which most of the time didn't end up being especially
serious. In fact the pope's court sometimes cleared entirely those who'd been so
accused, like the scholar of Hebrew, Johannes Reuchlin, whose case just a few
years before seemed at first glance something like Martin Luther's. No, the pope
had a lot bigger things to worry about than arguing friars or troublemaking professors, including a rebellion among his cardinals, and capturing Urbino for his
nephew, and making yet another plan for a crusade against the Turks, and trying
mightily to finish the cathedral of St. Peter, and of course hunting.

   But Leo had a look at the 95 theses anyway, and probably even at the 99 theses
against scholastic theology too. Like everybody else, he was alarmed most by the
95 and decided to take immediate action against them, since they were causing
the most immediate problem, as in damaging his new St. Peter's indulgence. And
he decided that the best way to take that action was not through Archbishop
Albrecht, who'd complained to him, but through Luther's superiors in the

Augustinian order. After all, Luther had taken a vow of obedience, which was very useful in situations like this.

And so on February 3, 1518, Pope Leo asked Gabriel della Volta, the general of the Augustinians, to order Friar Martin to silence, for spreading novel teachings among the people. Leo suggested the general send that order in a letter, or even through an agent, straight to Staupitz, head of the German Augustinians, as Leo knew they were about to hold their annual meeting in Heidelberg, in April.

That would take care of it, and the pope could get on with truly urgent matters. Like hunting.

STILL AUDACIOUS

The pope didn't bother to tell Albrecht about this plan, or what Albrecht ought to do himself about Luther, but just left the archbishop wondering.

Hearing nothing from Rome and fuming that the theologians of the University of Mainz wouldn't condemn the 95 theses, Albrecht tried recruiting the theologians of the University of Leipzig to do so. This time Albrecht even *demanded* that the theses be condemned, but this batch of theologians refused too, saying once again that it was a matter for the pope alone to decide, which everyone in the world but Martin Luther seemed to understand and accept.

In fact, as Archbishop Albrecht knew very well, Luther was still working diligently against the St. Peter's indulgence in February and March 1518, despite all the criticisms and warnings that had already come his way to just leave it alone.

4

Not Exactly Ivory Towers

Wittenberg, St. Mary's Church. A Sunday in February or March, 1518, When Stone Buildings are Still Cold.

The wooden pulpit of the city church stood at the front of the nave, to the congregation's left, set flush against a pillar just in front of a wall. A few feet to the pulpit's right was a tall archway that led the congregation's eyes on through to the not-quite-centered and slightly elevated choir, where the high altar stood.

The pulpit was decidedly modest—not all that wide around, set atop a single narrow pillar, its tallest splinter eight feet high. But it was lovely too, with colorful painted panels encircling the preacher from his feet up to his waist and featuring a very German-looking Matthew in his study and an equally German-looking John in his, both fussing with newfangled books instead of the scrolls that the actual evangelists would have fussed with. Nobody was going to worry about little anachronisms like these, though, because the panels were pleasant to look at, especially if you got tired of looking at the preacher.

Luckily the preacher today, Dr. Martin, wasn't all that wide around either; in fact he was a little gaunt and hollow-cheeked from years of fasting and blanketless sleeping and otherwise ascetic living, so he would fit inside the pulpit just fine. Any flashes of light reflecting off the larger-than-usual tonsure on top of his fleshy head would have only added to his austere look as he climbed the few steps up the pulpit.

Dr. Martin wasn't just a professor, and confessor, and occasional preacher around town, see, but since 1514 the official city preacher of Wittenberg. In fact, until his 95 theses were published, this was how most people who knew him,

knew him. He preached at St. Mary's, the city's one
and only parish church, at least weekly and sometimes daily, especially during Lent and Advent, so
that by now he could practically make in his sleep
the six-minute muck-filled walk over from the friary.
It was Staupitz who'd pushed the town council to
appoint this young friar they really didn't know,
partly because Staupitz saw his protégé's potential
as a preacher, partly because it would give Brother
Martin yet another thing to do besides fret over
his soul, and partly because it would be good for
the friary and order. Hundreds of city churches in
the empire had official preachers now, besides their
regular Mass-serving pastors, and Staupitz wanted
Augustinians in as many of those pulpits as possible,
instead of rival Dominicans or Franciscans, because
the reputation—and, yes, the temporal well-being—
of an order perpetually depended on how enthusiastic laypeople were about it. And few things made
them more enthusiastic than a good preacher. That
was one reason Staupitz made all of his friars study
theology, or even get a doctorate—so they'd be more
qualified than other sorts of friars when city pulpits
came open.

Luther's pulpit.

Not every friar who studied theology could preach,
and not all who preached could preach to the liking
of laypeople, but Staupitz assured the town council
that Dr. Martin could do just that, and the council
had gone along. And so far most people in town seemed happy with him, and
thought him well worth the piddly eight gulden or so that he cost each year.

The people of Wittenberg surely appreciated that his clear tenor voice reached
them just fine inside the big (but not gigantic) church, carrying at least the 80 or
so feet experts said a good preaching voice ought to carry. And surely they appreciated too that he avoided excessive spitting and sniffing and throat-clearing, and
didn't overdo his gestures. But surely they appreciated most of all that he worked
hard to reach their hearts and minds.

Dr. Martin got this position because of his learning, but he kept it because he saw quickly that the twin towers of St. Mary's weren't made of ivory any more than his *cloaca* tower was. No, all these towers were made of plain old earth, just like the mist-breathing crowd before him, and if he wanted to move their hearts then he needed a big dose of earthiness too. And so he saved complicated explanations for the *Klueglinge* ("clever little ones") at school, as he fondly called them, and worried here at St. Mary's about reaching "Hansie and Betsy." He used imagery the audience understood, like comparing ungrateful Christians to chickens who eat grain in one place but then lay their eggs in another, or referring to lazy and gluttonous Christians as "knights of the belly" but not of the spirit, or saying that if good works could get you to heaven, then asses would get there for sure because they did so many. He skipped the long-winded introductions so many preachers loved, and got to the point. He didn't speak too fast or too slow, or worry about fancy phrases and techniques, but just said things plainly, and used phrases they could remember, and explained ideas clearly, and all this in German too, which was no easy thing mind you when you'd learned and talked about religion exclusively in Latin for so many years. Oh, he could have trotted out all his learning to impress his listeners, but the most learned preacher of all, Jesus Himself, had never preached that way, said Brother Martin, who reminded himself that there were young girls and women and old men and farmers in the audience, and they were most likely to be moved by God's True Word if they heard it in a way they understood, even more than if they read it, which most of them couldn't do anyway.

And people reported that he often moved his audience indeed. Even one of his students, an always tough crowd, said that Dr. Martin was kind, mild, and good-natured in the pulpit, and had a gift for speech, and whoever heard him once wanted to hear him again, unless the person was made of stone. Others said his voice could be either sharp or gentle as needed, and that he was full of wit, and moved so naturally from one point to the next that you couldn't imagine thinking about the subject any other way than the way he explained it.

Before climbing into the pulpit, he usually organized the points he wanted to make in thesis-like fashion (he couldn't help it), but he would never just read them out or decide in advance exactly how to say things. Instead, he found that he spoke best if he prepared well on a subject but then just let God speak through him or, as he put it: if he just tried to get out of God's way. And on this wintery day his speaking went something, but not exactly, like this:

Liebe Freunde Christi, Dear Friends of Christ. You should know that some modern teachers say that penance has three parts: contrition, confession, and satisfaction. No one can prove this from scripture, but let's set that aside for now and speak their way, to note that an indulgence is supposed to remove the third and least important part of penance, which is satisfaction, and that satisfaction includes praying, fasting, and almsgiving. But if an indulgence removes these good works of satisfaction, then what is there left for us to do?

So, he was preaching on indulgences again, which he'd already preached on a few times over the past year. Some in the crowd knew about his 95 theses, and a few may even have been clutching a copy, since they had spread around Wittenberg too. If they did know the 95, they also soon realized that Dr. Martin wasn't going to recite every one of them today. Instead he would reduce them to around 20, emphasizing the ones he was sure were indisputable and also the ones he thought were most relevant for the audience—meaning especially the ones that didn't say a thing about the pope. He didn't want anyone getting the idea that he was somehow against the pope! Because that just wasn't true: he'd even already promised to say something for laypeople that was more positive about indulgences than his 95 theses had been, and maybe this was it today.

Except that the first point he'd just made hadn't sounded all that positive. Neither did many of the points that came after. No one could prove from scripture, he went on, that God's righteousness and forgiveness demanded anything more from the sinner than heartfelt contrition. Look at how Mary Magdalene was immediately forgiven, and the adulteress, and the lame man, without a pile of penitential deeds! But they shouldn't get him wrong: he wasn't against good deeds. In fact they should all do good deeds to fulfill their punishments, and do their satisfaction, but they should remember that those deeds couldn't possibly pay back God or save them, and that satisfaction maybe wasn't even actually part of true penance. They should also quit trying to escape their punishments, or satisfaction, by buying indulgences, because the suffering that came with punishment turned them to God. It would, in fact, be a thousand times better if no Christian would buy this new indulgence at all, because it was better to do the good deeds that went with punishment than to avoid them. It was also better to give to a poor neighbor than to give for any building, including St. Peter's. They should give to St. Peter's only when no one in the city needed help and all local churches and altars were in good condition, and even then they should give to St. Peter's for its own sake and not for any indulgence in return. Of course it took money to build churches, but thinking that sin would be forgiven if you contributed to one was wrong every time.

The crowd may well have been riveted by these claims, but not even a good preacher kept everybody riveted all the time, including Dr. Martin. Sometimes he barely found the courage to climb into the pulpit, and then only by trusting that God was saying to him, "just go on preaching . . . and let me manage." Because no matter how well he preached, there were always those in the crowd whose minds wandered or who slept or who even snored, especially when he preached on justification, or forgot his usual earthiness and strayed a little too high into the heavens. But when he started telling stories again, he complained, the whole audience would wake up! Still, even when telling stories, it was hard to keep everyone's attention in a church like St. Mary's. It wasn't just big, but had an odd configuration, thanks to assorted not-entirely-harmonious enlargements added over the centuries, whenever there was a bump in population and whenever enough indulgences could be secured to pay for them. Yes, St. Mary's too, like so many other structures in the Christian world, was built on indulgences. And so the choir was off-kilter, and there wasn't a single nave but three, which made it hard for a preacher to find true center in the audience and sometimes for the audience to hear.

Up in the rear balcony, built just the year before to squeeze even more people inside, it was hardest of all to hear, especially when there was any competition going on with the sermon at the 16 side altars where other priests were saying private masses for the dead, and adding even more candlewax and incense to what was already smoking in the church. If you couldn't hear well, or were fidgety or bored, you could look around and admire all the wondrous things you and your forebears had helped build and pay for with your indulgences and offerings—the fine old baptismal font up front, standing on legs representing Peter, Paul, John, and Andrew, and with a cleverly arranged drain running down the middle to wash away your devilish original sin. Or if you strained your neck a little, you could see the four high arches of the naves, with all their monsters trying to storm heaven, and all the corbels on the pillars in the shapes of angels, dragons, monks, old men or women, or lute players. On the walls were fading murals of Bible scenes, and on the tympanum of the biggest portal you could spot the saints who were there for you in times of crisis: Mary, Peter, Paul, Dorothy with her basket, John with his cup, Nicholas with his crosier, and Catherine with her wheel and sword.

Dr. Martin's voice cut through at least most of the distractions as he warned against the easy grace that indulgences promised, completely ignoring the irony that he was saying all this in a church almost entirely built with them. His view of grace was firmly grounded in scripture, he repeated, and not in the speculations of the scholastics. If scholastics and their followers now called him a heretic, then it was because they cared about their donations from indulgences, not the salvation of their flocks. Their bawling didn't bother him, he insisted, because it came from darkened minds that never got a whiff of scripture. And if the audience wondered whether he was saying not to buy indulgences, then they needn't wonder anymore, because yes, that was what he was saying: don't buy them! No, they didn't need to go out and speak against indulgences, but they shouldn't speak *for* them either. The best thing they could do was run away from them. May God give them all right understanding. Amen. Then he climbed back down the little pulpit. He'd spoken for 20 or 25 minutes.

If he'd come to St. Mary's that day to preach the more positive message he'd promised to deliver on indulgences, well, you wouldn't exactly have known it.

A VERY PUBLIC EXPLANATION

By the time of this sermon in February or March 1518, Dr. Martin still hadn't heard a word from Archbishop Albrecht about his 95 theses.

Of course, Dr. Martin hadn't said much about them either since sending them off last October. He could have easily mentioned the theses in a letter he wrote to Prince Frederick in early November, but the letter was devoted instead to reminding the prince that he owed Brother Martin a new cowl, and urging the prince not to levy a new tax on his subjects just this moment, and pleading with the prince to forgive some unnamed offense by Dr. Staupitz. But not a word about the theses. And not a word in any letters or sermons in December or January either.

But by February 1518 Dr. Martin felt practically compelled to talk about his theses again, because of the heat he himself was starting to feel from the little fire the theses had started. The bishop of Brandenburg was telling him to be quiet, Tetzel was holding disputations against him and threatening to start a big fire with Dr. Martin in it, and Dominicans were raging against him in pulpits all over German lands, and now in Rome too. Even his own colleague on the theology faculty, Karlstadt, was saying the theses went too far, while his fellow

German Augustinians were worried that the theses were going to get them all in trouble with the pope—they who belonged to the only order ever founded by a pope! And of course there was the pope's command, sent through General Della Volta via Staupitz, that Dr. Martin be silent, although it wasn't clear at this point whether Staupitz had passed that command along.

Reactions like that were very unnerving for someone who was sure he was teaching nothing but orthodox theology, and who'd never had any other set of theses get so much attention before. "I have provoked all the people," he said in February, "the great, the average, the mediocre, to hate me thoroughly." To make it worse, some of those people were even blaming the 95 theses on Prince Frederick, saying he'd made his professor write them in order to justify keeping the St. Peter's indulgence out of Saxony. Brother Martin knew that the prince, with his legion of spies, would hear that rumor too, and not like it, especially since he didn't really like Dr. Martin's criticisms of indulgences to begin with.

But for all his worry, Brother Martin didn't ease up or back down. Instead he kept condemning indulgences and completely forgot about his plan to say something nice about them. He told George Spalatin on February 15, 1518, that he was sure indulgences were nothing but "a pure deception of souls," which was a lot more than he'd said in the 95 theses themselves, or his sermons. He also decided that with all the people who were now condemning him, he had to defend himself. "I see that the bean must appear among the cabbages," he said. He would have rather stayed in his little corner of the garden, he told Spalatin, and Spalatin and Prince Frederick both would have rather that he stayed there too. But now he felt that he had no choice but to answer, and not only in private but especially in public. He'd always thought of "public" as the cluster of people around his pulpit in St. Mary's, or the pulpit in his classroom, but the attacks on him had spread so far and wide that he had a much bigger public in mind now too. The usual lecture or disputation or even sermon just wasn't enough anymore.

He started out privately, writing back to the bishop of Brandenburg to complain that people were taking his theses to be absolute assertions of truth instead of the "disputable points" they, like all theses, were supposed to be—the truth was, he hadn't been sure at all about plenty of the theses, but was simply trying out ideas, as usual. He also sent the bishop a draft of the "explanations," or formal proofs, that he had prepared to support his 95 theses during the disputation he'd hoped to have about them. Since no disputation seemed likely to happen, he had in mind to print those explanations, and he would like his bishop's permission to do so (the bishop said they were "Catholic enough" but that Dr. Martin shouldn't print them).

Dr. Martin also responded privately to the *Obelisks* of Dr. Eck by sending in return a handwritten copy of a work he'd written, called the *Asterisks,* named after the symbol that scholars drew in the margin of a book to mark something especially good. But if the *Obelisks* were daggers, the *Asterisks* were more like hatchets. It claimed that Eck refused to ground his arguments in Holy Scripture, that his arguments smelled strongly of Aristotle, that he was a loyal dog to his masters the scholastic theologians, and that he was more interested in flattering the pope than in actually defending him. It was also the first time Dr. Martin had shown in writing his talent for name-calling and mimicking, like calling Eck Dr. *Dreck* (scum) and Dr. *Geck* (imbecile), and parroting back the tone and title his rival had thrown at him. But Dr. Martin wasn't any nastier than most other writers, who like him had grown up in the insult-heavy culture of disputation.

Dr. Martin's defense got more public with his sermon in St. Mary's in February or March 1518, of course, but what he really had in mind by "public" now became completely clear only when he published in March, in German, a short little eight-page pamphlet called *A Sermon on Indulgences and Grace,* surely based on his recent actual sermons. Here was something not just for the crowd in St. Mary's or the students in his lecture hall but all sorts of German-speaking people all over German lands.

He wasn't the first preacher (or printer) to think of publishing a sermon like this. Staupitz's predecessor as vicar-general had done the same thing with one of his and saw it go through 20 printings in about 20 years. But it wasn't a common thing to do either. And what surely gave Dr. Martin (or his printer) the idea to try it himself was the seemingly miraculous spread of his 95 theses: here was a subject (indulgences) that people were interested in. Oh, he still wasn't happy that his theses had been translated into German, without his permission, and that just anybody could see them now. But since they *had* spread far and wide, he felt an obligation to clarify what he'd meant about indulgences, especially to laypeople. He already had years of experience at clarifying ideas from the pulpit, so why not try it on paper as well, for an even bigger audience, and in just a few pages instead of the dozens that something scholarly would take? And printers loved eight pages, he learned, because that many pages were actually printed on a single folio of paper and then folded into a small pamphlet, making it almost as simple to set up as a leaflet, and

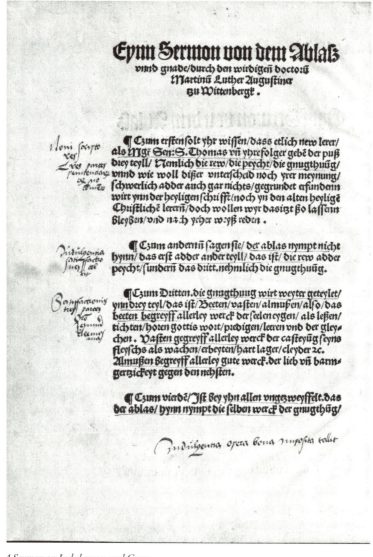

A Sermon on Indulgences and Grace.

almost as cheap to print. And so his printer fit his *Sermon on Indulgences and Grace* into that tidy little format, and folded it, and had it ready to sell to all sorts of laypeople and preachers, who could read it not only on their own but especially aloud to others.

Of course, just because something was short and cheap didn't mean people would buy it. It also had to capture their imaginations, and the *Sermon on Indulgences and Grace* did exactly that, even more than Dr. Martin could have dreamed. It was a huge success, even more than the 95 theses had been and for much the same reasons too—not just because people were dying to learn the true theology of indulgences, but especially because so many Germans weren't happy about the pope's influence in their lands, and this particular St. Peter's indulgence seemed to be all about that.

Even though the printed *Sermon,* just like the spoken ones, didn't have a single unkind German word to say about the pope, ordinary people understood just as well as elite people that criticizing indulgences and especially this indulgence meant you were criticizing the pope too. That might get you in trouble with some Germans, but it could also make you the hero of plenty others, like those thousands who seemed to be snatching up or listening to copies of Dr. Martin's *Sermon.* Of course some people might have bought or heard the *Sermon* for its theology and out of real concern for their salvation, but if that was the only reason then they might have also been expected to lap up as many copies of Brother Martin's earlier *Theologia Deutsch* or *Seven Penitential Psalms,* or even his 99 theses against scholastic theology, since those had even more to say about how you were saved than his sermon on indulgences did. But these others didn't come even close to the 14 printings the *Sermon on Indulgences and Grace* reached before the end of 1518, making it one of the first great bestsellers in German. And there would be 10 more editions in the next few years.

A VERY LEARNED EXPLANATION

The stunning success of the 95 theses and especially of the *Sermon* spurred Dr. Martin on to write even more, for learned and unlearned people alike.

In the first half of 1518 he wrote at what might have seemed to some a demonic pace, but which to him could have only come from God, because he produced some 15 new titles by the end of the year. He wrote on all sorts of subjects too, like a little eight-page tract in German on the Ten Commandments, and a longer Latin one on preparing for the Eucharist, and a long Latin sermon on penance, and a short Latin guide for confessors on consoling troubled consciences, and more. But as long as the controversy over indulgences kept raging, he felt he had to keep writing about that too, even beyond his *Sermon on Indulgences and Grace.*

He had to respond to Johann Tetzel, for example, who'd been so alarmed by the success of the *Sermon* that he'd challenged it with a short German tract of his own, called *Refutation Made by Brother Johan Tetzel . . . Against a Presumptuous Sermon of Twenty Erroneous Articles Concerning Papal Indulgences and Grace.* It countered every single one of Luther's points with proofs from scripture and authoritative sources: yes, maybe Christ could forgive on the spot the sins of contrite people like the adulteress, said Tetzel, but an ordinary priest couldn't and so he had to impose satisfaction too. And if satisfaction wasn't scriptural, then why did David have to do so ridiculously much of it for his sins? And why did Augustine say that God forgave sins "as long as the fitting and necessary satisfaction for the sin is not omitted"? And sure, maybe punishment was good for you sometimes, as Luther said, but there were endless examples in scripture of God relieving punishment too. And none other than Augustine said that the customs of the people were valid, even if scripture said nothing about them, so Luther needed to quit saying that indulgences weren't scriptural, because it didn't really matter whether they were. Saying that scripture was all that mattered, as Luther had, and that you could ignore the doctors of the church, would lead to chaos: then everybody could interpret scripture however they wanted. And finally, insisting that scripture was all that mattered was what the heretics Hus and Wycliffe had said too, but maybe Luther liked that company.

Tetzel's tract was a mere speck compared to the *Sermon on Indulgences and Grace*, as it was printed only once. Obviously it wasn't what most German-speaking pamphlet-buyers wanted to read or hear at the moment. But Brother Martin decided to respond to it anyway, maybe because this was the first time someone had publicly linked him to the dreaded Bohemian Jan Hus (Eck had linked him only in semi-private), the author of the dreaded Bohemian heresy that said the pope was not supreme over the church. And so in June Dr. Martin published in German his short *On the Freedom of the Sermon on Indulgences and Grace*, which refuted every single one of Tetzel's refutations (professors loved refuting refutations), and added a little personal invective too, like saying that Tetzel treated scripture the way a sow treated a feed sack. Still, unlike almost all other refutations of refutations, this one astonished everyone by running to at least nine printings by the end of 1518, showing again that the audience for German works that criticized indulgences was a lot bigger than the audience that supported them.

Friar Tetzel wasn't any more successful in trying to appeal to a learned audience on the subject of indulgences than he'd been to a German-reading one. Surely hoping again to imitate the success of Brother Martin, he had all of the

106 Latin theses from his Frankfurt disputation printed and distributed around the empire by the thousands, but like almost all other sets of theses they didn't exactly fly off the shelves. What's more, students in Wittenberg burned the 800 copies that came to their town (critics blamed Brother Martin for it, despite his denials). Then in April, Friar Tetzel wrote and defended 50 more theses against Luther for his doctorate at the University of Leipzig. This time, Dr. Martin insulted his rival even more by not even bothering to respond.

But what Brother Martin cared about most during that first half of 1518—more than about Tetzel's writings and disputations or even more than his own *Sermon on Indulgences and Grace*—was the tract he'd been working on since at least February, and which he'd already sent in draft to the bishop of Brandenburg: his thorough explanations of his 95 theses. This one went way beyond the very basic proofs he'd offered to general readers and listeners in the *Sermon on Indulgences and Grace,* because it was meant for experts—specifically for the biggest expert of all in the church, Pope Leo X himself.

Called simply the *Explanations,* or *Resolutions,* this book set out to supply proofs "for every single syllable" in the theses. It almost succeeded too, since the *Explanations* ran to 170 pages, way beyond the single page of the original 95 theses. Surely a work this thorough would clear up everything, thought Dr. Martin, and convince especially the pope of his good intentions.

But Brother Martin should have known from years of disputation that changing somebody's mind wasn't ever so simple, especially when he decided in the *Explanations* not just to add his long proofs to the theses but to rewrite some of the theses themselves and make them even sharper than before, which couldn't help but increase suspicions that he really did believe what the theses were saying, and also make him seem even more critical of indulgences, and the pope, than he was already suspected of being.

Thesis 49 in the *Explanations*, for instance, no longer said that indulgences were useful under the right conditions but instead that they were downright dangerous and "directly contrary to the truth." Thesis 50 no longer said that the pope would rather have St. Peter's burn than that his flock be robbed, but instead that "indulgences are the most worthless of all possessions of the church" and "deserve to be cursed." And 56 through 68 no longer just redefined the treasury of merits but denied that saints had any surplus merits to hand out at all.

Dr. Martin was also sharper about grace and faith now, which hadn't even appeared in the original 95: "We are justified by faith, and by faith also we receive peace, not by works, penance, or confessions." And also, "The bestowing of indulgences is a small matter compared to the grace of God." Thesis 7 had said that God wouldn't forgive anyone who didn't humbly confess to His vicar, the priest, but now it said that God's forgiveness came even before you made confession, from God Himself, and the priest was just a servant in the process: "it is not the sacrament that justifies, but faith in the sacrament."

The theses and proofs that criticized the pope went even further than that. "It makes no difference to me what pleases or displeases the pope. He is a human being just like the rest of us. . . . I listen to the pope as pope, that is, when he speaks in and according to the canons, or when he makes a decision in accordance with a general council." But otherwise? No. "The pope is only human and can err in matters of faith and morals," and it was therefore actually dangerous for the church to follow unquestioningly every single thing he said. The *Explanations* pulled back a little from theses 82 through 90, containing the irreverent questions that supposedly came from grumbling laypeople: now they said that the pope himself hadn't actually provoked the questions, but his evil treasurers instead. And they added that it wasn't really Brother Martin's place "to judge the will of the pope, but only to endure," which sounded downright submissive. Yet even that statement ended up being critical, because it concluded, "I cannot deny that everything which the pope does must be endured, but it grieves me that I cannot prove that what he does is best."

The *Explanations* also made the clearest explanation yet of how Brother Martin understood theological proof in general. Which authoritative texts should be trusted? he asked. Anyone who'd been paying attention so far could have guessed what he would say, but now he spelled it out: truth could only be grounded in (1) the Holy Scriptures, or (2) the writings of the church fathers, or (3) reason and experience. In that order. He wouldn't accept anything from Thomas Aquinas (d. 1274) or Bonaventure (d. 1274) or any other of the usual authorities unless it was based on these sources. And he was so sure of this approach and his proofs that he would gladly suffer the death by fire that some of his opponents were already so ardently wishing for him.

In sum, said the *Explanations*, a reformation was needed of the theology and practice of indulgences—again, not a reformation of the whole church, because it had never been perfect and never would be until God Himself came to make it so. "Only God who has created time knows the time for this reformation," but it would certainly be at the end of all time, when Jesus returned, which by the way Dr. Martin expected to happen very soon. Still, one thing the church could do at the moment, besides reform the university curriculum, was to fix this little problem of indulgences. Sure, even some of his friends were calling him a heretic now because of his 95 theses, but his purpose wasn't to oppose the church: "I cherish the church of Christ and its honor."

He finished writing the *Explanations* by the end of May 1518, and once his bishop gave the go-ahead he tried to get it in print as soon as possible, to answer all the latest criticism coming out against him, and all the rumors that the pope might soon take legal action against him. But the plodding Johann Rhau-Grunenberg was living up to his well-earned adjective: he'd printed the simple little *Sermon on Indulgences and Grace* fast enough, but he wouldn't manage to finish the complicated 170-page *Explanations* until August, even though he was working on nothing else at the time. Frustrated, Dr. Martin therefore sent on May 30 a presumably handwritten copy of the *Explanations* to Pope Leo, through Staupitz, with a cover letter to each man.

He recounted to Staupitz the story they both already knew, about how the false preachers of the new St. Peter's indulgence had come along, and how he'd written theses to challenge them, and how his opponents had cursed him, and how they were now pretending that he'd "spoken against the power of the Supreme Pontiff." So he asked Staupitz, please take this "foolish work of mine and forward it" to Rome, "where it may plead my cause against the designs of those who hate me." Then "Christ will see whether what I have said is His or my own."

Brother Martin's letter to the pope then recounted what the pope surely didn't know: all the "evil reports" that had put Brother Martin's name "in very bad odor with you and yours, saying that I have attempted to belittle the power of the keys and of the Supreme Pontiff," and accusing him of "heresy, apostasy, and perfidy" and 600 other nasty names that made his "ears shudder," were simply false. What had really happened was that preachers bearing the papal seal had come into the land and started teaching wild heresies about indulgences that made the church "a scandal and a laughing-stock," and gave people false hope, and plucked the flesh from their bones, until in taverns everywhere the pope was being blamed for the preachers' greed. Brother Martin knew it wasn't his place to "make any decrees" but he had offered a "gentle resistance" by privately informing a few bishops of the problem, and also publishing a few theses which he meant to be discussed among just a few people at his university. But then somebody published them, and they had gone out into "almost the entire land," and "lo, this is the fire with which they complain that all the world is now ablaze!" It was too late to pull all the copies back now, but what he could do was be "the goose that squawks among the swans" and offer these trifling *Explanations* of them, here enclosed, "though I am but an uncouth child." He hoped the Most Blessed Father would see in these *Explanations* "how purely and simply I have sought after and cherished the power of the church and reverence for the [papal] keys." Brother Martin left his fate in the hands of the pope: "make alive, kill, call, recall, approve, as it pleases you: in your voice I will recognize the voice of Christ who rules and speaks in you. If I have deserved death, I will not refuse to die."

It all sounded terribly humble and submissive and made Brother Martin again seem like the most vehement papist he still claimed to be. But it couldn't blunt the new sharpness of the accompanying *Explanations*, or his new confidence either.

THE *CLOACA* AGAIN

Just a few years earlier, Brother Martin had been utterly despondent about his soul, and if he'd still been in a state like that then he might have easily crumbled under the weight of all the attacks now coming his way. But instead he'd managed to meet them head-on and even counterattack and then even send off all sorts of daring statements to the pope, making anyone who knew him surely wonder, where in the world was this new burst of confidence coming from?

Unpleasant as the attacks on him had been, they actually ended up increasing his confidence, because those attacks forced him back into his tower again and again, to study and think and pray some more, to make sure sure he had things right. And he grew confident not just about his views on indulgences but about his whole approach to theology, and most especially about his favorite theological subject of all: justification by grace, through faith.

Yes, that was especially where his confidence was coming from.

Again, maybe his insight into justification came in the single life-changing flash he later said it came in—and in the *cloaca* no less. The *cloaca*? Just as he didn't say exactly when any such moment happened, he also didn't say what he meant by *cloaca*: the actual lowly place on the ground level of the tower, full of human waste? His little study upstairs in the *cloaca* tower? The filthy repository of guilty feelings inside overscrupulous friars like himself? This entire world, with all of its stink and corruption? But whether he was teasing about the actual *cloaca* or just being metaphorical, it was exactly the sort of irony he loved. Why *shouldn't* he get an insight from God in the actual *cloaca*, since it was just a tiny part of the bigger *cloaca* that this world was? If Christ could be born amid the filth of this world, and God's greatest glory came on the lowliest place of all, the cross, then why couldn't a divine insight come in the next lowliest place, the actual *cloaca*? And what better way than with an absurdity like the actual *cloaca* to make the point that God was master of all and above all?

But whatever he meant, it was obvious that Brother Martin was sunnier than ever in the spring of 1518, and that the insights just kept coming. His Hebrew was good enough now to know that the crucial word for God's righteousness in the Old Testament, *sdq* or *sdqh*, was used to mean that God's very righteousness was what led Him to mercifully redeem and sustain His erring people, despite all their erring. Again, God took the initiative, and generously too! He didn't just hand out what people deserved, but more. And mercy and grace might have defined His righteousness most of all.

Another insight emerged too. Theologians had long argued that love was the key to salvation. But like Augustine, Brother Martin couldn't see humans ever getting love (or any other virtue) right on their own, without God's help. And so he became convinced that faith in God's saving grace was the real key to salvation: when people got that, *then* they could truly love. He also seemed by the spring of 1518 to finally drop the idea that humility was a prerequisite to being justified; even in February he was still writing to Spalatin that you become acceptable to God by humbly confessing your sin. But then that idea disappeared.

This new confidence was also evident in how Brother Martin Greekified his name to Eleutherius—the free one. Spalatin had first given him the

Lucas Cranach, *George Spalatin.*

nickname in 1516, but Brother Martin signed his name that way especially from November 1517 on, in 27 different letters to friends. He was now free from the burden of having to prove himself to God.

His confidence was evident as well in the lectures he was still giving on the book of Hebrews all winter and maybe into the spring of 1518. These didn't focus on any humble attitude humans needed in order to win God's favor, or on their lowliness, but instead on how God's righteousness, once God bestowed it, absolutely transformed you. God created "our repentance and righteousness," so you weren't just a miserable sinner anymore, but instead your faith in Christ united you with Him and let you share His attributes, making you a new person, a new Adam. Oh, on your own you were still a miserable sinner, no question about it, but united with Christ you were justified: both sinner and justified at the same time.

It was evident in his new sermon *Two Kinds of Righteousness*, arranged in the same winning formula as the *Sermon on Indulgences and Grace,* with 20 thesis-like points propped up by dozens of scriptural texts. The first kind of righteousness came from outside yourself, from God, through your faith, and was given at baptism and whenever you were truly repentant, and allowed you to say, "Mine are Christ's living, doing and speaking," because just as a bridegroom received everything that belonged to his bride, and she everything that belonged to him, so did you now receive everything of Christ's. The second kind of righteousness came after you were justified, from the new you, now working under Christ's influence, just like in the Song of Solomon 2, "My beloved is mine and I am his." And the result of that union was that you weren't trying to impress God any longer, or worried just about your own salvation but instead you looked out for the welfare of others—you did what Christ and Paul wanted you to do, which was to become the servants of one another, and not to boast in your good deeds or to triumph over your neighbors, but to do good for goodness' sake. Brother Martin had been saying since the *Disputation Against Scholastic Theology* that your works didn't make you righteous, but now he showed that you didn't have to just wallow in the knowledge of being a humble, miserable sinner but could instead be filled with God's righteousness and do much good. Surely it disappointed him that this sermon, when it was finally printed in 1519 in Latin and 1520 in German, sold only about half what the *Sermon on Indulgences and Grace* sold, telling him again that people just weren't as interested in justification as they were in indulgences. In fact, maybe this latest sermon only sold as many copies as it did because of the popularity of his first one, he had to think.

Brother Martin's new confidence was also evident at the annual meeting of the Augustinians, on April 25 and 26 in Heidelberg. This was the meeting at which General Della Volta wanted Staupitz to command Brother Martin to silence, but instead Staupitz decided to give Brother Martin a loud voice there, by having him prepare the theses for the disputation Staupitz had planned, as part of Staupitz's neverending efforts to get his friars to be scholars. Brother Martin was glad to do so, and to make the 300-mile journey to Heidelberg mostly on foot. And what a reception he got there from the local count, who showed him some of the fine local relics at the local castle chapel, but even better was the reception he got from his Augustinian brothers, after all the grumbling they'd done earlier that year about him, because now they absolutely loved the 40 theses Brother Martin had prepared for the disputation, which didn't have a thing to do with indulgences (thank goodness, they sighed), but instead with those most Augustinian of subjects: salvation and grace. These 40 theses didn't so much attack the scholastic theology that supported the usual view of justification but instead offered a more positive vision of what Brother Martin thought should replace it, which he called the *Theology of the Cross*, and which went something like this: we all try to glorify ourselves with good works, and by doing all that lies within us. But God's glory came, to our absolute astonishment, in the most unexpected of places: the humiliation and suffering on the cross. And that is exactly how God's glory comes to us as well—not in our perfect and visible obeying of the law but in our failure and suffering. Suffering shouldn't make us despair: it should make us hope and seek the grace of Christ, the way we seek a physician only when we're sick. It's therefore good to despair of your ability to save yourself and to suffer. So don't be afraid to suffer, and don't think you can save yourself with good works, or that repeating good acts over and over again makes you righteous, like Aristotle said it does, or that salvation can be understood by reason, which says you get what you deserve. Salvation comes only by faith, as in Ephesians 2: we are saved by grace, through faith, not by works . . . lest we boast. The brothers were thrilled and decided not to censure him after all, or enforce any order from the pope to be quiet either. In fact many of the biggest spreaders of Brother Martin's ideas would now be his fellow Augustinians, which surely only made his confidence grow even more. The disputation at Heidelberg was such a triumph that someone even arranged for Brother Martin to ride home to Wittenberg in a cart, so he wouldn't have to walk, as he usually did.

And Brother Martin's new confidence came through last of all in his *Sermon on the Ban,* which he preached soon after returning from Heidelberg, amid rumors that he was about to be banned, or excommunicated, himself. In it he agreed with many other theologians and jurists who said that excommunication was usually used far too arbitrarily, and mostly against people who owed money instead of to help people improve, which was how it ought to be used. But most strikingly of all he concluded that the church's punishment wasn't necessarily equal with God's punishment, and so if the church excommunicated him, well, that didn't mean God necessarily had. Oh, the church still mattered, and he wanted to be part of it, but it wouldn't have the last word about his soul. The spies sent by Johann Tetzel to report on this sermon furiously scribbled all this down.

Not even Tetzel's spies could dampen Brother Martin's spirits though. Because his new theology of justification by faith, and the success of his 95 theses and especially of the *Sermon on Indulgences and Grace,* spurred him on to write even more here in the first half of 1518, and to realize that he wasn't any longer just a friar, preacher, confessor, and professor, but an author too. And now, having sent off so many of his new writings to the printer(s), and his *Explanations* to Rome, he waited to hear the judgment of his readers, especially that of his very most important reader at the moment, Pope Leo X himself.

5
The Lion Stirs

Way South of Wittenberg, on the Road. Early October, 1518, When Rain is in the Air.

At least it wasn't as cold as the last time he'd walked along this never-ending road, in the middle of winter. In fact the weather this time of year could be most pleasant, but if it was raining or snowing, then it wasn't pleasant at all, and according to an old saying it would have even been his fault: "when *Mönche* go walking," it said, "then storms are sure to follow." See, storms came from pressure, and pressure came from rising vapor, and rising vapor came most of all from *Mönche,* because all the beer they drank and all the sweating they did while walking escaped a lot more easily from the tops of their tonsured heads than it did from the heads of the fully haired population.

Dr. Martin knew it was a joke, and he could put up with a little or even a lot of rain, because it wasn't as bad as sleeping all winter without a blanket. But good weather would speed up his exceedingly long journey, so he surely would have been glad for some, because he absolutely had to get where he was going by October 7.

Maybe he'd cut things a little close by leaving so late in September, giving himself only nine or 10 days to get there, which meant he and the brother-friar with him would have to go faster than the usual 20 to 25 miles most walkers managed in a day. But he'd left when he did because he didn't want to neglect his duties in Wittenberg for too long: his long trip to Heidelberg last May had kept him away almost a month! Being gone that long was a bother to him, his students, and his prince, plus all the walking was sure, unfortunately, to take off some of the hard-won bit of plumpness he'd added on his trip to Heidelberg, and that everybody had been complimenting him on lately.

The road, running south through the middle of the empire, was level enough at first out of Wittenberg, with some small hills at most, until the two friars got past Weimar, where the mountains rose to over 2,500 feet. Then it was down again to flatland toward Coburg, then Bamberg, Erlangen, and Nuremberg, after which they would gradually climb another 1,000 feet, and then proceed gradually downhill toward their destination.

If Brother Martin and Brother Leonhard were traveling the way friars were supposed to, then they would have been moving in single file, thinking and pondering, instead of walking next to each other and prattling, the way worldly people did. But Brother Martin was an easy talker, and a little of it could have helped take his mind off the dangers that might await him.

The last time he'd been on this road, in 1511, he was in a cheerful mood despite the winter cold, because his brother-friars in Erfurt had asked him to conduct some business for them in Rome, and he was full of anticipation at the thought of seeing all the holy sites, and saying masses there, and getting his grandfather Heine out of purgatory, and of making yet another general confession, the one that would finally make him feel forgiven. And when he'd finally arrived he'd kissed the ground, and even almost wished that his parents were already dead so he could say masses for their souls, because everybody knew that masses in Rome were worth more than masses anywhere else. The trip didn't go exactly as he'd hoped: the business he'd gone for turned out to be a failure, the city was more dangerous than he thought, the old St. Peter's was crumbling and work on the new St. Peter's had been dormant for so long that the pillars were growing weeds, no one had been learned enough to take his confession, and Roman priests said the Mass so fast that it scandalized him (they said six masses in the time it took him to say one!). But he'd still loved seeing the city's seven famous churches, and the catacombs of the ancient martyrs, and the stairs of Pilate's palace, and all the other holy relics, and just Italy itself, where grapes and figs were bigger than the German sort and pants were better-tailored and the people more attractive and emotional and polite (although they could be a little snobbish toward north Germans). But on this present trip he had nothing like any of that to look forward to. What loomed ahead this time was maybe arrest, or worse.

The summons from the pope had stunned Brother Martin when it arrived on August 7, ordering him to appear in Rome within 60 days to answer for his writings. He, a professor of biblical theology who'd sworn to teach the truth! The *Explanations* he'd sent to the pope obviously hadn't done the trick. Even before the summons arrived, he'd heard rumors that he'd soon be arrested. The Count of Mansfeld, from Brother Martin's hometown, warned him not to set one foot outside Wittenberg, and at a dinner in Dresden where Brother Martin was present an eavesdropping Dominican stood outside the door and jotted down snippets of conversation that might be used against him in a trial. But Brother Martin was still full of resolve and decided to answer the summons anyway. "I fear nothing, as you know," he wrote Frederick's secretary, Spalatin, before leaving Wittenberg. "Even if their flattery and power should succeed in making me hated by all people, enough remains of my heart and conscience to know and confess that all for which I stand and which they attack, I have from God."

Brother Martin would have worried even more that summer if he'd known that a formal legal process had been started against him in Rome at least by June, probably even before his *Explanations* arrived at the papal palace to supposedly clear everything up: the truth was, the *Explanations* never had a chance. Rome saw by then that Vicar-General Staupitz wasn't going to take any real action against his protégé, that Prince Frederick didn't seem inclined to take any either, and that all sorts of other noteworthy people were clamoring for the pope to do something about this upstart friar—especially Archbishop Albrecht, who'd been clamoring since December 1517, and the Dominicans, who'd been clamoring almost as long as that. Soon even Emperor Maximilian would send a letter to Rome practically demanding that Luther be tried for his "most perilous attack on indulgences," lest "not only the people but even the princes be seduced." Maximilian had once been curious about this Luther, but after reading the version of the *Sermon on the Ban* produced by the spies of Friar Tetzel, the emperor was convinced that Luther was a heretic, and no ruler wanted to protect one of those—not only to avoid God's wrath or that of his fellow princes but because, as everybody knew, heresy always led to rebellion.

And so the pope's prosecutor, a Dominican named Marius de Perusco, sought permission from Pope Leo to bring Luther to trial for heresy, for disrespecting the church's authority, and for questioning the power of the papal keys. Leo agreed. Then he had his court theologian and Master of the Sacred Palace, 62-year-old Silvester Mazzolini, called Prierias (also a Dominican), write an expert opinion on the 95 theses, while the papal auditor-general, Girolamo Ghinucci, started the preliminary hearings. By late July there was enough evidence to send Brother Martin the fateful summons.

Along with the summons came a copy of Prierias's expert opinion, called *Dialogue on the Power of the Pope*—not, as you might expect from a work that was supposed to refute a bunch of theses on indulgences, *Dialogue on Indulgences*. Just like Dr. Martin's earlier critics, Prierias took one look at the 95 theses and decided they were really about the pope. And it was so easy to refute the theses, boasted Prierias, that he had his response ready in three days: the pope was supreme over everything in the church, it said, including over councils and scripture, because councils had erred and popes had corrected them, and because someone had to have the final say in interpreting scripture. Not only that, but the pope couldn't err when he made a decision, ergo whoever didn't follow the teachings or customs allowed by the pope could not possibly be anything but a heretic. Luther could have avoided becoming one himself if he hadn't insisted on ignoring the learned scholastic doctors of the church, especially (the Dominican) Thomas Aquinas, who had thankfully done so much to define the office of the pope.

Brother Martin was stunned by the tract almost as much as by the summons, first because it said on the cover "Master of the Sacred Palace," which made him think, "Good God, has it come to this that the matter will go before the pope?" And second because it was so sloppy, which even Prierias's colleagues at the papal court soon grumbled about. In fact, Dr. Martin thought the tract so bad that he didn't even bother to refute it at first, but just had it reprinted and let it condemn itself. Still, he couldn't resist putting out something of his own, on August 31, once his plodding Rhau-Grunenberg finally had the press cleared of other things. Brother Martin's response, written in two days to outdo Prierias, focused on condemning indulgences instead of questioning papal authority, which was dangerous to do, but it came close a few times anyway, like when quoting Augustine to say that only the Bible—not the pope—could be called infallible, and when quoting canon law to say that nothing could be taught in the church except scripture, and when quoting also the famous old jurist Panormitanus (d. 1445) to say that not only councils had erred but popes too. And Dr. Martin reminded Prierias that since the church hadn't yet defined indulgences, it was perfectly permissible and even laudable for a professor of theology to dispute them, since it was his job to settled unsettled things. Besides, his criticism had obviously not been of the pope but of the greed for money in Rome.

Naturally Brother Martin's new tract didn't make his summons go away any more than his *Explanations* had. Rome still thought he was wrong, not only (partly) on indulgences and (entirely) on the pope but in his whole approach to theology, especially his insistence that the Bible was supreme. That just baffled his critics. Of *course* the Bible was supreme, they said: the question was, who had the supreme right to interpret it? Scripture didn't just interpret itself, as Luther seemed to think. The pope had always had that right, but popes had also long valued the insights of acceptable theologians. Why would Luther want to ignore them, since the Bible was so hard to interpret? Wouldn't it be better to have more reliable interpreters instead of fewer, especially since so many of the old reliables had been declared saintly? Not only that, but insisting that the Bible was above the pope, the way Luther constantly did, could get people thinking that everybody was free to interpret the Bible as they pleased, and that the interpretations of saintly doctors and even of the pope himself weren't to be trusted! "All Christendom will come into spiritual danger when each individual believes what pleases him most," Tetzel had already warned.

If Brother Martin's critics were offended by his criticism of the pope and baffled by his approach to theology, they were downright alarmed by his willingness to argue about sensitive matters in print, in the vernacular. Yes, as a preacher he was free to preach in public, but his sermons should be based on settled theology and not on controversies involving the pope, and for God's sake they shouldn't be printed! That was why the short and German *Sermon on Indulgences and Grace* was even more troubling to Rome than the Latin 95 theses had been. Once Brother Martin willingly printed that sermon and took the disputing outside the usual academic and churchly forum, he'd crossed the proverbial Rubicon and in his critics' eyes lost his usual professorial right to dispute. "Rustics" didn't have enough sense to make sense of such arguing, said critics, and appealing to them upset the divine order of things. And claiming that indulgences were an unsettled subject when the church had long allowed them could make people unaccustomed to such discussions think the church (and pope) was wrong. Plus saying that satisfaction wasn't scriptural would surely make people do fewer good works.

All that explained how Brother Martin came to be holding in his hands on that dreaded August 7 a summons from Rome that made him feel like he was an enemy of the church, and how he and Brother Leonhard came to find themselves on the road south again.

THE PRINCE'S DIET

At least Brother Martin wouldn't have to go all the way to Rome this time, all the way through the Alps in winter, as he had in 1511. And he could thank Prince Frederick for that.

A day after receiving the summons, an anxious Brother Martin had written George Spalatin to ask for Prince Frederick's help. Of course Brother Martin didn't want Frederick's reputation to suffer for protecting him, and in fact he would gladly accept punishment and recant everything if somebody could show him where he'd been wrong. But he wasn't a heretic, he insisted, and "shall never be." That was why he needed help fast: would the prince possibly be willing to arrange for a hearing on German soil? It wasn't just the distance, or the rigors of a trip to Rome that worried Brother Martin. No, it was more the absolute certainty that any such trip there was bound to end with his execution.

Luckily for Brother Martin, Prince Frederick was not only willing to try but in a better position than ever to arrange such a thing. For most of the summer, he and his courtiers had been in Augsburg, at the imperial Diet, or assembly (from the medieval Latin *dieta*, which referred to a daily diet of food as well as the daily meetings of the assembly). The Diet met every few years or so, in one of the great imperial cities, to banquet and joust and manage the empire's business, which usually involved the emperor asking for more taxes and power and the three "estates," or colleges, doing their best to resist him. These estates included (1) the seven electors, (2) over 300 bishops and counts and lords, and (3) representatives from more than 60 free imperial cities. Even though an old joke said that every single Diet was the same, each one had its twists, and here in Augsburg there were two: Emperor Maximilian (and the pope) wanted a new tax to pay for a war against the Turks; and the emperor (but not the pope) wanted his grandson Charles elected as his successor.

Maximilian was the most powerful emperor in 250 years, but he was still less powerful than most

Lucas van Leyden, *Maximilian I.*

kings around Europe, and he couldn't just decree as he pleased: he had to convince the three estates to go along with his plans. And both Maximilian and the pope knew that the chances of convincing the estates improved exceedingly if they could get Prince Frederick of Saxony on their side: he wasn't just the senior and most influential voice in the college of electors but probably the entire Diet. Frederick understood his position perfectly, and knew he could use it to get things he wanted from both Maximilian and the pope—like a favorable hearing for his professor.

And so when both emperor and pope came looking to court his support for the Turkish tax, Frederick played even harder than usual to get. Maximilian waved Frederick heartily over when he first saw him at Augsburg and pulled him in close, in front of everybody who was anybody, exclaiming how glad he was to see his old bosom cousin and childhood friend and jousting partner: even though they'd had a falling out years before, surely Frederick could be counted on for something as important as the Turkish tax! The pope, uneasy at how close the Turks were coming to Italy, wanted the tax as much as Maximilian did, and so he came courting Frederick's influence too, mostly by sending a special agent to Augsburg, Cardinal Tomasso de Vio (called Cajetan), with a wagonload of gifts: Albrecht of Mainz was to be made a cardinal (for free this time), Maximilian was to get the crusading helmet and dagger that proclaimed him a Protector of the Faith, and Frederick was to get two more indulgences for his castle church in Wittenberg. But Frederick wasn't impressed. He knew that Maximilian, for all his dash, was remarkably bad at war, and had wasted plenty of Diet-granted taxes in the past. And he wasn't about to do the pope's bidding either, even for more indulgences, until the pope did something to address the many grievances the estates had against Rome, the *Gravamina*. And so when Cajetan made his big Turkish-tax speech to the estates on August 5, Frederick led the resistance, saying that they wouldn't consider any such tax without some action on their *Gravamina*, especially those that complained about all the German money which in complete violation of nature kept flying across the Alps. Like the recent "false, blasphemous indulgence" for St. Peter's.

Frederick stood firm as well on the second great matter at the Diet: the election of Maximilian's successor. Most kings in Europe were born that way, but the German king, named "king of the Romans" because of the old alliance with the pope, had for centuries been elected, by seven princely electors. Members of the Habsburg family had won the election since 1440, but it was no sure thing they would win again, as no family since the first, Charlemagne's, had won more than four times in a row. To guarantee another win, Maximilian wanted his sole heir and grandson, Charles, to be elected even before Maximilian died, which he would gladly tell you was about to happen any day. Maximilian had had 15 health crisis in the last little while, and he'd traveled with a coffin since 1512, when one of his 23 physicians told him that the next eclipse of the sun would mean his end was near. On June 8, 1518, just before the Diet began at Augsburg, an eclipse occurred, and sure enough Maximilian started to fade. He had to hurry. By August 27, he'd persuaded five of the seven electors to vote for Charles, through offering the usual monumental (and forbidden) bribes. But the most important elector of all, Maximilian's old bosom cousin, Prince Frederick, would, as usual, not commit just yet. Yes, he was just one vote, but he had enough influence to possibly change the minds of the five electors who'd committed, and also to keep postponing the election until after Maximilian died, which would start the whole process over again.

The pope and Cajetan were highly interested to learn about Frederick's in-decision, because much as they wanted Maximilian to get the Turkish tax they didn't want him to get this election for his grandson at all. It wasn't anything against Charles personally, mind you—no, Pope Leo was just against the idea of such a powerful emperor as he would be. Thanks to a slew of fortunate marriages and hugely unfortunate deaths, the now 18-year-old Charles was the sole heir of not just Maximilian Habsburg but three other great noble families too, and had already inherited Spain, the New World, Sicily, Naples, the Netherlands, and Franche-Comté; when Maximilian died, Charles would inherit Austria too. If he were elected emperor besides, well the pope might fall off his favorite white horse in shock, because then Charles would rule over more territory than any-body had since Charlemagne, and he would become the pope's neighbor in Italy too. "Do you know how many miles it is from here to the border of Naples!" Leo yelled at his courtiers. "Forty! Therefore Charles must never become King of the Romans!" Leo wanted Francis I, king of France and Charles's main rival, to be elected instead. Maybe Prince Frederick, thought the pope, could be persuaded to want Francis too. The new indulgences hadn't moved Frederick, but maybe something else would—like something to do with Martin Luther.

Both the pope and Cajetan had written harshly to Frederick for months for refusing to arrest "that son of iniquity" Martin Luther, reminding Frederick (with a little exaggeration) just how loyal his princely family had always been to the pope and that he should therefore follow that example. But now, with the specter of Charles looming, Cajetan and the pope softened their approach. The cardinal asked Frederick whether he was interested in getting, in addition to the two nice indulgences already gotten, the Golden Rose of Virtue, consecrated and fragrant, which the pope handed out every year or so to a prince or church or town who'd shown extraordinary service to the pope. Oh yes, Frederick was interested indeed, even if he pretended not to be. But Frederick also saw, in the pope's eagerness to please him, how he could help Dr. Martin.

Naturally Frederick didn't want it said that he protected heretics, but he also didn't want outsiders interfering with a subject whose heresy wasn't obvious enough to justify sending him to Rome in chains. And so Frederick proposed a compromise: let Dr. Martin at least be heard by a committee of German bishops, on German soil, so he wouldn't have to go all the way to Rome. And let it be just a hearing too, instead of a real trial. And let the committee include Frederick's friend, the elector of Trier, who was also an archbishop, and who happened to be the other elector, besides Frederick, who was wavering about Charles.

The cardinal was suddenly all ears. Not a bad idea, he replied. But he suggested another compromise: the friar could indeed be heard on German soil, right here in Augsburg in fact, but the cardinal himself wanted to do the hearing. Could Frederick accept that? Since Cajetan struck Frederick as more open-minded and learned than he'd expected, and since the cardinal promised to make it a "fair and fatherly" hearing and to not arrest Luther no matter the outcome, Frederick agreed. Maximilian, who also wanted to keep Frederick happy, went along with the plan too, and even promised to protect the friar during his journey south, even though Maximilian had recently sent a nasty letter about Luther to the pope.

Cajetan wrote the pope for approval, and the pope wrote back on August 23 to agree that Luther could go to Augsburg instead of Rome, but only on certain conditions—conditions that Cajetan didn't bother to tell Frederick or Luther, and that weren't nearly as favorable as what Cajetan had promised Frederick. Leo was already convinced that Luther was a "notorious" heretic instead of just a suspected one, and notorious heretics didn't get trials. And so the pope told Cajetan that he could receive Luther in Augsburg, but not discuss or dispute anything with him, as if they were in some university classroom, or even as if this were some sort of mere hearing: instead the cardinal should just give Luther a chance to recant. If he did recant, then Cajetan could absolve him. But if he didn't, then Cajetan was to have Luther arrested right away, and was free to pronounce a formal judicial judgment against him. If Luther didn't bother to come to Augsburg at all, then Cajetan should automatically declare that not only he but also his protectors—like Frederick—were all heretical, and excommunicated, and banned.

Again, Frederick didn't know about these new conditions from Rome. And so he had Spalatin write Dr. Martin with the good news that his prince had managed to arrange a nice, fatherly hearing for him in Augsburg so that Dr. Martin wouldn't have to go to Rome. That news probably got to Wittenberg around September 11. Since the summons had arrived on August 7 and gave 60 days to appear, Dr. Martin still had until October 7 to get there.

The Diet would be over by then, and Prince Frederick would already be gone, having bade his last farewell ever to his once-dashing cousin Maximilian, now so old and ailing that his reddish-blond hair was stringy gray, and that he dragged one of his legs when he walked. But even with Frederick gone, Brother Martin would at least be heard on friendly ground.

IN THE PALACE OF THE FUGGERS

There hadn't been any serious incidents along the way, thank goodness.

In Weimar the local Franciscans, usually Brother Martin's rivals, had kindly hosted him and begged him not to continue his journey, because he would surely be burned in Augsburg. Frederick and his courtiers were in Weimar then too, on their way back from the Diet, and they asked Brother Martin to preach in the local castle church. They also let him know that Frederick had left two councilors behind in Augsburg for protection and support. Then in Nuremberg,

Augsburg. Holzschnitt aus Hartmann Schesdels, *Weltchronik.*

Brother Martin's old friend and fellow Augustinian, Wenceslas Link, joined the traveling party and gave (or loaned) Brother Martin a new cowl to wear instead of the usual shabby one he had on.

Late in the afternoon of October 7, the very day he was due, Brother Martin was only three miles from Augsburg but so exhausted and sick he couldn't walk another step. Luckily a man with a cart came along and agreed to take him the last little way, and he made it through the gate in time. Surely part of his sickness was due to the difficulty of the trip, but much was due as well to his worry about the upcoming meeting, and to the question the Devil was always tormenting him with: "Are you alone wise and all the ages in error?" How could he be so sure that he was right about indulgences?

Although too unwell to go see the cardinal right away, Brother Martin did send a messenger to say he'd arrived. Then he went to rest in the Carmelite convent where he was to stay, which Prince Frederick had also arranged for him. Brother Martin didn't see the cardinal the next day either, because some friends of Spalatin in Augsburg were horrified that Brother Martin didn't have an imperial safe conduct and insisted that he get one before going to any meeting with the cardinal, to protect him from arrest. That would take a few days, and it also offended Cajetan, who thought his promise to Frederick not to arrest Brother Martin should have been enough.

During those few days of waiting, Brother Martin had a strange visit from an Italian ambassador named Urban de Serralonga, who had been at the Diet and knew both Frederick and Cajetan. His advice was simple: the friar should renounce his wicked claims and come back to the church. But he hadn't left the church, replied Brother Martin, and wasn't he allowed to defend his position, or at least be shown where he was wrong? "No," said Serralonga: Did the friar think this was some game? And did he really think Prince Frederick would protect him if he didn't recant? And where would he go if Frederick didn't protect him? "Under heaven," replied Brother Martin. Serralonga scoffed and left. The visit was Brother Martin's first clue that maybe the cardinal didn't have an open and friendly hearing in mind after all.

On October 12, five days after he'd arrived, and with the safe conduct in order, Brother Martin finally made his way to the palace of the Fuggers, the pope's bankers, where Cajetan was not so coincidentally staying. The palace was actually a series of adjoining houses that had been linked together with a common façade and fresco, a style that Jakob Fugger had seen in Italy and that also showed off just how wealthy he was, because houses were taxed on how much of them fronted the street. The cardinal's rooms were somewhere deep inside this complex, and no doubt looked into one of the palace's four inner courtyards with their arcades and mosaics and Tuscan-marble water basins.

Brother Martin entered the palace, apparently alone, and was led to the cardinal's room. His friends had already told him the protocol. He was to prostrate himself and wait for the cardinal to tell him three times to stand up. Then he should rise only to his knees before finally standing on his feet. He did so, which seemed to please the cardinal. And at first Brother Martin seemed pleased too, as the cardinal didn't seem to be one of those "extremely harsh bloodhounds who track down monks." Tomasso Cajetan was, in fact, a learned doctor of theology, just like Martin Luther. Not surprisingly, Cajetan was also a Dominican, in fact the most important Dominican on earth at the moment: the head of the order itself. He was therefore in all ways perfectly capable of having the sort of detailed discussion about indulgences that Dr. Martin was itching to have with somebody from Rome. And the two men would have even agreed on a few things about them, such as that they weren't necessarily of divine origin. But the problem, of course, was that Dr. Cajetan wasn't supposed to get into any sort of argument or discussion with Dr. Martin, and Dr. Martin didn't know it. And that little misunderstanding got the meeting going in the wrong direction fast.

The way Brother Martin remembered it, after the happy politenesses, the cardinal came right to the point: "I do not wish to argue with you," he said, "but to settle the matter peacefully and in a fatherly fashion," just like he'd told Prince Frederick. And as far as he was concerned the way to do that was for Brother Martin just to submit and do exactly what the pope wanted: come to his senses and retract his errors, promise not to repeat them, and don't trouble the church again.

Brother Martin was stunned. He could have retracted and promised and not troubled right in Wittenberg, instead of coming all this way down to Augsburg. In fact he could have refused to come at all on any number of legitimate pretexts, such as that he'd already explained his views on indulgences in his *Explanations*. No, he'd come all this way because he assumed the pope and cardinal wanted actually to hear still a little more about his theses. And so instead of submitting, he now asked, as humbly as possible, to at least be instructed, to know "in what matters have I been wrong, since I am not conscious of any errors?"

Maybe the cardinal was as stunned by this answer as Brother Martin had been at the cardinal's. Was he serious? He didn't know how he'd been wrong? Even though Cajetan had been ordered not to start arguing with the friar, the theologian in the cardinal couldn't resist: disputation was his language too. Plus he didn't want to seem like one of the harsh bloodhounds people like Luther feared, and he had after all promised Prince Frederick a fair hearing. So, against the pope's orders, he decided to argue a little. Specifically about the 95 theses.

Okay, said the cardinal, he would name two errors: thesis 58, which hinted that the treasury of merits wasn't the excess merits of Christ and the saints, and thesis 7, which said that the Eucharist was useless for those who took it without faith, while those who took it with faith could be sure of their absolution. These had to be retracted, said the cardinal: 58 contradicted the papal bull *Unigenitus* that established the treasury of merits, and thesis 7 contradicted the church's teachings that you could never be sure about grace, and that the sacrament worked because of the authority of the priest and not the state of the person taking it.

Were those two theses really more offensive to the cardinal than 82 to 90, with all their scurrilous criticisms of the pope? Very possibly Cajetan picked theses 7 and 58 because they seemed the easiest to pin down as heresies. To convict somebody of heresy, you had to show that he had contradicted a settled doctrine, and of all the theses numbers 7 and 58 seemed most obviously to do just that.

The men in the cardinal's entourage were sure too, and, according to Brother Martin, they smiled and giggled, because they thought Cajetan had him now. Surely Brother Martin didn't know about *Unigenitus,* from 1343, since it was part of the collection of bulls known as *Extravagantes* (or "wandering outside"): these bulls weren't always included in collections of canon law, or *Decretals,* but they were still binding, even if you didn't know them. And *Unigenitus* proved that the church had indeed settled the doctrine of the treasury of merits, and indulgences, contrary to what Brother Martin claimed. And so in denying that doctrine, he'd stated a heresy.

But Brother Martin did know *Unigenitus,* and the other *Extravagantes* similar to it, especially *Romani Pontificis* of 1477, and neither bull was the least bit conclusive, he replied, because they "distort the Holy Scriptures" so wildly that they contradicted their meaning. Thus, "nothing is proven" or settled in these bulls, since they depended solely on some claims by Thomas Aquinas, and that wasn't enough, he told the cardinal. With respect. And so he couldn't be accused of contradicting anything.

This wound the cardinal right up. Aquinas wasn't just another Dominican but one of the greatest of all, and Cajetan wasn't just a theologian but a specialist on Aquinas himself: he would not have him, or the pope, ridiculed like this! Once again the argument was turning right toward the throne of Peter and away from indulgences. The cardinal insisted that Aquinas had it absolutely right about the treasury: since the pope was above any other authority, including scripture and councils, he certainly could declare such a thing. Brother Martin responded that if the pope was above a council, then why had the exceedingly orthodox theologians of the University of Paris just this past March appealed a recent decision by the pope to a council? And the university should have been punished, shot back the cardinal! Now words were fired back and forth about grace, especially regarding thesis 7, a thesis Brother Martin had always thought so harmless that surely no one would ever object to it.

The two men were disputing a lot more than Pope Leo or Cajetan himself had intended, and seeing it was going nowhere, a flustered Brother Martin asked for time to think, then stormed into the nearest Fugger courtyard with the cardinal's master of ceremonies running after him. He kept right on going, all the way to his lodgings.

Brother Martin came back the next day more subdued, no doubt because Staupitz was now present at the hearing too. He'd made the 130-mile trip from Salzburg as fast as he could when he'd heard about the hearing. A notary, four imperial councilors, and a couple of witnesses were also there this time. Surely at the advice of Staupitz, Brother Martin had prepared a written statement, to help prevent any more outbursts like the one he'd had the day before.

The cardinal permitted him to read it. The statement didn't continue the arguing the two men had done over theses 58 and 7, but just affirmed Brother Martin's absolute loyalty to the church: he obviously felt it was in some doubt and wanted to make it clear before they went any further. "Above all I, Brother Martin Luther, Augustinian, declare publicly that I cherish and follow the holy Roman Church in all my words and actions—present, past and future. If I have said or shall say anything contrary to this, I wish it to be considered as not having been said." But he also couldn't simply recant and go along with the pope's demands, he continued, without the sort of proof he trusted, which did *not* mean Thomas Aquinas or any other scholastic theologian standing all on their own without any support from scripture or the church fathers. "I declare publicly that I am not conscious of having said anything contrary to Holy Scripture, the church fathers, or papal decretals or their correct meaning," with the key being those last two words. Still, if he saw proof he trusted, then he would submit to it, because of course he was as fallible as anyone. He would also like to elaborate now for the cardinal his views on theses 7 and 58 (and more), and have them judged by the University of Basel, or Freiburg, or Leuven. And if the cardinal didn't want to allow that, then he would still like to set his views down in writing and present them.

Luther before Cardinal Cajetan.

The cardinal turned the request for other judges right down, but before he could even turn down the request to elaborate in writing, Staupitz interrupted to asked the cardinal to please let Brother Martin do just that. This irritated the cardinal, who started complaining again about thesis 58, but finally he agreed to let Brother Martin present something the next day.

That afternoon and probably evening Brother Martin worked feverishly on his piece, and the next morning he walked to the Fugger palace to present it. This time Prince Frederick's councilors were present too, and before things even got started they reminded the cardinal of their prince's wish for a fair and gentle hearing, as promised. The cardinal may have noted that reminder, or not, before he started reading Brother Martin's writing aloud, or had it read.

It was a highly elaborate answer for an interview that wasn't supposed to include any such thing, with numerous points and subpoints so typical of disputations. Brother Martin explained that even though he knew about *Unigenitus* and the other relevant *Extravagantes,* he'd refrained from mentioning them specifically in his theses or his *Explanations* because he wanted "to save the honor of the pope" by not opposing them in writing. But he'd had to say *something* about the treasury of merits the bulls treated, because they were contrary to scripture: scripture taught that every single human was deficient, even the saints, and so it wasn't possible for anybody to have any excess merits to pass around. He simply couldn't ignore so many important clear scriptural proofs "on account of a single ambiguous and obscure decretal of a pope who is a mere human being."

Ah, so he was going to go there now after all—to the matter of the pope's authority and fallibility that he'd avoided in his earlier writings. Yes, he repeated, the pope could and did err, and yes a council was superior to a pope, as Galatians 2 made clear, recounting how Paul the mere apostle reprimanded Peter the chief apostle, and also how Peter's teaching wasn't approved until James the bishop of Jerusalem and the entire church agreed to it. And anybody who bothered to look could see for himself how many papal decrees had been corrected by later ones. Still, this didn't mean Brother Martin was necessarily against the pope: he now tried mightily to show that even though he disagreed with the pope about the treasury of merits he still acknowledged the pope's authority in general. But he soon gave up and ended his response by coming back to indulgences themselves: once again, they were useful only for the truly penitent, but the truly penitent didn't really need them.

As for thesis 7, surely the cardinal knew Augustine's famous saying, "When the Word is coupled with the element, it becomes a sacrament, not because it becomes a sacrament, but because it is believed." Yes, faith mattered most in a sacrament, not the power of the priest, as anyone who studied scripture would see. Then in three points and 11 subpoints laden with verses from Romans, John, Matthew, Mark, Genesis, Isaiah, Hebrews, and even James, Brother Martin dared to question priestly authority, and more specifically papal authority, with a startling overhaul of the passages in Matthew 16 that gave Peter and his successors the power to bind and to loose, both on earth and in heaven, and that had for so long been taken as the basis of the papal keys. Brother Martin now said that the usual interpretation was all wrong: the keys were faith, not papal authority, a conclusion that came right out of his new ideas on justification. "Show me how I may understand this doctrine differently, instead of compelling me to revoke those things which I must believe according to the testimony of my conscience," he continued. "As long as these scripture passages stand," he couldn't believe them any other way, "for I know that one must obey God rather than men" and he was reading them as God intended, he was sure.

In conclusion, Brother Martin pleaded for the cardinal to intercede "with our most holy lord, Leo X, in my behalf so that he will not proceed against me with such stern rigor that he cast my soul into darkness." Brother Martin sought only the light of truth in his writings, and he was prepared give up everything and revoke everything, if he could be shown a better way to understand. But if he couldn't, then he would reject even a papal bull that went against scripture—a recantation for sure, but not quite the one the cardinal had hoped for.

When the reading of Dr. Martin's response was finished, the cardinal said it was worthless—"mere words." He agreed to send it on to Rome, but he was sure it wouldn't do any good: Luther had accused the pope of wrongly using scripture, he hadn't disproven *Unigenitus*, and he'd based his certainty of justification on Bible passages that the church had interpreted otherwise for centuries. Soon the cardinal was yelling again and demanding again that Luther recant, and threatening him and his friends and supporters with the ban (excommunication) and the interdict (no sacraments), and invoking Aquinas again to say that no one should wish to know more than the church did. Brother Martin tried interrupting him more than once, but the cardinal shouted him down.

Finally Brother Martin was able to yell out a suggested compromise: "If it can be shown that the bull *Unigenitus* teaches that the merits of Christ are the treasure of indulgences, I will recant." The cardinal quickly asked for a copy of canon law and started reading aloud until he came triumphantly to the part that said Christ acquired the treasury by his suffering! Brother Martin interrupted the "Most Reverend Father," and asked him carefully to consider the phrase "Christ has acquired." If Christ "acquired the treasury by his merits, then the merits are not the treasury; rather, the treasury is that which the merits earned, namely, the keys of the church." Faith. Therefore, his thesis, that the merits of Christ did not equal the treasure of indulgences, was correct. He puckishly added something about Germans not being as ignorant of languages as the cardinal might have supposed, making Staupitz wince, and Cajetan blow up: the cardinal had had enough, and was done with being fatherly. Mad at himself for being led into the very sort of disputing he didn't want to be led into, and for losing his usual cool, he yelled, "Go, and don't come back to me unless you want to recant." At least he kept his promise to Frederick not to arrest Brother Martin, even if it meant disregarding his orders from the pope.

Of course, this was Brother Martin's version of events. Who knew how Cardinal Cajetan would have described the hearing, if he'd bothered to write an equally long account? Maybe he would have told of a rebellious friar, and a long-suffering cardinal listening patiently to him, trying to save his soul.

OLD NAG

The unpleasant interview ended at lunchtime. Brother Martin went to eat with Staupitz and Frederick's two councilors, who all said that, except for the little crack about Germans, Brother Martin had argued very well.

After lunch, Cajetan sent word to Staupitz and Wenceslas Link that he wanted to speak with them, alone. When the two Augustinians arrived, they saw that Urban de Serralonga was there too, and for two hours the two Italians tried to convince the two Germans that they needed to get their brother to recant. Staupitz said that he'd tried more than once, but without luck, since Brother Martin knew scripture better than he did and was smarter: no, it was up to the cardinal to convince him. The four men also discussed what a possible recantation might look like. The cardinal wanted Luther especially to take back his view of Matthew 16, on the papal keys: make him recant that, he bargained, and everything else (the treasury of merits, certainty in the sacraments, and so on) could be settled in the usual way—through a lot of academic disputation. But by the end there was no agreement on any plan.

Within a day or two, a rumor spread around Augsburg that Cajetan was trying to get civic leaders to arrest Luther, and if they wouldn't do it then Augustinian leaders would have to. This alarmed Staupitz, since he was the biggest Augustinian leader in town: he hustled over to Brother Martin's rooms, took him aside in private, and absolved him of the vow of obedience he'd taken when he'd become a friar 11 years before. That way he wouldn't have to obey if Staupitz were forced to come arrest him. Staupitz also gave Brother Martin some money to flee somewhere else, like Paris, home to a famous Augustinian friary. And to protect himself against having to make any such arrest, Staupitz got out of Augsburg as fast as he could, with Link alongside him.

Brother Martin didn't leave town right away, though, just in case Cardinal Cajetan wanted to summon him again. But he frustratingly heard nothing, and finally took the advice of Frederick's two councilors still in town and went to see a notary so he could draw up an official appeal to the pope. Cajetan hadn't issued any formal verdict after the hearing, as the pope had said he could, but obviously Brother Martin was expecting the worst. He also sent an apology to the cardinal, for speaking abruptly and disrespectfully. He should have been more modest, he said, and he promised that he wouldn't say another word about indulgences (a subject he didn't like anyway) as long as his enemies didn't either. But he couldn't recant unless he was proven wrong. With real proof.

When the cardinal still didn't call him, Brother Martin wrote again on October 18 to say goodbye. He was wasting his time, he saw, and had to go "somewhere." It still wasn't clear where—if he went home, he might taint Prince Frederick. And at this point he couldn't be sure that Frederick would even want to protect him, or the prince might be condemned too.

Two days later, on October 20, after still hearing nothing from the cardinal but all sorts of rumors that the cardinal planned to throw both him and Staupitz into jail, Brother Martin finally made plans to leave. First, he posted a copy of his appeal to the pope on the door of the cathedral, to make it public, then sent a copy to the cardinal too, adding that it was nothing personal. Then he went to find his horse.

Thinking way ahead, about this very moment, Staupitz had borrowed the horse on his way over from Salzburg to Augsburg, from the prior of the Augustinian friary in Ramsau. The prior didn't know that the horse was needed for an escape, and so he hadn't loaned Staupitz his speediest creature or even put a saddle on it. But Brother Martin climbed up on it now anyway, wearing at least some knee breeches and spurs to help him control it, then rode off through one of Augsburg's gates. Staupitz had also arranged in advance for someone to ride with Brother Martin for a while, to show the way.

By the end of October, the weather in and near Augsburg was close to freezing at night, and the chances for rain or snow were good. And so it couldn't have been an easy night, or even an easy decision about which way to go. To Paris, 480 miles due west? Or back to the uncertainty of Wittenberg, 300 miles north?

He decided quickly on north. That night he made it 40 miles, all the way to Monheim, where he got off his horse and collapsed. He was in Nuremberg by the 22nd, and soon after that he ran into his old acquaintance the Count of Mansfeld, who had a good laugh at Brother Martin's unfriarlike appearance. He got lost near Leipzig, stopped at the Augustinian friary in Kemberg to say Mass, then finally arrived in Wittenberg on October 31, sort of safe and sort of sound, and not sure at all how long he would, or could, stay.

It was exactly one year ago that day that he'd sent off his troublemaking theses to Archbishop Albrecht.

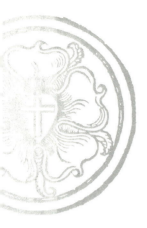

6

The Rose of Gold

Wittenberg, the Refectory of the Augustinian Friary. December 1, 1518. The Feast of St. Eligius, Who was Generous.

If Prince Frederick's court had been in town, then Spalatin could have brought along some of the good wine from the castle for this latest farewell dinner, but the court wasn't, and so the group of friends had to raise their cups to each other with the ordinary stuff instead.

The first farewell dinner for Brother Martin had been back in 1505, in Erfurt, when he'd left the world to enter the religious life. And now tonight was another, because tomorrow he was leaving Wittenberg, maybe for good, and, some wondered, maybe the religious life too. After all, he'd already been released from his vow of obedience, and given all the trouble he was now in, who knew but that he might decide to quit everything else as well?

Even if they'd had the castle's heavenly wine to drink, the friends gathered here at the friary surely weren't as lively as they might have been if they'd been at the castle itself, because dinners here were supposed to be quiet, except for the brother who read out something edifying amid the chewing and smacking and swallowing. But the mere presence of the friends just as surely made the meal warmer than usual, and maybe there was even dispensation for them to stay later than usual for a few final drinks, because God only knew when they all might ever see each other again.

Even before Brother Martin arrived back from Augsburg on October 31, Cardinal Cajetan was writing Prince Frederick to tell his brief version of the hearing, which he concluded was a disaster and had solved nothing. Surely the prince would now see that Luther had to absolutely be arrested and sent to

Rome: the man wasn't just tossing out disputable theses anymore but making misleading and openly heretical claims, including in print "in the German language," for everyone to see. If Frederick couldn't bring himself to arrest Luther, then at least he should throw him out of Saxony: "Your highness should not let one little friar" stain the reputation of his family, warned the cardinal. "I saw your father Ernest in Rome, who was a very obedient son of the church," and "Your Serenity" should be likewise.

Brother Martin knew about the cardinal's insistent letter because Prince Frederick sent him a copy, and asked for ideas on how to respond. That gave Brother Martin a chance to write the prince with his own version of what had happened in Augsburg, to repeat his regret that the prince had been dragged into this big mess, and to say once again that if somebody could show him that he was wrong then the prince should most certainly expel him from the land, and the university most certainly dismiss him, and Jesus Christ most certainly destroy him. But until somebody showed that, he hoped that the prince would keep shielding him from Rome.

Writing that letter to Frederick, and remembering how much attention some of his writing was getting, and also considering how thoroughly disillusioned he was about his interview with Cajetan, surely gave Brother Martin the idea to put his version of events in Augsburg into very public print. One of the highest theologians in the church wouldn't even discuss things with him, but just tried to shut him up instead. And the "monstrous" Roman instruction to Cajetan, of August 23, which Brother Martin saw for the first time only when Frederick sent it along too, proved that somebody in the curia had decided he was a heretic even before the hearing took place, which made it not much of a hearing at all. Surely Pope Leo, whom Brother Martin held in "the highest regard," wouldn't have judged him in advance like that: surely that instruction was a forgery by Cajetan and the papal prosecutor Girolamo Ghinucci. Brother Martin wrote out all this and much more, and had his account ready for the printer in mid-November, under the title *Acta Augustana*. It was in Latin, so his learned critics couldn't say he was trying to stir up "rustics" again. In fact, it even begged his learned readers to forgive him for becoming against his will "the talk of the people," and for wearying readers again with his trifles, which he did now only "very reluctantly" because so many lies were being told about Augsburg. He had to defend himself, and his prince too.

But Prince Frederick wasn't happy when he found out about the plan to print the *Acta*, because it didn't just tell Dr. Martin's version of events but added some vinegar to the whole dispute with Rome—like that the papal *Extravagantes* were dead wrong, and that by relying on them the popes did violence to Holy Scripture, and that Brother Martin didn't just have a few doubts about indulgences anymore but was instead sure they were wrong too. "Bear witness to this, my reader. I revoke" indulgences. The *Acta Augustana* also explained, in even more detail than Brother Martin had offered in Augsburg, how popes could err and why Matthew 16 on Peter and the papal keys had nothing at all to do with popes. That level of boldness was too much for Prince Frederick, especially at the moment here in November 1518, because he was still negotiating with Cajetan about Brother Martin, and a book like this wasn't going to help. And so the prince told Spalatin to ask Brother Martin to hold off printing it for now. Brother Martin agreed, but not just out of respect: he was sure he would have to leave town soon anyway, and so he would just print it once he got to wherever he was going.

While preparing himself in late November to leave, Brother Martin also decided to make another appeal about his case—not to the pope this time, but to a council of the church. After all, such a council had just ended in Rome the year before, and so there was reason to think that maybe another would assemble soon. But popes didn't like appeals to councils, because they suggested that a council was higher than a pope. Pope Pius II in 1460 had even expressly forbidden monks and friars from making such appeals, since they of all people should know that the pope was supreme. But Brother Martin either decided he wasn't a full-fledged friar anymore or just didn't care what the pope had decreed, because he marched over to the little Corpus Christi chapel next to St. Mary's church and before what was surely a modest audience announced his latest appeal. He wasn't against the church or the pope, he explained, just a badly informed pope, as was any pope who thought popes were supreme.

Oh, Brother Martin sounded as confident as one of Prince Frederick's leaping forest stags, but doing something this bold was unnerving too. Around the time he did it, he told his brother friars that he might have to leave town fast, without even saying goodbye, and he'd dropped the same sort of hints to his flock at St. Mary's in recent sermons. He also wrote on November 25 to Spalatin to say that he was expecting the papal ban any day, and that when it came he would definitely leave Wittenberg and Saxony, so as not to be a bother to his prince. Spalatin responded on November 28 that he and the prince weren't opposed to that plan. Maybe they were even relieved.

A lukewarm answer like that helped to explain why Brother Martin, even though no ban from Rome had arrived yet, now made firm plans to leave Wittenberg, very possibly for Paris, on December 2. At least this farewell dinner on the 1st was giving him a chance to say a real goodbye to his friends instead of having to ride off in the middle of the night.

But suddenly a messenger came into the refectory and interrupted all the health-drinking by handing yet another letter from Spalatin to Brother Martin. He opened it and read: Prince Frederick didn't want him to leave Wittenberg after all.

So much for the farewells.

The letter didn't explain why. And it didn't necessarily calm Brother Martin, who still leaned toward leaving, so his prince wouldn't be in the difficult position of having either to protect or arrest a subject accused of heresy. Yes, Frederick had already protected him some by arranging for a hearing in Augsburg instead of Rome, but a dutiful prince like Frederick might have done that for any of his subjects. How far would his protection go when the charges of heresy and the demands to arrest got even heavier, as they were sure to get?

Further than Brother Martin ever imagined, was the answer. On December 7, Frederick finally replied to Cajetan's October demand that Luther be arrested. In a rare fit of frankness, the prince made his position absolutely clear: the friar still hadn't been properly heard (no, the hearing at Augsburg didn't count), the pope or cardinal still hadn't forced the friar to recant anything, plenty of sworn-to-orthodoxy theologians agreed that his teachings weren't unchristian, and so in Saxony Martin Luther still wasn't considered a heretic. Frederick therefore couldn't possibly send him to Rome without damaging his own reputation, and his university's too. If Brother Martin ended up being convicted of heresy, after a fair hearing, then the prince would of course send him along. And by fair hearing Frederick meant one held on German soil before a panel made up of Dr. Martin's fellow scholars, not a bunch of Roman churchmen.

When Brother Martin, still muddling over whether to leave town, got a copy of that letter from Spalatin, he was ecstatic, and gladly decided to stay. He didn't have to be unsure anymore about Frederick's support, or whether he should flee Wittenberg. "I have seen the admirable words of our Most Illustrious Prince. . . . Good God, with what joy I read them and read them over again!" When the University of Wittenberg also came out and supported Brother Martin's right as a professor of biblical theology to dispute unsettled matters of faith, which indulgences most obviously were, he felt even more secure—secure enough to go ahead and publish his *Acta Augustana* right then and there, even though Prince Frederick still didn't want him to. Brother Martin placated the prince a little, by having the printer black out the most offensive part, at the front of the book, which accused Cajetan and Ghinucci of forging things, but the rest was readable in bookshops by mid-December. So was Brother Martin's appeal to a council, which Prince Frederick didn't like either, because printing a vinegary book about a cardinal and an upstart appeal to a council wasn't how you went about making things right with Rome, or making life easier for your prince. It was probably best that Frederick didn't know Brother Martin had another new work in mind too, on the current reign of the Antichrist in Rome, by which he meant the pope himself.

Despite these latest books, Frederick decided to stand by his professor, even when a new papal bull on indulgences, probably authored by Cajetan and called *Cum Postquam*, appeared in print as well on December 13. Now Dr. Martin could no longer say that the topic of indulgences was still unsettled, or that his theses were orthodox, because the bull plainly contradicted him. Yes, the bull said, just like the 95 theses, that indulgences were about forgiving satisfaction only and not guilt or sin. But unlike the 95 they declared once and for all that the treasury of merits was indeed the surplus merits of Christ and the saints, that the pope was absolutely in charge of those merits, and that anyone opposing indulgences would now be excommunicated. That last part kept Brother Martin from condemning the bull in public, because he didn't want anything to do with excommunication. But he wasn't going to take back anything he'd already written on indulgences, especially now that his prince was behind him—and not just any prince either, but one of the greatest among the 250 or so who ruled the impossibly shaped principalities of the improbably named Holy Roman Empire.

HEFTY

Frederick's power came of course in the first place from his exceedingly lucky birth as the eldest son and heir to the elector Ernest Wettin, the 30th or so duke of shape-shifting Saxony.

In fact, the Wettins as a whole had been exceedingly lucky just to become dukes and electors of Saxony in the first place, thanks to the horrifying luck of the previous ruling family, the Ascanians: in 1419, the castle where they were sleeping collapsed, killing them all. Soon afterward, the emperor exercised one of his few imperial powers and named Ernest's grandfather, Frederick I, as the new duke and elector of Saxony, in thanks for Frederick's ferocious fighting against the duchy's ferocious neighbors, the Bohemians, which had also earned the new duke the nickname, the Warlike. Saxony threatened to change shape yet again after Frederick died in 1428, when his sons, the ingloriously named Frederick the Meek and the more heroically named

Frederick the Wise.

Wilhelm the Brave, fought for long over the inheritance. The nasty struggle finally ended in favor of Frederick (now the II), when the emperor exercised one of his few other powers and stuck his nose in to intervene, but only of course after the Wettins had damaged themselves enough to make them a less formidable rival to the emperor's own Habsburg family.

When Frederick II died in 1464, his eldest son and successor Ernest tried to avoid a repeat of brotherly wars by ruling Saxony jointly and chummily with his brother Albrecht, which worked happily for many years. But the arrangement fell apart in 1480, when the pope gave only Ernest the Golden Rose and not Albrecht, and when Ernest went to Rome to fetch it and left Albrecht only partly and not totally in charge. The ill will got so ill that in 1485 Ernest proposed solving their argument in the tried and tested brotherly way of drawing a line down the middle of everything and dividing it. Their dear father had forbidden any such dividing, as had the famous Golden Bull of 1356 that settled the system of seven imperial electors for good, but the brothers divided things anyway, and thus were born Ernestine Saxony and Albertine Saxony, thus changing the old duchy once more. Because Ernest kept the title of elector, his territory was also called Electoral Saxony while Albrecht's was also called Ducal Saxony. And since Ernest was the one who drew the dividing line, Albrecht, as per hallowed brotherly rules, got to choose which part(s) he wanted—except for Wittenberg, which was the electoral city and thus had to stay with Ernest. Against Ernest's expectations, Albrecht chose slightly richer and more urban parts of the duchy, even though whoever did that had to pay 100,000 gulden to the other. Albrecht also surprisingly chose a thoroughly patchwork half, instead of a tidily contiguous one, so that by the time the brothers were done the two Saxonies looked something like a limp *X* lying on its side. The Ernestine/Electoral part lay mostly southwest to northeast, and the Albertine/Ducal part northwest to southeast. When Ernest died in a hunting accident in 1486, just a year after the division, he at least knew that his 23-year-old son, Frederick III—the future patron of Martin Luther—would succeed him, and that Electoral Saxony was still one of the great principalities of the entire empire.

But Frederick's power didn't come from just his lucky birth or position: instead it came especially from how well he learned to wield and build it, with no small thanks to the fortune in silver that now seemed to be oozing out of Saxony's countless mines.

Frederick built that power tangibly starting with the patching and mending and even complete rebuilding he did of the dozen or so castles he inherited, partly so none of them would fall down like they had on the Ascanians, partly so he could move and eat and hunt his way around all of his lands, and especially so he could make clear who was in charge, because nothing said you were in charge like a massive castle did. Frederick tried to avoid playing favorites among his castles, but surely he had one at Torgau, where he was born, and where he might spend half the year, and from where he could easily get to his dear hunting lodge at Lochau. He also tried to spread his wealth widely around, employing tailors, shoemakers, weavers, cooks, locksmiths, guards, doghandlers, falconers, stable hands, masons, carpenters, jesters, horn players, drummers, singers, and many more, to dress and liven up all his castles, which were always noisy from all the work and music going on.

He also built his power tangibly by laying down roads, and putting up bridges across even tricky rivers, and repairing and improving fortifications around towns, and of course by rebuilding and endowing churches and monasteries and shrines, because like many rulers Frederick understood that the best way to be in charge of something was to pay for it, and he wanted to be in charge of the church in his duchy even more than his predecessors had been. Oh, he didn't want to provoke the pope, who granted him indulgences for his projects and charters for his university and precious Golden Roses for his pious rule, and who also ordered the churches of the empire to send their excess relics to Frederick, for his growing collection in Wittenberg. But Frederick would always push his authority as far as he could, and he managed church matters so well that he made people like Martin Luther begin to wonder whether princes might not be just as good at running the church as any pope was.

Frederick did his tangible building most grandly of all in, of all places, puny little Wittenberg, which was the official but never sentimental heart of Electoral Saxony. In fact, if Saxony hadn't been divided, Frederick might have ignored the place as much as his predecessors had, but after the division Wittenberg was about his only choice left to build in: he no longer had a grand city, or grand residence, or a university, or even a cathedral city, even though parts of eight bishoprics ran through Electoral Saxony. And so he decided to put all he could into humble Wittenberg, even if he wouldn't be there as often as all the furious building suggested he might. Around 1490 he razed the old and decrepit castle and started a brand new one, a big *U*-shaped, three-winged, 35-room fortress on the southwest corner of town, built right into the town wall, and styled by all the great names in German art—Dürer, Cranach, Burgkmair, and more. He even built a full church instead of just the usual chapel, on the whole north wing of that castle, because if Wittenberg couldn't be a cathedral city it could at least be the religious center of Saxony. The castle church became exactly that, with its 20 altars, and its altarpieces and paintings and organs, and its 9,000 masses and 40,000 candles per year, not to mention all its relics and all its pilgrims who bought enough indulgences to pay for 31 people to run the church and 24 more people to do things like teach at Frederick's new university in Wittenberg. He opened that university in 1502, because even though he'd had the usual education of a Saxon duke (horsing, jousting, hunting, fighting), he was interested enough in the new learning to get some Latin and French too, and stylish enough to see that a great prince needed a great university, and not just for show but because he was sure that the more wise men he had around him the fewer disasters there would be. And so Frederick recruited the wisest people he knew to start it, starting with the Augustinian Johann von Staupitz, which was why in 1502 Frederick started building a whole Augustinian friary in Wittenberg too, at the southeast corner of town, so that other Augustinians could attend and teach at the university. The university grew into a respectable place, with 37 faculty and 400 or so students, but in the last year enrollment had grown all the way to 552 thanks to the growing fame of Dr. Martin, which was a not-to-be-underestimated reason for the prince to protect his professor from any unwarranted arrest, beyond his usual sense of obligation he felt toward any subject.

Frederick built his power in intangible ways too, because building and learning and art and even silver-oozing mines didn't guarantee a prince's authority. After all, Emperor Maximilian and probably Albrecht of Mainz too had even more churches and castles than Frederick did, but both of those princes also had intangible flaws that led to tangible debts and thus a tangible crippling of power. No, what a prince needed most were intangibles, and Frederick's were considerable. His piety, for example, went beyond just building churches and collecting relics: he'd been a big supporter of religious reform since the start of his reign; he joined humbly in processions, like at the Diet of Nuremberg in 1491, where he astonishingly walked on foot while all other princes and the emperor rode on horseback; and he went on pilgrimage to the Holy Land in 1493, a trip that cost 14,000 gulden and was full of peril. That Frederick had no wife but a mistress, his dear Anna, and two sons by her, wasn't seen as contradictory to his piety at all, because for over a thousand years the church's position was that a prince could have either a wife or a mistress, but not both, and Frederick's choice was clear by 1500. Maybe he didn't marry Anna because she wasn't noble, or because not marrying anybody would help keep peace with his brother Johann, who did marry and soon had a son: Frederick and Johann would rule together, and Johann's son would be their joint heir, and they would avoid all brotherly wars. Whatever Frederick's reason for not marrying, in 1514 the Fifth Lateran Council in Rome ruined everything: it decreed that a prince could have only a wife at court, not a mistress. Plenty of princes still kept both, but Frederick, as a champion of religious reform, couldn't blatantly ignore the rule, and he reluctantly sent Anna away that same year—the year his physical ailments got worse too. Expelling her was surely his most pious act of all.

Besides pious, Frederick was also cautious, and patient, and clever, and tactful, more like a hare than a wolf, said some, but sometimes like a stubborn, angry bulldog too. He was also thrifty: yes, he spent like a prince at times, on relics and jousting and music and feasting, the way his subjects almost expected the great to do (within limits), maybe to help them feel great themselves through him, but instead of spending without counting, Frederick counted; instead of betting thousands at the gaming tables that were set up wherever princes got together, Frederick bet hundreds; instead of eating his way ravenously around his castles, Frederick noted carefully at each how much he and his court consumed. He also listened: instead of relying on his own judgment alone, he had at least five councilors at court at all times, and took the attitude, "I believe the shoemaker about the shoes, the tailor about the trousers, and the smithy about the iron," and so the theologian about theology too. And Frederick tried to be fair: even though there wasn't even a hint of any sort of representative assembly in Saxony to rein in or challenge him, he made sure to compensate any farmer whose grain was trampled by one of his many hunting parties, for instance, because he knew he needed his subjects' unofficial good will, even if they didn't have any official voice in how they were ruled.

Maybe most importantly of all, Frederick understood better than anyone just how tenuous all the power that he'd built up truly was, both in Saxony and the empire, and just how many threats there were to it. That was precisely why he was so cautious. Neither he nor any other German prince was great enough to resist all by himself an attack from his fellow princes, if they all suddenly decided he was breaking one of their precious princely rules. Yes, Frederick socialized and in his younger days jousted with the emperor and other princes, and cooperated with them when it suited him. And in a real way the princes all needed each other. But under the right circumstances, say like if one of them was protecting a heretic, they could turn on each other too, whether they really even cared about the particular heretic in question or not.

There was first of all the threat of Frederick's untrustworthy cousin, Duke George, in Ducal Saxony, who would have been only too glad, and on the flimsiest pretext, to take over Frederick's part of Saxony.

There was the threat of Frederick's own brother Ernest too, who Frederick started feuding with in 1506 because Ernest called Anna a whore (even though Ernest was already suffering from the syphilis that would kill him in 1513 and that put Albrecht of damned Brandenburg in his place), which feuding got even worse when Ernest entered into a nefarious plot with Cousin George to take over Electoral Saxony.

There was even the threat of Frederick's other and usually cooperative brother Johann, with whom he so carefully and jointly ruled, so as to avoid brotherly feuds, but the two started feuding in 1513 anyway, to the point where they divided the territory that each would rule (but at least they didn't officially divide Electoral Saxony itself).

There was further the threat of his princely neighbors, the Hohenzollerns of damned Brandenburg, in the persons of Joachim the elector and Albrecht the archbishop (and elector) of Mainz, who would have also been glad for some excuse to attack Frederick.

There was the threat of the nearby king of Bohemia, another of the seven electors, who was still fuming that the electors of Saxony, Brandenburg, and Mainz had voted for Maximilian as emperor all those (31) years ago, and had even recently seized some of Maximilian's lands in Austria—maybe he would come after one of the maddening electors next.

There was also the imperial threat of Frederick's old bosom cousin Maximilian himself, who didn't want any family in the empire growing more powerful than his own.

And finally there was of course the threat of the pope. Yes, the pope was at the moment treading a little less heavily than he might have against Frederick, and Brother Martin, because of the looming election, but if Frederick didn't vote the way the pope wanted, then the pope might decide to tread heavier than ever and excommunicate not only Brother Martin but anyone who protected him, including his prince. That would free Frederick's subjects from obedience and also give the emperor a chance to appoint another new ruling family in Electoral Saxony, say like Cousin George. This was the biggest reason of all why Frederick couldn't be seen as an obvious supporter of Brother Martin but instead as just his fair-minded prince.

Brother Martin wasn't exactly gifted at matters of state and politics, but he understood very well the predicament Frederick was in with the pope. In his worst moments, Brother Martin would sometimes call Frederick, still without a nickname, the Great Hesitator. But most of the time, and especially now in this time of peril, he thought Frederick an excellent prince—and his habit of hesitating was a big reason for that excellence. It meant, among other things, that Frederick wouldn't act rashly and quickly when someone came along demanding the arrest of one of his subjects on suspicion of heresy.

THE POPE'S MOST SAXON MAN

Even though the pope wanted Prince Frederick to arrest or expel Luther, he couldn't afford to be any more arbitrary in how he proceeded than Frederick could, and for the same old reason: there were threats to his power too.

Leo and his predecessors had already lost some power in France and England and Spain, where strong kings were able to bargain and threaten their way into having more control over the church within their borders than ever before.

German princes weren't as big and strong as those rulers, but what if enough of them joined together and started to resist him, the way they'd already and so alarmingly done at the Diet of Augsburg? That was why Pope Leo had to take care in how hard he pushed Frederick to do something about the "little friar."

And so in early September 1518, about the same time that he agreed to let Luther be heard in Augsburg by Cardinal Cajetan, the pope also decided to approach Frederick another way. Not only would Leo give Frederick the much-desired Golden Rose, but he would send a member of the papal household, who happened to be a Saxon nobleman and therefore one of Frederick's own "loyal subjects," to deliver the Rose in person, and, while he was at it, solve the Luther problem, Saxon-nobleman to Saxon-nobleman. If the pope's Italian agents couldn't fix things, maybe a local fellow could.

Like most people making judgments about places far, far away, Pope Leo didn't have the local flavor quite right. The nobleman in question, Karel von Miltitz, was indeed from an old Saxon family with lands near Meissen, but those lands were now in *Ducal* Saxony: Miltitz was therefore a subject of Duke George, Frederick's cousin and rival. Still, that was close enough for Leo.

The 28-year-old Miltitz had ended up in the papal household as a chamberlain and notary thanks to his uncle, the Dominican Nicholas von Schönberg, who knew all the right people in Rome, including Cardinal Giulio Medici, Leo's trusty advisor. But the young nobleman himself wasn't particularly gifted: six years of law hadn't made him learned, ordination as a priest hadn't made him pious, and four years in Rome had mostly increased his interest in good wine. He was also just one of many notaries in the papal household, and only a titled chamberlain instead of an actual one. Still, he was Saxon, and noble, and officially close to the pope, and so he seemed suited for the job.

Miltitz didn't leave Rome right away, maybe because the pope was having second thoughts about his choice, or was just hoping for a happy outcome from Cajetan's meeting with Luther. Only on October 15, the very day that the cardinal and Brother Martin were yelling at each other in the palace of the Fuggers in Augsburg, did Leo finally give Miltitz his commission, and only in November did Miltitz finally head north with the precious Rose, and a letter for Frederick explaining what he still had to do to get it.

The look of the Golden Rose changed often, depending on the pope and craftsman involved. It might stand anywhere from six to 22 inches high, but it was always made of pure gold, always included thorns and red tint and a red ruby to remind everyone of Christ's Passion, and always had some heavenly fragrance about it. For centuries, the pope had blessed the latest version of the Rose every fourth Sunday of Lent in a rose-colored (instead of Lenten-purple-colored) ceremony, then handed out that Rose to whichever shrine or church or ruler he wanted to honor at the moment. As the "flower among flowers, the fairest and most fragrant on earth," the Golden Rose symbolized the Kingly Majesty of Christ and the "most precious blood of our Savior," as Leo explained, but it also bestowed the sort of prestige that princes in Europe could never get enough of. Isabella of Spain got it in 1493, Henry VIII in England had already gotten it twice, Frederick's own father, Ernest, got it in 1480, and now it was Frederick's happy turn.

But like any other lucky prince, Frederick wasn't going to get the Rose for nothing. Besides hoping that the Rose would spur Frederick on to vote against Charles Habsburg as emperor, Leo didn't want Frederick to actually receive the Rose until he'd arrested or expelled Martin Luther. Miltitz wasn't to take the Rose all the way to Saxony at first, but leave it in Augsburg with Cajetan instead: only when Frederick did his duty was Miltitz to go fetch the Rose and present it. Leo also instructed Miltitz to report to Cajetan on his talks with Frederick, and to take any further instruction on the matter from Cajetan as well. None of that thrilled the chamberlain, since the cardinal wasn't exactly his favorite person at the papal court.

When Miltitz reached Augsburg in late November, he dutifully gave the Rose to Cajetan, who put it in a vault in the Fugger bank. Miltitz also had a pleasant dinner with Frederick's councilor Degenhart Pfeffinger, at the latter's estate nearby, and, surely thanks to Pfeffinger's wine, the chamberlain blurted out more than Cajetan or the pope would have liked—such as that maybe the arrest of Brother Martin could still be avoided. He didn't clarify what he meant by that, and maybe he wasn't in any state to clarify, but it certainly gave a hint that maybe Rome, through Miltitz, was still willing to negotiate about Martin Luther. Pfeffinger sent that information to Frederick right away.

That piece of intelligence may well have been why the cautious Frederick, after agreeing on November 28 that maybe it would be best for everyone if Brother Martin left Saxony soon, decided suddenly on December 1 that he should stay right where he was. Of course, Frederick could have changed his mind because he'd heard by now that Maximilian was fading fast, which meant there would be no election before his death after all and that the pope would be trying to please

Frederick even more than he already had. Or Frederick could have changed his mind because his own health wasn't sparkling, with his gout and fading eyes and growing melancholy now that dear Anna was gone, so what did he have to lose by defying the pope a little? But the most likely reason Frederick changed his mind and decided to keep Brother Martin in Wittenberg was the very loose tongue of Karel von Miltitz, who seemed determined to impress and please whoever he happened to be talking to.

The chamberlain's tongue got even looser, in fact, the closer he got to Saxony. Councilor Pfeffinger, surely hoping to hear more, accompanied Miltitz on the rest of his journey north and did indeed hear plenty. One moment Miltitz opened his pockets to show off the papal dispensations he planned to hand out as incentives in the Luther case, the next moment he said he had three papal instructions ordering him to capture Luther, and the moment after that he volunteered sensitive information on the case in order to get on the good side of his hosts. At Nuremberg on December 18, for instance, Miltitz revealed that the papal court had found the indulgence sermons of that "dirty dog" Tetzel "coarse," had been unhappy about Prierias's sloppy response to Luther, and had said there hadn't been such an upsetting case as Luther's in a thousand years and they would gladly pay 10,000 ducats to be done with it. All this was relayed ahead to Prince Frederick too.

Maybe Miltitz opened up not just to find favor and good will or because he'd drunk a little too much Bavarian wine, but because the farther he traveled the more he saw how much support there was for Luther, in every tavern he entered. It would be hard, he realized, to get anyone to arrest the friar, which was the main point of his mission. Hoping to salvage the situation, Miltitz decided to try another plan instead: he, and not the annoying Cajetan, would be the one to heroically reconcile Luther with Rome. Miltitz hinted at this plan to Christoph Scheurl in Nuremberg, and once Scheurl heard it he sent yet another letter racing toward Saxony, telling Brother Martin to of course stand firm but please do not antagonize this papal nobleman who, unlike Cardinal Cajetan, was ready to talk and compromise. Please find a way to please the pope and your conscience, and avoid the church's excommunication and the empire's ban. Plus Miltitz wasn't such a bad guy, added Scheurl.

Miltitz finally arrived in Saxony the day after Christmas, at the town of Gera, and announced himself to Prince Frederick, whose court was only 20 miles farther away at Altenburg. By December 28, Miltitz was at the court in person, ready to talk.

Frederick had already been discussing with his councilors how to proceed, at their usual almost-daily meetings inside his seven-towered castle at Altenburg, with its 13-foot-thick walls, where his father and uncle had been kidnapped as boys by an angry noble rival, and which sat atop a high hill that dominated the mere 250 or so souls below. If Frederick followed his reported custom, he would have asked to hear his councilors' views on the subject at hand, then closed his eyes and listened. Among the various views offered about Brother Martin was an old rural parable: that of the sheep who at the advice of the wolves sent away the watchdogs. That was what they would be doing if they left Brother Martin unprotected, said the councilor. They should refuse to hand him over unless he was proven guilty of heresy, which only confirmed what Frederick had already written to Cajetan.

And Frederick stayed with that view when Miltitz arrived at the palace, was granted an audience, then started in on his usual hard-to-follow song and dance. First he tried to intimidate Frederick, demanding that he expel Luther from Saxony or, better yet, arrest him and let Miltitz take him back to Rome. Frederick sometimes had a hot temper, but this bluff was too obvious for him to waste any fury on: instead he just refused. Then Miltitz tried to smooth things: what if they found some sort of solution that might satisfy all sides? That sounded better to Frederick. But what Miltitz meant by "solution" wasn't what Frederick meant. Miltitz explained that if Frederick handed Luther over for trial, then the pope would reward Frederick with the long list of things contained in the letter that Miltitz now handed over, for Frederick to read himself.

First, said the letter, Frederick would get the already-promised Golden Rose, which he would be very lucky to get by the way, and it would now also come with even more plenary indulgences than Frederick had already received. Second, he would also get the right to legitimize the illegitimate births of two people of his choosing—obviously meaning Frederick's two sons by Anna. And third, Frederick would get the right to name a cardinal, which Miltitz took to mean Martin Luther himself, although that was a questionable conclusion, since in the next breath the pope ended the letter by saying that all Frederick had to do to get these benefits was to cast out that "infected, scrofulous sheep," that "son of perdition," Martin Luther.

It must have all been at least a little tempting for Frederick, especially if Miltitz pulled the relevant dispensations out of his pockets to put them within very easy reach. But these offers also showed just how alarmed Rome already was at Brother Martin's growing popularity, if they were willing to grant gifts like these. Maybe Frederick could live without the Rose: he wrote to Cousin George to say that the pope was refusing to give it to him "unless I banish the *Mönch* and say he is a heretic," but then Frederick jokingly added that maybe he should just do as his favorite court fool, Claus Narr, advised, which was to "go on drinking my wine and being a heretic all my days," Roseless. And would legitimizing his sons maybe start a fight with Brother Johann over the succession, since they had already agreed how it should go? As for naming a cardinal, it just wasn't tempting enough.

And so Frederick stuck to his original position: he would not arrest Luther, he told Miltitz, until he was proven guilty. Yes, as a Christian prince, he would protect the church, but he must be sure that Luther had harmed it. Frederick repeated his already stated hope that Luther should be heard by a panel of qualified German judges—they didn't all have to be scholars, he conceded now, but could be churchmen instead, preferably learned bishops, or they could even be one bishop, who could be trusted to judge impartially. But until then, there would be no arrest. Seeing that Frederick wouldn't budge, and wanting to save the mission, Miltitz now suggested the last-ditch plan he'd had in mind, and that Cajetan probably wouldn't like: what if the chamberlain spoke with Brother Martin himself, and convinced him to recant, and reconcile?

Frederick wasn't against it. But there was no way he was going to be anywhere close while Miltitz tried, because he had to maintain his appearance of neutrality in the matter. And so while Spalatin asked Brother Martin to come quickly to Altenburg, Frederick and most of the court left as fast as they could, for Lochau, where the prince might still get in some good winter hunting.

THE KING IS DEAD

Spalatin stayed behind in Altenburg to watch over the talks, which would be held in the house that he had there, as a canon of the local church.

He also spoke with Miltitz while they both waited for Brother Martin to arrive, and took the chance to speak ill of Friar Tetzel. True to his usual ingratiating self, Miltitz went right along, and even had Tetzel summoned to Altenburg from Leipzig in order to answer charges being made against him and to hear just how furious the pope was with him. Tetzel refused to budge from Leipzig though, saying it was too dangerous for him to travel anymore, as "a great

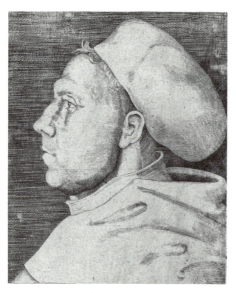

Lucas Cranach, *Luther with Doctor's Cap*.

number of Luther's partisans have sworn my death." But Miltitz was determined to blame Tetzel for the entire mess over indulgences, and soon after leaving Altenburg he would visit Tetzel in Leipzig, formally charge him with embezzlement and living an immoral life, and generally yell at him. It was all his fault, not the pope's, insisted Miltitz.

Brother Martin arrived in Altenburg just after New Year's Day, 1519, and probably stayed at the Augustinian friary there, but for his talks with Miltitz he walked over to Spalatin's house, just below the castle. At their first meeting, Luther and Miltitz were both stunned at how young the other was. They ended up talking for two days, in the presence of Frederick's councilor cousin, Fabian von Feilitzsch, and possibly Spalatin too.

Just as he had when talking to Spalatin, Miltitz again blamed Tetzel for everything, and now heaped some blame on Archbishop Albrecht too. Yes, the good Dr. Martin had misled people about indulgences in a few ways, but Tetzel had misled them more, and it had all been because of Albrecht's endless need for money. No, even though Albrecht had been made a cardinal, Rome wasn't happy with those two men, Miltitz said. Miltitz also recounted how he had heard at inns all along the way just how popular Brother Martin was among so many people!

But Brother Martin wasn't going to fall for flattery. He agreed that Albrecht was partly to blame: if the archbishop would have spoken to him with a little courtesy "in the beginning, this affair would not have made so much noise." But Brother Martin was sure by now that Rome had played a role in the shady St. Peter's indulgence business too, and he said so. But Miltitz wouldn't have that, and he attacked: "Did you know that you have taken the whole world away from the pope, and attached it to yourself?" But Dr. Martin wasn't fazed: "God stops the waves of the sea" with something as simple and stubborn as sand, which was all Brother Martin was. Miltitz asked whether Dr. Martin wouldn't restore what he had taken—namely some of the reverence and honor due the pope. Brother Martin said he wanted to know specifically what Miltitz meant by that, and added that he was willing to have his writings judged by a panel of German bishops, just as Frederick had suggested. He now nominated three: the archbishop of Trier (Frederick's friend), the archbishop of Salzburg (Maximilian's friend), and the archbishop of Friesing. No one could accuse him of weighting the panel to his side with a group like that.

After two days of talking, Miltitz and Dr. Martin finally agreed on four things. Brother Martin would (1) stop criticizing indulgences if his critics stopped criticizing him, (2) write the pope and apologize for speaking so hotheadedly and explain that he'd only meant to protect the church, (3) publish a tract saying that very thing to a wider public too, and (4) allow the archbishop of Salzburg alone to judge his case.

On January 6 Miltitz hosted Brother Martin at a final dinner, where the two men hashed out some details and took leave with kisses and tears, according to Miltitz, but Brother Martin claimed he wasn't fooled by the kiss of Judas or the crocodile tears. "I pretended not to see through this Italian act of insincerity," he said of his fellow Saxon: even though he'd admired Italy on his 1511 trip to Rome, it wasn't the first time since then that he'd spoken ill of Italian manners. He also doubted whether the pope would go along with this agreement anyway, especially since the new bull on indulgences now made it impossible for any judge to see indulgences any other way than the way the bull prescribed.

But Miltitz was ecstatic over the agreement, and wrote the pope to tell him the good news: Luther was ready to submit! That was of course overstating things. The agreement didn't say that at all, only that Luther admitted to having spoken a little heatedly, and would stay quiet for the moment. Still, Brother Martin tried to do his part. He stopped arguing about indulgences. He was presumably ready for the archbishop of Salzburg to judge him. He soon wrote up *Doctor Martin Luther's Instruction on Several Articles [or Theses] Which are Ascribed and Assigned to Him by his Detractors,* which urged people to follow the church even though he'd pointed out some abuses and problems, and which explained that he'd meant only to defend the church. And the very night he ended his talks with Miltitz, he very probably drafted the required letter to Pope Leo, apologizing for his hotheadedness, and saying that he had simply meant to defend

Jacob Cornelisz van Oostsanen, *Charles V* (right) *and Maximilian I* (second from left).

true doctrine. He really couldn't bear feeling the pope's anger, he wrote, but he couldn't give up his views either, because if he recanted he would be recanting truth, and something like that would only hurt the church in the long run. It was the indulgence-preachers who needed to recant, he insisted. To him the Roman Church stood above everything in heaven and on earth, except Jesus Christ himself.

But Dr. Martin never sent that letter. It could have been, again, because he thought the pope wouldn't approve of the agreement with Miltitz. But more likely it was because of the world-changing event that now intervened.

On January 12, 1519, between 3 and 4 a.m., the Emperor Maximilian finally died. He'd gone to bed back on December 15 with a fever, and heart pain, and had long talks with a Carthusian monk about death. On January 2 had come horrible pain and diarrhea and more fever, for three days, then yellow eyes, and alternating constipation and diarrhea that contained rivers of blood and slime. After a week of that, Maximilian expired. Gallstones followed by bowel failure, diagnosed his last doctor as the cause of death.

Maximilian hadn't been able to see his grandson Charles elected king after all, because Frederick of Saxony had been able to delay the process. The campaigning for the next king would therefore start from scratch very soon, in the form of new bribes and threats, including from the king of France, Francis I, who immediately started offering favors to Frederick, while at the same time hinting to the electors of the Palatinate, Mainz, Trier, and Cologne that he might just invade a few western German territories, where they all happened to be located, if he didn't get his way at the election.

Maximilian's death gave the pope new hope that Francis could win, and it also made Frederick the most important man in the empire at the moment: not only was he by imperial law the interim ruler, as the elector of Saxony, but his usual heavy influence would make his vote more crucial than ever at the upcoming election, to be held in June. At least until then, the pope absolutely couldn't afford to act hastily and harshly against Martin Luther. Maybe Brother Martin would even get some rest now. Unless of course one of his enemies decided to criticize him in print again.

7

Cooked Goose

Leipzig, at the Grimma Gate. June 24, 1519. The Feast of St. John the Baptist, Who Preached in the Wild.

The 50 or so miles from Wittenberg were flat enough, at least if you took the road that went around the wooded hills instead of over them, but even if you did go over them you had to climb and descend only a few hundred feet at most, so if things went the way they ought then whichever road you took gave you a good chance of getting to Leipzig in a single long and grueling day, especially so near the summer solstice when the sun was up before 5 early and down only around 9:30 late.

Of course things didn't always go the way they ought, especially when two wagons were involved instead of just one, which increased your chances of breaking a wheel or axle or animal, particularly since one of the two wagons was creaking with chests full of dead-heavy books. The eight people also in the two wagons, and maybe even the innkeepers along the way, most certainly hoped that the trip would take just a day, because walking alongside the wagons was an unofficial escort of 200 eager-for-action students, and heaven only knew how any inn or even group of inns would ever sleep, much less feed them all. Just in case things didn't go as they ought, the wagons had left a whole three days before their most important passengers, Dr. Martin and his colleague Dr. Karlstadt, absolutely had to be in Leipzig.

Dr. Martin was finally going to get the big public disputation he'd been hoping for ever since his troubles began. Well, maybe. Karlstadt would definitely be disputing in Leipzig, that was certain, and everyone assumed Dr. Martin would join in too, but that still wasn't certain, even this close to the big day. Of course Dr. Martin badly wanted to dispute: Rome still hadn't agreed on where or even whether he would have the hearing he'd agreed to with Miltitz, and next to a hearing a big public disputation like the one he was now going to was the next best way to defend himself against the ever-louder accusations of heresy his critics were firing at him.

Many of those in the traveling party had already been to Leipzig and knew what to expect: rows and rows of three-story buildings for the city's 8,000 or so inhabitants, a bunch of mostly cobblestoned streets, the four colleges that made up the university, the brothels that some people called a fifth college, the local beer that students called *Rastrum* after a farmer's rake because that was what it did to your stomach, the big main market where the famous Leipzig fair took place, and of course the grand castle, the Pleissenburg, next to the market, where the disputation would actually be held. And thanks be to God, the city indeed came into sight on that very same day of St. John the Baptist.

The Wittenbergers entered through the Grimma Gate, on the city's eastern wall, with the wagon carrying Dr. Karlstadt going through first, since he was holding the passport for all of them. A crowd of curious people had already gathered near the gate, most of them locals but some of them come from all over the empire to watch the disputation. The local guilds and guards officially greeted the Wittenbergers, then started leading them to their lodgings. But after just a few turns of the wheels, and right in front of the Dominican friary, the axle of the first wagon suddenly snapped, surely from the weight of those dead-heavy books hitting the cobblestones too hard. The wagon and books went down in a violent heap, as did the wagon's main passenger, Dr. Karlstadt, who had to be led ingloriously on foot the rest of the way.

Karlstadt was badly shaken from the fall, but unfortunately for those who would attend the disputation and have to endure the long passages he read from them, the books survived just fine. Fortunately for Dr. Martin, he was in the second wagon. He and his friends, including Johann Lang (a fellow Augustinian friar), Nicholas von Amsdorf (a fellow Wittenberg theologian), Philip Melanchthon (a professor of Greek), and Duke Barnim of Pomerania (the rector of Wittenberg University), made sure that Karlstadt was attended to before going on to their own lodgings. Dr. Martin and Melanchthon were staying with the printer Melchior Lotter, who had recently published some of Dr. Martin's works.

The champions from Wittenberg had made it in plenty of time, but it wasn't exactly a promising start.

NOT THE TALK OF THE TOWN

After Maximilian died in January 1519, people almost stopped talking about Brother Martin, it seemed. For weeks and even months they had another favorite subject instead: Who would be the next Holy Roman emperor?

Brother Martin was surely glad for the respite, because he had plenty of other things he would rather do than worry about his ongoing legal case before the pope.

He was still a preacher and teacher in Wittenberg's city church, and "every day toward vesper time"—every day—he recited the Ten Commandments and Lord's Prayer with children and laypeople.

He was still saying Mass every day, and still (usually) singing the seven Hours of the Divine Office at the friary too, even though he'd been released from his vow of obedience.

He was still lecturing at the university, on the Psalms again, and organizing disputations, such as the 15 theses he prepared recently on *Whether the Books of the Philosophers Are Useful or Useless for Theology.*

He was still involved in town-and-gown sorts of business, most recently over whether students should be allowed to carry weapons to defend themselves against local apprentices; the faculty and students all said yes, but the town and Dr. Martin said no, which caused more than a few students to threaten him with stones and even with the weapons they weren't supposed to be carrying.

He was writing more things than ever for publication, including a Latin *Commentary on Galatians* but also a burst of new German sermons for laypeople.

He was still reminding Prince Frederick about cowls the prince owed him, like the black one already promised, and surely after the Galatians commentary, he deserved a white one too, he thought.

He was about to take his turn as dean of the faculty of theology, so that by March 1519 he was (like so many professors) complaining that he had "absolutely not time enough" for his work.

And he was still working to drive Aristotle and the scholastics out of every last crevice of the theology curriculum and to bring in more Greek and Hebrew instead. Prince Frederick and Spalatin went along with him too, even though changes like that always cost a university plenty and also led to plenty of grumbling among the faculty. Still, it was worth the trouble, thought Dr. Martin, because the changes included among other things a new professorship in Greek (only the second such position in German lands), which was filled by the young and gifted Philip Melanchthon. Even though Brother Martin had at first been skeptical of the man, what with his mere 21 years and five-foot frame and odd shoulder-hitch when he walked and his speech impediment, Master Philip's very first lecture knocked just about everybody over, because it explained even more clearly than Brother Martin had that to understand the Bible you had to stop reading scholastic theologians and start reading it in its original Hebrew and Greek instead. The two became fast friends, and Brother Martin liked to imagine that the short and scrawny Melanchthon looked like St. Paul. He also worried that the small professor would grow tired of Wittenberg and be stolen away by some other university.

But of course Brother Martin couldn't completely ignore his legal case in Rome, because other people just wouldn't let him. Pope Leo himself wrote personally in March 1519 to say how thrilled he was to hear from Karel von Miltitz that Brother Martin had finally realized he'd gone too far and was ready to recant. Would he then be so kind as to put on paper the recantation that Cardinal Cajetan had prepared for him at Augsburg, last fall? Then maybe they could all consider this whole unfortunate matter settled.

Ah, but the pope was badly misinformed again, Brother Martin surely sighed: Miltitz had given his usual overly optimistic account of things. At least this time Pope Leo had referred to him as "My beloved son" instead of his more usual "son of perdition," but Brother Martin had to correct the pope on the matter of any recantation: he had indeed said he would recant, but only if he were proved wrong, with real proof, and that still hadn't happened, he wrote Leo. And he wasn't simply being contrary: the last thing he wanted, he explained, was to break fellowship with the church. Yes, certain things in Rome needed improving, but "there is not—nor can there be!—any reason for tearing oneself away from the church in schism," he insisted. In fact, the worse things got in the church, the more a person should be ready to stand by it and help, "for by schism and contempt nothing can be mended." The church had never been perfect, and never would be as long as humans were involved, but it could be improved. And that was all he was trying to do with indulgences and justification—not to break away. But he still couldn't recant.

Even though Miltitz had given Pope Leo the wrong impression about the meeting in Altenburg, Brother Martin had to give the chamberlain some credit for continuing to try. On May 3, 1519, Miltitz even met with Cardinal Cajetan in Koblenz and supposedly convinced him to let Brother Martin be heard once and for all on German soil by Frederick's old friend, the archbishop of Trier. Surely that would resolve the matter at last. Miltitz wrote Brother Martin immediately and told him to get to Koblenz as fast as he could, before the cardinal changed his mind. But Brother Martin said no, mostly because Miltitz had again painted an overly rosy picture: Cajetan would sit in on the hearing, it emerged, and no archbishop was going to give anyone a fair hearing with the cardinal sitting there and intimidating him, which Brother Martin knew all too well from his interview with Cajetan in Augsburg. Brother Martin also wanted to know in advance exactly what he would be expected to retract at such a meeting. And how in the world would he ever get a safe conduct to Koblenz when there was no emperor at the moment to hand them out? Plus wouldn't the archbishop of Trier, who was an elector, now be busy electing one? Brother Martin himself was busy preparing for the big disputation in Leipzig, so he wasn't about to leave Wittenberg and run off to Koblenz for some unpromising hearing.

Yes, the disputation. In Brother Martin's mind, it had come about because his enemies had broken the silence on indulgences that he and Miltitz had agreed upon. First had come, in January, Prierias's new tract on the subject, which repeated that Luther was a heretic and schismatic and which Brother Martin had just ignored. But when the much more formidable Johann Eck published a new tract against him too, he couldn't hold back any longer.

Or maybe the disputation was even Karlstadt's fault, because back in the summer of 1518, he'd gotten hold of a copy of Eck's *Obelisks* and decided he didn't want to be left out of the arguing. In his usual exuberant way that would later cause Dr. Martin to say Karlstadt swallowed the dove-like Holy Ghost, feathers and all, Dr. Karlstadt had 380 theses printed, mostly against the *Obelisks,* and challenged Eck to a disputation. Eck wasn't interested, and wished that Karlstadt would have kept his overflowing theses private, but now that they were published Eck couldn't very well turn him down or he would damage his reputation and his university's too. He therefore finally accepted, and even said Karlstadt could name the place. Karlstadt suggested either Erfurt or Leipzig, and Eck chose Leipzig, in Ducal Saxony—220 miles from Eck's Ingolstadt, and 50 miles from Karlstadt's Wittenberg.

But after that conciliatory gesture, Eck turned sneaky. He wrote to Leipzig to ask permission of the town, the university, and its prince, Duke George, to come there and defend the true faith against not just Andreas Karlstadt but Martin

Luther and his most unchristian 95 theses too. The news thrilled Duke George: what a great way to boost the university's prestige, he thought, thinking of Luther's recent notoriety. Leipzig had the sixth oldest university in the empire (1409) but had faded some, thanks to newer Wittenberg. Yet when the theology faculty at Leipzig heard this news they said they wanted nothing to do with an accused heretic. George was furious. This was their big chance! All they had to do was

Johann Eck. Copper engraving.

host, not dispute, and if they were afraid to do that, then they were a bunch of lazy, overeating, worthless fellows who should be replaced with a bunch of "old women," the lowest insult he could think of. The chancellor of the university, who happened also to be the bishop over Leipzig, was against it too, but George overruled them all: on February 1, 1519, he forced the university to invite Johann Eck to dispute, and presumably the opponents of his choice too.

By then Eck had already printed an announcement of the disputation, including the mere 12 theses he wanted to dispute (instead of Karlstadt's 380). And these were sneaky too, as Dr. Martin realized immediately when he saw them in February, because all 12 were obviously meant for him, not Karlstadt. They were on indulgences, and purgatory, and the treasury of merits, *not* on free will, which was what Karlstadt's 380 were about. And Eck wanted to dispute these topics because he was sure they would lead to the topic he wanted to dispute with Luther most of all: the authority of the pope. He had his eye especially on Luther's assertion in his *Explanations* of the 95 theses that the pope's authority over the church wasn't established until the sixth century, which proved, said Luther, that it was of earthly rather than divine origin. Showing that Luther was wrong about that would be a much bigger achievement, thought Eck, and a much bigger service to the church, and a much bigger grabber of the pope's attention, than merely vanquishing Karlstadt would.

Dr. Martin had been itching for a disputation on indulgences, of course, but he was angry at how he'd been practically dragged into this one. His spat with Eck had until now been private, and he'd promised Miltitz to keep quiet about indulgences, but now he had to dispute, or *his* reputation and *his* university's would suffer. Dr. Martin therefore drew up 12 countertheses to Eck that summarized the many, many theses he'd written in the past couple of years against indulgences and scholastic theology. Then he showed them to Karlstadt, and suggested that Karlstadt lead the disputation but that he, Dr. Martin, should join in as well. When Karlstadt said yes, Dr. Martin had his 12 countertheses published, and announced that he, too, was going to Leipzig to dispute with Eck.

The theology faculty at Leipzig just about shed their professorial robes, Old-Testament style, when they heard that, and not just because they despised Luther: no, it was because a professor couldn't just invite himself to dispute at someone else's university. He had to be invited. Maybe Duke George wouldn't listen to the faculty's other complaints against Luther, but he had to listen to this one. The faculty was right, admitted the duke. Luther should write a letter of apology for being presumptuous. But George still wanted Luther to dispute, and so he left up to Eck the decision of whether to invite him, or not. Eck wanted Luther to dispute, obviously, or he wouldn't have tricked him into it. But he took advantage of his new power and let Luther sweat, by not sending any invitation. For months. On March 14, Eck even republished his 12 theses and now added a 13th, on free will, as if he were turning his attention to Karlstadt, and as if Karlstadt could then argue the other 12 too, which was no doubt enough to make Luther pull out even more hair from his already generous tonsure.

Even though he still had no invitation, Dr. Martin had to prepare as if he were still going to participate, or he'd be beaten badly when the big moment finally came. He decided to surprise Eck: instead of avoiding and sidestepping the question of the pope's authority, which everybody always did and which Eck surely expected, he would take it straight on, by learning everything he could about the subject, and by showing everyone just how right he was. Yes, the pope was important in the church, Dr. Martin had no problem admitting that. But he was already sure that the pope wasn't what most people claimed he was—more specifically, his office had never even been established by God.

Here was exactly how not to win the disputation or save your life, thought Brother Martin's friends. Stay with safe subjects, they said, like the free will that

Karlstadt so boringly wanted to dispute. But he pressed on anyway, studying more church history and canon law than ever before. And what he learned was so disturbing that he told Spalatin in the midst of his studies, in March 1519, that he wasn't sure "whether the pope is the Antichrist himself or whether he is his apostle, so miserably is Christ (that is, the truth) corrupted and crucified" in the centuries of papal decretals that made up canon law. The popes had more than once issued decrees that went against scripture, their office wasn't authorized by scripture, and when the church was founded there wasn't any pope in sight: it was a human institution invented much later, as in six centuries later.

In May, after all his study, Dr. Martin not only republished his 12 countertheses to Eck's but, like Eck, added a 13th thesis too—and it wasn't about free will. Instead it summed up what he'd been learning, and dropped a big hint of what he had in mind for the disputation: the only evidence for the claim that the pope was supreme over all Christian churches came from the popes' own decrees of the last 400 years, *not* from scripture or the church fathers or church history. In fact these three all proved that the pope wasn't supreme at all.

Brother Martin's friends didn't like the sound of this either. Why go out of your way to volunteer a statement like that on the pope's supremacy when there was no reason to? they asked. Forget the pope! But Dr. Martin wouldn't budge. What he was saying was bold, he knew, but he wasn't wrong to say it, or wrong to be bold. He'd have been burned at the stake by now, like his enemies wanted, if Christ hadn't been with him so far, so he would trust Christ to keep being with him, he said. And if Christ decided not to do that, and his days were numbered, then he was going to be bold instead of timid. Which after all was his job as a professor of gospel truth.

But that all assumed he'd be invited to dispute, of course. Because in early June he still wasn't, and the disputation was supposed to start on June 27. Now worried that the invitation might not actually come, and that he wouldn't be able to present his hard-won ideas in public, he decided to outfox Eck again: he would publish not only his upsetting 13th thesis in advance of the disputation but also all the proofs and arguments he'd found for it so far. When that tract appeared, Dr. Martin's friends wrung their hands and shook their heads some more, while his enemies seized on it as indisputable proof that Luther absolutely was a heretic. Eck himself, as badly as he wanted to dispute his rival, even urged Pope Leo to condemn Luther immediately, even before the disputation began, so nobody would have to hear his disturbing ideas. Just like the pope had said to Cajetan, a heretic shouldn't get a forum, especially not one as public as this disputation was going to be.

But the pope let the disputation go on, and all of churchly Europe now turned its eyes toward Leipzig. On June 24, Dr. Martin still didn't have an invitation, or even a safe conduct from Duke George. He was also having more of his *Anfechtungen,* wondering again how in the world he could be right and everyone else wrong. But he decided to climb aboard one of Karlstadt's wagons anyway and go along with him to Leipzig.

THE SPECTACLE BEGINS

Eck arrived on June 22, two days before the Wittenbergers, to give himself plenty of time to be feted.

He was so sure of good hospitality that he brought just one servant along, and his supporters were so sure of victory that the town council and Duke George treated him like he'd already won, giving him lodgings, and guards, and a horse, and a riding companion, and a place to say Mass, and a stag, all for free, while they would give Karlstadt only a doe and Luther absolutely nothing, except his share of the usual gift of wine. That Eck carried a letter of recommendation from the Fuggers didn't hurt either, and neither did his impressive display of piety in the Corpus Christi procession on June 23. The theologians of Leipzig, especially Hieronymus Emser, a chaplain at George's court, loved him as much as they hated Luther.

When the Wittenbergers came so crashingly to town on June 24, the bishop of Merseburg tried to stop the disputation: he had a sign posted on the church door prohibiting it, and right next to the sign he posted the new papal bull on indulgences too, as if to say that the subject had already been decided, so no talking was necessary. Duke George had someone run over to the church and take the sign straight back to the bishop, and the town council threw the fellow who'd posted it into jail.

Soon after arriving in town, the students from Wittenberg got into a scuffle with some local students. Certainly the Wittenbergers loved Dr. Martin more than the Leipzig students loved Eck, but mostly they were as always just eager for some action. The scuffling got so bad that first night that 34 guards had to be posted near the lodgings of the Wittenbergers, who were of course blamed for everything.

Eck and Karlstadt finally came together on June 26 to confirm the rules they'd already agreed on in writing. Karlstadt hadn't recovered from the injuries he'd suffered in the wagon-crash, or from the bleeding he'd undergone to try to mend himself, which probably explained why he got so mad when Eck tried to change the rules. The plodding German style of disputation—in which notaries wrote down every word so that judges somewhere else could render their verdict later—was too slow for Eck. He said now that he wanted the give-and-take Italian style of disputation instead, which was about memory and quick jabs and winning points with judges who sat right in the room and ruled on the spot. Karlstadt wasn't good at that style. He preferred to read long passages from the dead-heavy books he'd brought, to prove his points, and wanted absolutely zero judges, because where in the world would they find any judges now who were sympathetic to his and Luther's theology? But Eck wanted no books, and live judges. They finally compromised: (1) they would dispute German-style, with four notaries; (2) there would absolutely be judges; (3) but the judges would be chosen after the disputation and thus not be there to hear it in person; and (4) Karlstadt could read from his books, for now.

Pleissenburg, During a Non-Verbal Battle.

The festivities began early the next day, at 6 a.m., in the main auditorium of the main university building on the Ritterstrasse, where law professor Simon Pistoris greeted everyone on behalf of the university. With banners waving and guards walking alongside, the crowd then moved procession-style, two by two, over to the St. Thomas church for Mass, then at last to Duke George's Pleissenburg palace, which he'd offered when it was obvious the university didn't have a big enough hall to hold everyone who wanted to watch. Everybody finally settled into the palace's Hall of Princes, where walls and benches and tables and the upper gallery were covered with banners and tapestries that made it look like a jousting tournament. But even this bigger hall overflowed, especially since besides the regular onlookers 76 guards had to stand inside, supposedly to protect Eck from Wittenbergers and Bohemians. Two tables stood in the middle, with a pulpit on each, the one for Eck covered with an image of St. George slaying the dragon, and the one for Karlstadt (and presumably Luther) covered by St. Martin. The Leipzig theologians all sat behind their man, while the Wittenbergers sat behind Karlstadt. The still-not-invited Martin Luther watched like an ordinary spectator from the upper gallery.

For the next two hours, a Leipzig professor of Greek named Petrus Mosellanus gave a speech on the "Art of Disputation, Especially on Matters Theological," because no one from the theology faculty would give it. He'd been sick, and so was hard to hear, but as best he could he urged the disputants to show gentleness and humility, to resolve disagreements instead of heightening them, to state an opponent's argument fairly instead of distorting it, to refute clearly instead of vaguely, and to avoid false charges and shouting and anger and hate and hair-splitting—in other words to do and avoid what almost no disputant ever did or avoided. When he finally and blessedly finished, he asked everyone to kneel and listen to the St. Thomas choir, accompanied by the local fife corps, sing *Veni, Sancte Spiritus,* or Come, Holy Spirit, because boy did they need it.

During the lunch that followed, rumors spread that more Bohemians were in town than expected, and so Duke George, despiser of all things Bohemian, increased the guard still more. When everybody was back from lunch, Karlstadt and Eck both formally took an oath of orthodoxy, with Karlstadt adding on his own that he didn't intend to deviate one iota from Catholic doctrine, and with Eck—not to be outdone—adding that he was totally loyal to the pope and would not stray one tiny bit from scripture or holy mother church.

Finally the disputing began, and continued the rest of the afternoon, and then for five more days, entirely on the question of free will, with Eck saying that by nature you certainly could use free will to cooperate with grace, and Karlstadt supporting Luther's position that you could not: salvation was entirely in the hands of God. Eck hemmed and hawed over whether you needed grace first to do good works, because if he said yes he'd be supporting Luther and if he said no he might look Pelagian, but Karlstadt was still too woozy from his fall to trap him into some contradiction of logic or dogma, which was how you actually won a disputation. Instead Eck confused Karlstadt with sarcasm, and Karlstadt alternated between looking frantically through his notes and reading out long dead-heavy passages from his dead-heavy books. Some students from Wittenberg soon headed home, disappointed that there wasn't more action than this, and even Dr. Martin admitted that the disputing had been "wretched." Oh, Karlstadt knew scripture better than Eck, but if people were asleep then how could they notice?

THE CHAMPIONS AT LAST

Just before Eck and Karlstadt had started their disputation, on that June 27, Eck had summoned Luther and at this last possible moment finally officially invited him to join in, and to discuss the rules the two of them would follow.

Surely Eck left Luther waiting all these months not just to annoy him but also so that Eck would be sure of disputing with Karlstadt first, so that he could vanquish him and win the audience to his side before he even took on Luther.

Eck and Dr. Martin agreed on rules similar to those Eck and Karlstadt had agreed on too, except Dr. Martin was even more against the idea of outside judges than Karlstadt had been, and he wanted absolutely no notes of the disputation sent to Rome as possible evidence against him. But both Eck and Duke George insisted on judges: they and everyone else and in fact all of Christendom wanted a clear winner, and a once-and-for-all declaration on Luther's theology. Brother Martin's friends finally made him realize that if he refused judges, it would look like he refused to be judged at all, which would hurt his reputation. At last he said fine: then no Dominicans or Franciscans. Fine, said Eck: then no Augustinians either. Dr. Martin also wanted judges to come from all the faculties of the universities that would do the judging, not just the theology faculty, because he knew that most professors who liked his theology were young, and most young professors were in the colleges of Arts and law, not theology. Why not let "shoemakers and tailors" judge them then? asked Eck sarcastically. The two men agreed that the judges would come from the universities of Erfurt and Paris, but when they still couldn't agree on which faculties should be included they agreed to leave the matter until the disputation was over.

Eck and Dr. Martin were supposed to start disputing on July 4, the day after Eck and Karlstadt broke off. Very early that morning, before the action began, Dr. Martin for some reason visited the church of the Dominicans. Did he want a glimpse of the ailing Johann Tetzel, who was still hiding out at the friary there out of fear that the Wittenbergers had come to kill him? Dr. Martin actually felt for the man, he said, writing in February 1519 that "I regret that Tetzel has been reduced to such misery, that his doings have been brought to light, and that his safety is in danger." Dr. Martin also later claimed that he wrote Tetzel a letter of comfort, telling him not to take all the blame for the mess over indulgences, because some of the very people who were now mad at him were more responsible than he was, including Archbishop Albrecht and the pope. Whether Tetzel got any comfort from this or not, he soon died—very possibly during the disputation—with his prophecy unfulfilled that he would live to see Luther burn at the stake still.

It was also possible that Dr. Martin went to the Dominican church just to hear Mass. But if he did, then when word spread that he was in the church, all the mass-saying priests at the altars supposedly grabbed up all the holy vessels they could and fled so that they wouldn't be contaminated by the presence of such a heretic.

The new round of disputing between Dr. Martin and Eck was to begin at 7 a.m., with the swearing of oaths. The excitement, long gone from the Hall of Princes thanks to Karlstadt, now returned as the two champions entered: this was the battle everyone had come to Leipzig to watch. "In the name of the Lord. Amen," swore Dr. Martin, who couldn't resist adding that "out of reverence for the Supreme Pontiff and the Roman Church" he gladly would have avoided the subject of papal supremacy, because it "creates an astonishing amount of odium against one," but he was drawn into it "by the excellent Dr. Eck." Dr. Martin looked thin again, said Petrus Mosellanus, who later described the scene, so thin that you could almost count his bones. But he was also vigorous and lively and witty and "full of learning" and would soon show that he seemed to have the whole body of scripture at his fingertips—which by the way never impressed his enemies, who said that the Devil and every heretic knew scripture inside out too. Dr. Martin would also show himself to be courteous and friendly when he wanted to be, but everyone agreed that he had a couple of annoying habits: he was "somewhat too violent and cutting in his reprimands," and during the disputation he always held a flower or two in his hand, which drove some people crazy. He also wore a silver ring with a capsule on it, instead of his usual gold one, and at least one person in the audience guessed that the Devil was inside that capsule. But in fact Dr. Martin used these items to keep the Devil away: roses were known to be good against the evil one, and so was the amulet that was almost certainly inside the capsule, rather than the Devil himself.

Eck swore his orthodoxy next, and he couldn't resist adding something either, which contradicted what Luther had said about how this whole argument had started: it was actually Luther's doing, insisted Eck, because he'd first raised the question of the pope's authority in his *Explanations* of the 95 theses. Eck's 13 theses were a *response* to that, and thus not first. Eck, 33 and thus three years younger than Luther, was an even more impressive figure, with his taller and more powerful body (his enemies called it bloated and flabby), his fuller voice, his superior reputation as a disputer, and a longer and wider-ranging education too: Eck had started university at 12, was ordained a priest earlier than usual, was a doctor of theology at 24, and had studied every theological tradition plus ancient languages. He especially possessed one gift everyone could agree on: a phenomenal memory, compared to Luther's merely excellent one (at least for scripture). Eck was a little more charismatic than Luther too, coming into every session smiling, and bowing, and trading smart remarks, and sparring with George's fool, and even walking in one day with a whip to show that he'd just come in from a ride, as if he never needed to prepare for mental combat. Even his enemies admitted that he was funny and told good stories and was fast on his feet, but he used scriptures "promiscuously," they said, without regard to context, and if you stopped to look at what he said, you might think he was just "throwing dust" into the eyes of his audience.

After taking their oaths, the two men started disputing, as they would do for the next 10 days (except feast days). Eck launched immediately into the only subject that really seemed to interest him: the supremacy of the pope. He argued at length, with proofs from scripture and the church fathers, that God Himself had founded the papacy and that the pope was therefore universally supreme over the church from the start, contrary to what Dr. Martin had asserted in

Max Seliger, *The Leipzig Disputation 1519*.

his *Explanations* and then more elaborately in his 13th thesis. But Dr. Martin responded that Eck was interpreting scripture wrongly: the usual proofs of papal supremacy—Matthew 16 ("you are Peter, and on this rock I will build my church") and John 21 ("feed my sheep")—didn't refer to Peter's (or his successors') particular authority or charge but to the faith of the entire church. Faith was the rock, just as he'd told Cajetan in their meeting at Augsburg, but now he said it in public too. Faith was what fed the sheep. And he was absolutely sure of this interpretation, even though Eck presented evidence that the church fathers had said otherwise. Brother Martin explained why: yes, the church fathers had to be respected, but they didn't carry the same weight as scripture, especially on this subject, and they hadn't relied on convincing passages from scripture to support their view. No, to understand the office of the pope you had to interpret scripture properly, realize that scripture was superior to the fathers, and study some church history, which he had been doing for the past few months.

This had to surprise Eck. He'd expected Luther to rely on both scripture and the church fathers, but he hadn't expected him to say that scripture and the fathers weren't equal, or to rely so heavily on all the church history that he now eagerly trotted out. The early Greek and African and Asian churches were independent of Rome but everyone still considered them part of Christendom, explained Dr. Martin, so how could the pope have been universally supreme? Ah, countered Eck, those churches made appeals to Rome, suggesting they recognized its supremacy. Dr. Martin explained those appeals away, and concluded as he had before: the popes could certainly be granted the honorary leadership of the church, but the papacy itself was an earthly institution created by humans rather than directly by God.

This went on all day, back and forth, neither champion yielding an inch or leaving any argument unchallenged. Only on the next day, July 5, did Eck see his chance. If Luther wouldn't accept the usual scriptural proofs of papal authority, and if Eck couldn't come up with any other proofs that would satisfy Luther, then Eck would try another tactic: guilt by association. And Eck guessed that the association he had in mind would play exceedingly well with his audience. Suddenly Eck asked rhetorically, guess who else questioned the divine right and supremacy of the popes over the church? None other than John Wycliffe, the English heretic, and Jan Hus, the Bohemian heretic.

BOGEYMEN

Even though there wasn't any formal charge of heresy from Rome yet against Dr. Martin, just about everyone, especially in Saxony, where the Hus-loving Bohemians had wreaked so much havoc a century before, knew that Hus was a terrifying heretic. If Luther could be made to sound like him, then that could be enough proof to show that he was a terrifying heretic too.

The Bohemians hadn't been the only people in recent centuries to complain about the authority of the pope, but they had been some of the few willing to do something forcible about it, as in make war and shed blood among their neighbors. Brother Martin understood how deep this memory was in Saxony, which was why he'd been insisting he was no Bohemian ever since Johann Tetzel first called him one in 1518. Still, for many years he didn't really think much more than anybody else about what the label meant: as a boy he'd heard goosebump-raising stories about Bohemians, and as a young friar he'd heard his fellow brothers proudly tell how one of their very own from the friary in Erfurt had been the lead denouncer of Hus at the Council of Constance in 1415. And all the friars in Erfurt, including Brother Martin, had even taken their final vows while lying upon the tombstone of that brother, just in front of the high altar. Like everybody else, Brother Martin just knew that a terrifying label did-n't really need explaining, or detailed knowledge and proof: they all just knew in their bones that Bohemians were bad.

Then, to his surprise, he'd begun to doubt that. After a few years as a friar, he'd nervously read some of Hus's sermons and was stunned to see that they weren't as bad as he'd supposed. Then these last few months of studying church history, he'd been even more stunned to see that some of Hus's teachings condemned at Constance weren't so bad either, and that there was reason in scripture to agree with them. Surely everybody else would see that too, if they would just look at the evidence, and stop calling him a "Hussite" like it was something bad. And so in response to Eck's little question, Dr. Martin decided to risk saying so out loud: Some of Hus's condemned teachings, he began, were actually perfectly Christian, such as that the church was the entire communion of the elect and not just the pope, and that believing in papal supremacy wasn't necessary for salvation.

Thump. If any boredom had crept back into the room since the champions began, or any drowsiness from the summer heat, it was gone in an instant and replaced by breath-robbing tension. Maybe Dr. Martin sensed that, because he quickly started explaining what he meant by such a statement, and presenting

Workshop of Lucas Cranach, *Portrait of George of Saxony (1471–1539)*.

all the indisputable evidence from canon law and church history that supported Hus, like the papal historian Bartolomeo Platina (d. 1481) saying that popes received their authority from the Roman emper-ors, not God. But Dr. Martin was trying to bring nuance and evidence to a term (Bohemian) that just couldn't bear it. No matter how much explaining he did, or how many authoritative sources he offered, all most Saxons in the audience heard him say was that terrifying and heretical Bohemians weren't so bad after all.

Duke George nearly lost his surely sub-stantial breakfast when he heard it. He shook his head, put his hands on his hips, and shouted, "Now there's the Plague!"

George had actually liked Luther at first, partly because he'd had some tussles with the pope himself. And in some ways George was theologically adventurous: after all, he hadn't been afraid to host this disputation, which his cousin Frederick of Saxony wouldn't touch. But at heart George was orthodox, and these statements about Hus proved to him that Luther wasn't. George was also possibly more afraid than anyone of things Bohemian, since his part of Saxony bordered that kingdom more than Frederick's part did, and since his mother was the daughter of a Bohemian king, which meant he had to worry about guilt-by-association himself.

But while everyone else was gasping, Eck couldn't believe his good luck. Instead of outfoxing Eck, Luther had fallen into his trap. Or to use a more fitting metaphor, his goose now looked to be about as cooked as Jan Hus's had been (in Czech, the language of Bohemia, "Hus" meant "goose"). Luther had been accused of Bohemianism for over a year now, but for him to more or less admit it in public was more than Eck could have ever hoped for. And he didn't miss his chance. As Dr. Martin remembered it, Eck "the reptile swelled up, painted my crime in the darkest colors, and almost drove the audience wild with his rhetoric," shouting in his strong voice that it was highly unchristian of Luther to call any of Hus's teachings Christian. Dr. Martin now saw clearly the trouble he was in, and protested this "shameless calamity" against him. *Obviously* he hadn't meant that Bohemians were wholly Christian, just that some of their teachings were! No one listened. Eck went on: Bohemians claimed to understand scripture better than not only popes, but councils too. Wasn't Luther saying the same thing, when he said that the Council of Constance back in 1415 had wrongly condemned some of Hus's teachings? For a whole day and a half, Eck kept denouncing Luther as a Hussite, and so upsettingly that Dr. Martin twice did the unthinkable in a disputation and spoke out of turn, to protest, and to deny that he was "a patron of the Hussites!"

He got another chance to speak properly again only on July 7, when he did another thing unthinkable in a disputation: speaking in German, at least briefly, so that those whose Latin was a little rusty would understand perfectly well what he had to say. He did not mean to attack the primacy of the pope, he explained, but to clarify the office's origins. He did not mean to encourage anyone to disobey the pope, but to follow scripture. He did not think Hus's genuine errors were Christian, he repeated, but only that some of his teachings were. In short, Dr. Martin was clearly nervous about what he'd said regarding Hus. And he still wanted scriptural proof that his statements were wrong, instead of just being linked to Hus. He also tried changing the subject, by insisting they return to the question of just exactly what sort of proof Eck had to offer for the divinely instituted primacy of the pope.

Eck was willing to change subjects indeed, but not to that, because he was sure he had scored all the points he needed on the question of the pope. He wanted to turn instead back to the subject of church councils, on which he was sure he could score more. Anyone who contradicted a legitimately gathered council, like Jan Hus had, had to be in error, said Eck. And wasn't Luther, like Hus, contradicting a council, by saying that the Council of Constance had been wrong to condemn Hus? Dr. Martin tried to explain this too: the council had condemned, among other things, an idea of Hus's that had also been taught by Paul, and Augustine, and Gregory of Rimini. So were those blessed men all wrong too? Eck had to prove that a council couldn't err, and not just assert it. Dr. Martin wasn't any more against councils than he was against the pope—after all, he'd appealed to a council just last year! And the first four councils of the church might even be rightly considered infallible, like scripture, he said. But councils held ever since those four were subject to scripture, just like popes, and they had made mistakes, just like popes: the just-concluded Fifth Lateran Council, for instance, had overturned some of the decrees of the Council of Constance, and even declared the entire Council of Basel null and void. All he meant in saying that councils could err was that they had to be understood correctly, just as the position of the pope had to be understood correctly.

Whether Dr. Martin was right or not about his history, what he was saying about popes and councils was absolutely contrary to the way both of them were understood at the moment in the church, and Eck kept exploiting it. Believing that a council could err, said Eck, was just as heretical as believing that popes weren't divinely instituted, and automatically put you outside the fellowship of the church!

The two men finally stopped discussing popes and councils only when each realized the other wasn't going to yield, and when Eck believed he'd exposed Luther as a soon-to-be-flaming heretic. After that, there were fewer sparks. On July 8 and 9, they disputed Eck's theses on purgatory but agreed with each other at times, and nothing ruins the drama of a disputation like agreement. On July 11, they disputed indulgences and agreed some more, so much that Dr. Martin even said that if indulgence-preachers had preached what he and Eck agreed on then "the name of Martin would be unknown," while Eck said that if Luther hadn't questioned the authority of the pope then they would have agreed on everything. On July 12 and 13, they disputed penance, without enthusiasm. Pausing for the notaries always took some of the drama out of things, even when the drama was high, but pausing now, when the arguing was dull, was utterly deadly. Now even more students from Wittenberg went home, since the event had turned into a nightmarish version of class, with the disputants making their tenth mind-numbing rejoinder to the fifteenth eye-closing distinction.

Eck and Dr. Martin finally finished their disputing rather anticlimactically at eight in the morning on July 14. Dr. Martin and most other Wittenbergers then left right away, which caused some to think he'd fled in disgrace: he hadn't even stayed around to find out who the judges would be!

Karlstadt, now feeling better, stayed behind a couple more days to continue his unfinished disputation with the tireless Eck. Eck finished that disputation too, then stayed in Leipzig another nine whole days, to soak up the praise and gifts lavished on him by those who were sure he'd won, gifts that included a coat of camel and goat hair, and a mounted deer from Duke George, just what every professor needed. Rumor spread that he also spent some time among women and got plenty drunk.

By the end, the three men had disputed for some 17 days, but Dr. Martin and also Karlstadt thought it still hadn't been long enough: sure, they had gotten through the 13 theses laid down for the disputation, but the treatment had been superficial, and the ending too sudden. Like most professors, they could have gone on much longer, but Duke George told them they had to be done by July 15 because he needed the Pleissenburg to host the elector Joachim of Brandenburg, who was coming through town on his way back from the election of the emperor, in Frankfurt am Main.

No, the disputants and their audience hadn't forgotten about the election.

LONG LIVE THE KING

On June 28, the second day of the disputation in Leipzig, Charles Habsburg was elected as the next king of the Romans, just as his late grandfather Maximilian had long hoped.

And just as the coronation always happened in Aachen, so the election always took place in Frankfurt am Main, where the elector-archbishop of Mainz, now Albrecht, had ritually summoned the other six electors to gather, in June 1619. But efforts to sway the election had been going on long before the electors ever got to town, both before and after Maximilian's death in January. Since the five electors who'd promised their votes to Maximilian had been released from that promise by his death, the campaigning, or better yet bribing, had been fiercer than ever. As Maximilian put it to Charles before dying, the key wasn't to stand on his Habsburg name but to promise "much money." And Charles did so during these six months, handing out almost a million gulden, most of it as usual borrowed from the Fuggers.

Francis I of France handed out huge amounts too, so huge that by May it looked like he might have enough votes to win: the electors of Brandenburg, Trier, and the Palatinate were on his side, and Francis was promising a nice French marriage to the elector Frederick of Saxony—if Frederick went along, Francis would have a majority. Cardinal Cajetan was pushing Frederick toward Francis too, by saying that how Frederick voted would have a lot to do with how "that only son of Satan, Martin Luther," would be treated, and with whether Frederick finally got the Golden Rose that had long been promised to him. But much as Frederick might have wanted to thwart the Habburgs, in the end he decided to turn down all the French and Roman offers and begin negotiations with Charles. An open alliance between France and the pope, with the king of France on the German throne, wasn't necessarily better than having a Habsburg on that throne, he seemed to say. Or maybe the Habsburgs just made Frederick a better offer than Francis had.

Of course the principled Frederick claimed never to have taken a bribe for his vote. No, all the Habsburgs offered him, he insisted, was simply to repay an old debt they already owed Saxony, and to marry Charles's sister to Frederick's nephew and heir, Johann Frederick. Frederick supposedly even turned down a chance to become emperor himself: when it was clear in June that Francis wouldn't win anymore, the papal nuncio started pushing for Frederick to be elected, even though he was the protector of Martin Luther. The English envoy to the election even claimed that Frederick was elected for three whole hours. But if that was true, Frederick finally declined: he would have had to bankrupt himself to pay off the electors, and he was sickly, and he had no real ambition anymore. No, the best or least worst thing for the empire and the Wettin family, he decided, was neither for him nor for the king of France to be emperor, but Charles Habsburg instead. And so Frederick persuaded all six electors present to vote for Charles, to make it unanimous, even though Charles had never set foot in the empire and even though his first language wasn't German, but French, just like Francis's. The tocsin rang three times in Frankfurt announcing the decision, 22 trumpeters blew their horns, and the fierce imperial knight Franz von Sickingen got his army together around Frankfurt am Main to discourage any angry invasions from France.

What all this intrigue around the election of Charles V had to do with Martin Luther was that Pope Leo X didn't need Frederick of Saxony anymore. Leo still wanted the Turkish tax, of course, but the election had been an even bigger matter, and on that Frederick had let the pope down. Now Leo could go after Luther however he pleased.

Outside Rome, a Very Large Hunting Lodge. May 2, 1520. The Feast of St. Athanasius, Who Hated Heresy.

The Castello della Magliana stood on low ground a mile from the Tiber River, and eight miles down that same river from the seemingly Eternal but actually only 2,000-year-old City of Rome.

The castello had been erected decades before as a country retreat by the ever-building Pope Sixtus IV, then was expanded and walled and moated by later owners to help protect it. Inside it was more like a palace than a lodge, with murals by Raphael Sanzio and Giovanni lo Spagna, including a big colorful scene of Perseus slaying Medea, which was only fitting given all the real-life slaying that went on around the castello seemingly all the time.

Making most use of the place lately was Giovanni di Lorenzo de' Medici, son of the Magnificent Lorenzo, of Florence. Giovanni had a lot of interests, all of them hugely expensive and most of them involving a belly-stretching dinner and some stirring music or theater, but it was possible—just barely possible—that his biggest interest of all was hunting, especially here at La Magliana, where the low and damp and only partly forested terrain was hell for catching fevers but absolutely divine for the chase.

Hunting was practically mandatory for great princes like Giovanni, or Frederick of Saxony, and not even the sometimes critical Martin Luther would have begrudged either man his beloved pastime, especially since Dr. Martin himself was occasionally the grateful recipient of a piece of nice game from Frederick. Princes were born and raised to such things, so how could he object? But plenty of other critics begrudged Giovanni's hunting, because he wasn't just a great prince but a great churchman—in fact the greatest churchman of all at the moment: Pope Leo X himself.

According to canon law, churchmen, especially the greatest of them, weren't supposed to do such bloody or sporting things as hunting. But Dr. Martin might have been able to overlook even that rule, because every man sinned in some way, and because he was beginning to wonder whether churchmen really needed to have different rules from laypeople anyway, and maybe finally because Leo was at least killing animals and not people, unlike the previous pope.

Besides, a lot of cardinals in Rome, the highest sort of churchmen after the pope, hunted too; in fact it was as a young cardinal that Leo picked up the bloody habit. Still, hunting was harder to justify when you were the pope: that was why Leo's hunting-inclined predecessors had after their elections put down sword and spear and just watched the violent action, and why Leo himself had even resisted at first, declining one invitation from a cardinal by saying, "Oh, that I could but enjoy your own freedom, so as to accept your offer!" But within a year of becoming pope, Leo was hunting again, forced to it, he said, by his doctors, who insisted that he get some fresh air and exercise for his ever-expanding corpus.

And what a devout patient he had become, making hunting an almost daily sort of liturgy, to go along with the traditional sort of liturgy he did in church. He was soon the first pope in history to have a regular band of hunters, gamekeepers, dogs, and horses, plus all the traps and tools and tricks needed to ensure that (almost) every hunt was a big success. Sometimes he even spent weeks away from the papal court, hunting. Here in 1520, at age 44, he couldn't hunt much himself anymore, as his spindly legs and huge stomach and bad eyes and long frame and profuse sweating and nagging fistula all made it exceedingly hard for him to ride. But he watched enthusiastically, from his stationary white horse, or from a platform constructed for him nearby, or (in marshy areas) from a litter carried close to the action, his ever-present spyglass raised alertly to his large head while he yelled advice, and encouragement, and insults, and warnings, and praise. Sometimes he even got the chance to climb down and amble over to deliver the coup de grâce himself to some braying, stuck beast.

Yes, he loved birding too, going in early autumn to Viterbo to watch his prized falcons from Crete and eagles from Spain and raptors from Armenia soar after partridges and pheasants and other prey. And fishing was a fine sport as well, which he did energetically from boats on Lake Bolsena, with hooks and nets, just like St. Peter. But in November, and, come to think of it, at many other times of the year as well, he could always be found at La Magliana doing what he liked most of all, which was leading a good frenzied hunt full of deer and wild boar and wolves and goats and rabbits and whatever else his gamekeepers could arrange without of course depleting the supply.

Days before the hunt a gamekeeper and dog would sniff out which part of the *campagna,* or plain, was thickest with wildlife, then on the chosen morning Leo's men would create a big semi-enclosure nearby, open on one side. The semi-enclosure was six feet high, and made from long pieces of sailing cloth hooked together and fastened to poles, to contain the animals that would soon be forced inside. While this was going up, the hunting party waited alertly nearby, including Leo and usually a few cardinals dressed in gray wool coats instead of their usual scarlet robes, with Cardinal Sanseverino even wearing a lion's skin over his shoulders, like Hercules. Even though he was only conducting and not actually hunting, Leo wore hunting clothes too, right down to the riding boots that gave his Master of Ceremonies fits: how in the world were people supposed to kiss the papal feet if he was wearing those?

Hunting the Wild Boar.

When everything was ready, Leo gave the sign to start. A relay of horns followed, telling strategically placed gamekeepers and archers and musketeers and peasants to start yelling and shooting and drumming and setting fire, all of which shooed the game from its hiding places and toward the semi-enclosure, where the hunting party was heart-racingly ready with spears and javelins and swords—no guns because animals and hunters alike would soon be running in every direction. Right on cue, the terrified animals soon enough came rushing into the semi-enclosure, realized the seriousness of their predicament, and tried frantically to escape. Rabbits had some luck turning back into the fields, while dogs chased furiously behind them, but most bigger game stayed blocked in by hunters on the open side and by the makeshift fence on the other sides, which was held tightly at the poles by peasants and Swiss guards. Then the slaughter began, all animatedly directed by Leo.

Most people agreed that Leo was usually a pleasant, easygoing, fun-loving fellow, but all those characteristics somehow disappeared during a hunt. A bad hunt—one with accidents, not enough animals, and weak fighting—was one of the few things guaranteed to turn him lemon-juice sour, so that he might start taunting even the greatest noblemen present about their failures. But a good hunt—one with everyone safe, and a lot of game, and much slaughter, like the day the party brought in 50 stags and 20 wild boar—sent him into ecstasy, and everyone knew that if they wanted some document signed or some favor granted then that was precisely the moment to approach him, right there in the sometimes muddy field. Or during the riotous dinner that followed.

Maybe no one could have predicted, when Leo was born as Giovanni in 1476, how much he would love hunting as a man, but probably at least a few people could have predicted that he might grow up to become pope. The Magnificent Lorenzo had started him, as the second son, on an ecclesiastical career at a tender age, and for a son of Lorenzo "career" wasn't going to mean becoming just a village priest or even the local bishop. Giovanni received the tonsure at seven, soon became an abbot and archbishop thanks to King Louis XI of France (until it was realized the current archbishop was still alive), and was given canonries in every cathedral in Tuscany, so that by the age of 13 he already held 27 different church offices at once.

Surely all these offices were enough to qualify at least this particular 13-year-old to be a cardinal, insisted Giovanni's Magnificent father to Pope Innocent VIII, even though Innocent had sworn not to elevate anyone to that position who was under the official minimum age of 30. But Lorenzo won that argument, and Giovanni became the youngest member of the college of 24 cardinals. He soon entered the service of Pope Julius II, and when Julius died in February 1513, most observers agreed that Giovanni had an excellent chance of becoming pope himself, despite his young age (37) and variable health, because his well-polished courtliness was exactly the opposite of the rough son-of-a-peasant Julius. And so when he heard about Julius's demise, Giovanni got himself from Florence to Rome as fast as his litter-carriers could run, even though his fistula was as usual killing him. He arrived on March 6, two days after the papal conclave had begun; luckily for him, though, no one else had won enough votes yet. When several more ballots still failed to produce a winner, the younger cardinals started pushing the older ones to choose Giovanni, and for once his fistula might have actually helped him: the deadly smell of it, and the surgeon who had to make an emergency intrusion into the conclave to operate on it, were very possibly enough to convince the unconvinced to vote for Giovanni as a sort of compromise can-

Raphael, *Portrait of Pope Leo X* (detail).

didate, because if he turned out to be a bad choice, well, at least he surely wouldn't last long. He was elected on March 11.

He chose the name Leo (Latin for lion), he said, because his mother had long ago dreamed of giving birth to a huge but tame lion and when he was born his mother wanted to name him that, but her Magnificent husband wouldn't hear of it: now Giovanni would fulfill her dream. He was quickly ordained a priest (despite all his church offices he still wasn't that), then bishop of Rome, and then on March

19 he received the papal triple crown. He waited until April 11, the Feast of St. Leo, to be publicly enthroned, because a huge celebration like that took time to plan. In fact it was the biggest thing Rome had seen since the defeat of the Goths a thousand years earlier, said some: the long procession was full of images of lions, tapestries, flowers, arches, and the golden balls of the Medici; cardinals dressed their households in matching outfits; the pope's musicians wore red, white, and green; his Swiss guards looked more severe than ever; and the new pope himself sat atop his favorite white horse. Leo sweated rivers under his new crown, even though a big canopy was held over his head, because riding was now hard for him and he'd had to be lifted onto his horse. Still he tried to be his usual friendly self, stopping several times to bless the cheering crowd with his bejeweled and perfumed and gloved hand, that was surely meant to prevent the crowd from getting a whiff of his fistula. People thought he was a good choice as pope, with good personal morals, and a taste for fine art and literature, as a banner on the crumbling façade of St. Peter's stated: "Leo the Tenth, Supreme Pontiff, Protector of the Arts and Patron of Good Works," the last part of which Martin Luther would have completely agreed with, in an ironic sort of way.

Despite that unforgettable day, by 1520 Leo had not exactly compiled a scintillating record as pope. Oh, he was a dazzling patron of the arts—saying yes to everyone even when he couldn't come through, and collecting ancient books and manuscripts for the Vatican library, and appointing men of letters as his secretaries and librarian, and founding presses to print in ancient languages, and revitalizing the University of Rome by recruiting top professors and paying them high wages, and competing with his own poets in composing impromptu verse in the good classical Latin he loved. He was a dazzling nobleman too, with all his castles, and generosity, and courtesy, and noble sports and jokes, and he could have been an excellent prince since he, like his predecessors, was not just the spiritual head of the universal church but the political ruler of the Papal States, which took up much of central Italy. And he was arguably a most conscientious priest, as he piously attended Mass daily, even in hot weather, when you would have thought the sweating would be unbearable for him.

But Leo was not a scintillating pope, or even prince, mostly because, like Maximilian of Germany and so many other great ones, he always spent more than he took in. He managed in record time to exhaust the surplus that Julius II had left, thanks partly to Leo's endless dinners (one featuring 65 exhausting courses), and endless commissions to artists, and his endless music and theater.

Oh, he liked liturgical music, which could make him weep. He had a good voice, and even dabbled at composing, especially liturgical music, which could make him weep, but he liked bawdy music and theater just as much—and all of it was expensive, like the farce written by his secretary, which Leo directed himself, and during which he as usual sat up above the crowd, with his spyglass, so he could see everything, and then laughed so hard at the raciest parts that according to witnesses even the French were scandalized. He also loved to gamble for stakes that were as high as heaven, and his generous habits of flinging winnings into the crowd and paying off losses right away shrank his purse. And of course he loved hunting, which was maybe his most expensive pastime of all, because hundreds of people at court had to move with him to his lodge, so that he could have his usual dinners and music and theater and fools in the countryside too.

In short, Leo broke most of the rules about thriftiness that his Magnificent father had laid down for him when he'd first left for Rome as a new cardinal decades before. Yes, if you were great you had to spend, or you'd get a reputation for stinginess, but the solvent among the great, said his father, always kept an eye on expenses and didn't outspend their income. Leo did: and when he ran out of money, he just borrowed more, including from everyone's favorite bankers, the Fuggers, at tiara-breaking interest rates. He also sold whatever he could to raise money, including church offices and of course indulgences, until a whole third of the pope's annual income of 500,000 ducats came from these. But no matter how much he fell behind in his debts, he was sure that heaven would always provide for someone as important as he was—helping to explain why he once happily said, "Since God has given us the papacy, let us enjoy it!"

As a war-waging prince, Leo wasn't all that different from many other war-waging princes. In fact, he and his predecessors felt that the pope absolutely had to wage war, or he would be attacked by some greater prince and lose his position not just as local head of the Papal States but spiritual head of the church universal. Still, many believers expected more of a pope than just being a prince, and so were disappointed with Leo, and his recent predecessors. Some in Rome, including some cardinals, were disappointed with him for other reasons, like not delivering on some of the promises he'd made when elected, and they even tried to poison Leo. He put down their revolt and levied some huge fines (of 150,000 ducats), but it didn't quiet all of his critics, or pay off his debts.

Dr. Martin was one of those troubled by the pope's failings and excesses, but unlike most others he didn't focus on them, since the man had again mostly been raised to do what he was doing, and since every single person was a sinner.

No, it was the pope's doctrine, and the practices that resulted from it, that bothered Dr. Martin most. And Dr. Martin's brazenness in complaining about both (but especially the doctrine) was what bothered Pope Leo most about him in turn: Leo was willing to put up with wisecracks about his plays or his free verse or his hunting, but he bristled when somebody had the nerve to start correcting doctrine, and to criticize accepted church practices, which in Leo's mind were the exclusive domains of the pope. Even Lorenzo Valla, that earlier great critic of popes, understood this: like many other reformers of the last century, he attacked the morals and the dubious historical claims of the popes—but never their doctrine—and he ended up with a nice plummy position as papal secretary because of it. But Luther's attack on doctrine made Leo and plenty of others in Rome feel like the man had gone too far.

And so when a horseman rode up to the castello today, May 2, with a draft of a papal bull that the horseman and other members of a special commission had drawn up against the heretic Luther, Leo was glad to see it, especially the imagery that came straight out of La Magliana: a wild boar from the (Saxon) forest was running amok in the fields of the Lord, it said, and he had to be stopped, if necessary even as forcefully as the boar that ran around near the castello. Yes, Leo would have liked that image, especially if it had been a good hunt that day.

THE WINNER PLEASE

The Leipzig disputation of 1519, now almost a year in the past, was supposed to have answered the nagging question: Was Martin Luther a heretic?

But by the spring of 1520 the official judges *still* hadn't decided. Since Eck and Dr. Martin hadn't even been able to agree on who the judges should be, Duke George finally decided for them, the day after the disputation ended: they would, he said, come from the faculties of theology and canon law (not arts or medicine) at the universities of Erfurt and Paris. But that was the only thing decided for months, partly because it took time for the official notes from the disputation to be compared and collated and copied and sent off and then read, and mostly because the judges didn't exactly seem keen to render a verdict. While all of learned (and parts of unlearned) Europe waited, plenty of observers were glad to offer their unofficial verdicts in the meantime.

Plenty of people were sure Dr. Martin had won, starting with Philip Melanchthon, who printed a tract quite predictably saying that even though Eck

had an obvious gift for speaking, Dr. Martin was clearly the best of the disputants. More surprising was that Erasmus was calling Eck a *Jeck*, or fool, and that
the Leipzig professor Petrus Mosellanus was writing that the scholars present all
thought Dr. Martin had won while the unlearned and easily duped were with
Eck. When Eck claimed that only a few unlearned canons thought Luther was
the winner, the theologians Lazarus Spengler and Johann Oecolampadius published a sarcastic response called *From the Unlearned Canons*, which explained
in highly learned detail why Dr. Martin had indeed won. Maybe the best sign
of support for Dr. Martin came in the form of the ever-growing enrollments
at Wittenberg University: the student body was up to almost 600 now. Prince
Frederick was certainly happy about that, even if it did cause a housing crisis in
the town of 2,300.

Dr. Martin himself was also sure that he had won, although he and Karlstadt
feared that most people who'd attended the disputation had the impression that
Eck had, which frustrated them both no end: if the disputants had been able to
treat everything more thoroughly, and if Eck had cared more about getting at the
truth than about scoring points with the crowd, then surely most people would
have seen things otherwise, Dr. Martin was sure. Yet he seemed less troubled by
the perception of Eck's victory than by the uncomfortable fact that the disputation had forced him to admit to himself, as well as to the public, just exactly
what he thought about the papacy. Oh, he wouldn't take back what he'd said, and
eventually he was even glad he'd been shaken up the way he had. "Eck made me
wide awake," he said later. "He gave me my first ideas" about the pope. Thanks to
Eck, he'd gone from simply questioning (in his 95 theses) the pope's authority over
purgatory, to questioning (at Leipzig) whether the pope had any divinely sanc-
tioned authority over anything at all. And thanks to Eck, he was now sure that
scripture was a more dependable source of God's divine will than a very earthly
and fallible pope was, who sometimes even interpreted scripture wrongly. Still,
admitting just how far away his heart now was from Rome was highly unsettling,
after all the mental acrobatics he'd done before the disputation to insist that he'd
always just been defending the pope. And it was dangerous to admit that too. But
it also had the effect of making him even bolder, or at least more desperate than
before: he was going to keep saying and writing what he knew was true, instead of
dancing carefully around. If his time was up, then so be it; if it wasn't, then God
would protect him. And so just weeks after the disputation in Leipzig ended, he
published in August 1519 his *Explanations* for all 13 of his countertheses from the

disputation, so the whole world could see all of his proofs. He was proud of them, and of how his enemies were now so furiously attacking him, because it was a sure sign the Devil was after him, and anytime the Devil was after you then you must be onto something good. And he also took the trouble in these *Explanations* to note what a pathetic disputant Eck had been, with his contradictions and theatrics—so pathetic that Dr. Martin began referring to him as the pig from Ingolstadt, intent on ruining and trampling everything, the way pigs did.

Eck himself was, of course, equally sure that he'd won at Leipzig. When he finally made it back to Ingolstadt, he boasted that he'd slain two monsters from Wittenberg, and he had letters from the University of Leipzig, the theology faculty at Leipzig, and Duke George, to prove it. Actually, by the end of the first disputation, with Karlstadt, Eck had conceded almost every single point, but nobody noticed or really cared about that contest, and everybody just assumed Eck had won. He'd conceded many points to Dr. Martin too, except on papal supremacy, and councils, and Bohemianism, and since Eck was sure that those points were the ones that mattered most, and that he had won them, then he'd obviously won everything.

The longer everybody waited for an official verdict, the more a few people kept arguing over not just who had won but the issue that the disputation had so dramatically brought out: the authority of the pope. Eck wrote Prince Frederick to urge that he finally do something about his irresponsible professor. Hieronymus Emser of Duke George's court published a tract expressing his fear that the anti-papal Luther and his frightening followers would join up with the anti-papal Bohemians. Dr. Martin responded with a tract that poked fun at Emser's coat of arms, which included a goat, calling him the Goat of Leipzig, and soon the two had exchanged a tiresome number of tracts that always included something unflattering in the title about Bull Luther or Goat Emser. In fact more people than ever started writing about Dr. Martin's ideas after the Leipzig disputation, even more than had written about the 95 theses, because at Leipzig the office of the pope wasn't just a sideshow or incidental, as it had been in the 95, but the main event. Five different pamphlet battles on the subject broke out in the months after the disputation, involving 27 different pamphlets.

An argument between Franz Günther, Dr. Martin's former student who was now city preacher of Jüterbog, and the Franciscans of that town was also memorable, not only for drawing in both Eck and Dr. Martin but for Eck saying on the title page of his tract on the matter that it was meant to attack Günther and all other "Lutherans," the first time anybody had ever used that term. Eck gave a copy of the tract to the bishop of Brandenburg, who after reading it said, while sitting around a fire, that he wouldn't rest until he'd personally thrown Martin Luther into the blaze, just like he was doing with these logs.

Maybe most disturbing of all to Dr. Martin while he awaited the official verdict of the disputation was reading seriously for the first time the writings of Jan Hus. He'd glanced at some of the man's sermons years before, of course, and he knew the teachings condemned by the Council of Constance, but in the fall of 1519 Dr. Martin started reading all of Hus's collected works, thanks to a Bohemian organ builder who'd been at Leipzig and who afterwards sent him a copy. Dr. Martin was astonished at what he found: maybe "we are all Hussites," he wrote after reading the collection. All this time he'd been teaching Hus and hadn't even known it! He didn't agree with Hus on everything: Hus hadn't seen the difference between law and gospel clearly enough, and he'd focused too much on the moral failings of the popes instead of their doctrinal failings, and he'd thought the church could be made perfect through reform. But Dr. Martin agreed with Hus wholeheartedly about the earthly origins of the papacy. He agreed with him too that laypeople, just like the clergy, should be able to take the sacrament of the Eucharist in both kinds—thus both the consecrated wafer and wine, instead of just the wafer, as had long been the practice in the Roman church. And Dr. Martin decided to now say that in print too, and in German, in a tract of December 1519 called *The Blessed Sacrament of the Holy and True Blood of Christ, and the Brotherhoods*. The Bohemians loved the tract, because it agreed with the practice they'd followed ever since Hus, but Duke George and the bishops of Saxony hated it precisely because it sounded so terrifyingly Bohemian. It even made some priests in the city of Meissen suspect that Luther had Bohemian blood in him, and to cause them to say that it wouldn't be any sin at all to spill some of his blood. Not even Prince Frederick was happy about Dr. Martin's little Bohemian-sounding book, because in his view it had unnecessarily upset Duke George, but Dr. Martin responded to his prince by saying that you couldn't preach the true gospel without upsetting somebody. Many followers agreed, and soon they were adding a swan next to Dr. Martin's image, as if he were the fulfillment of the prophecy people claimed had been uttered by Hus at the stake in 1415: "Now they will roast this goose ['Hus'] but one hundred years hence they will hear the song of a swan which they shall have to tolerate."

Suddenly in the middle of all the arguing over who had won the disputation, a rumor spread that the University of Erfurt had reached a verdict—in favor of Johann Eck. Dr. Martin was furious at the news and quickly wrote his friend at the Augustinian friary in Erfurt, Johann Lang, to say that the university should never have interfered in the matter, and he would condemn their decision in another public disputation in both Latin and German as soon as he could. But it turned out to be only a rumor: what the judges of Erfurt actually declared on December 29, 1519, was that they didn't want to rule on the disputation at all. Now Duke George was furious. He ordered them to do their jobs: it was an honor to be a judge, so judge! Dr. Martin was actually relieved by Erfurt's refusal, because it meant that the University of Paris, the other judge, probably wouldn't dare rule alone on such a sensitive subject as the authority of the pope. And Paris was having trouble anyway: it had started out in the hallowed way of universities, by forming a committee of judges, who were each supposed to get 25 or 30 crowns for their work, plus a copy of the official transcript of the disputation provided for free by Duke George. But George didn't want to pay for all that, and so Paris decided not to decide either.

A couple of other universities who hadn't been invited to the disputation-judging party were kind enough to jump in anyway, and to render a verdict not on the disputation itself, but on Luther's writings in general. The Universities of Cologne and Leuven had each obtained a copy of his first set of collected writings, published in late 1518 in Basel, and by August 30, 1519, both condemned a long list of alarming excerpts they had found. For good measure, they condemned them again on November 7, and yet again in February 1520. Naturally Dr. Martin disliked that verdict, and now he added to his list of very fallible human institutions not only popes and councils but universities too. After all, he said, universities had also condemned Johannes Reuchlin, Lorenzo Valla, Pico della Mirandola, William Ockham, Johann Wesel, Jacques Lefèvre d'Étaples, and Erasmus too, and had had to retract them all, so that their condemnations weren't worth any more "than the cursings of a drunken woman"—another version of a favorite insult of the time.

Johann Eck was thrilled about the general verdicts from Leuven and Cologne, but he was as frustrated as Duke George that the Universities of Erfurt and Paris wouldn't carry out their duties to decide on the disputation itself. He therefore decided to publish more books against Luther, especially a new tract from early 1520 called *Three Books on the Primacy of Peter,* in which he elaborated on what he had said at Leipzig: if you rejected popes and councils, then you couldn't be sure of anything; no one was free to interpret scripture on his own; and you couldn't say scripture was the highest authority when Christ himself had said in scripture (John 21) that not everything was in scripture. It wasn't a matter of scripture versus the institutional church, as Luther kept saying, but scripture *plus* the institutional church.

But even more important than Eck's writings after Leipzig was how he pushed Rome to take serious legal action against Luther, more than probably anyone else from German lands had. Yes, he wanted Paris and Erfurt to render an academic verdict, but even more important was that Rome issue a juridical verdict. Wasn't it obvious from the now-printed transcript of the Leipzig disputation, and from Luther's 13 theses and countertheses there, just how dead-set he was against the pope, and thus just how big a heretic he was? asked Eck. No one understood Luther the way he did, Eck kept repeating, and if Rome knew what he knew, it would do something right away. At this very moment, big chunks of Saxony and even Brandenburg were threatening to follow Luther and break away from the pope, he warned, that's how dangerously popular he already was.

THE POPE'S NEW GERMAN MAN

In a meeting of the cardinals in Rome on January 9, 1520, an Italian church-man stood up and repeated what Johann Eck had been saying for months, with a twist: that it was time for Pope Leo to finally do something about not just Martin Luther but his protective prince, Frederick, elector of Saxony, before the two of them poisoned the entire church.

Rome had left Luther pretty much alone since his meeting in Augsburg with Cardinal Cajetan in 1518, mostly because Pope Leo wanted Prince Frederick's vote for a new emperor. Yet when Frederick didn't vote the way Leo wanted, Leo still didn't take immediate action: like everybody else, the pope was waiting for the verdict from Leipzig, which he hoped would go against Luther and be enough evidence to persuade Frederick to finally arrest him.

While he waited, Leo showed he was less than happy about the continued bun-gling of Karel von Miltitz. Among other actions, Miltitz finally handed over the Golden Rose to Frederick in September 1519, in Saxony—or more specifically, he handed it to Frederick's cousin and councilor, Fabian von Feilitzsch, whom Frederick sent so as not to look too eager himself. The pope hadn't wanted to give the Rose until Frederick promised to arrest or expel Luther, but he couldn't go back on his word, and so Cajetan finally instructed Miltitz to take it to him, along with another reminder to obey the church, just like Frederick's ancestors had (mostly) done. Surely Cajetan or at least Miltitz hoped that by accepting the Rose Frederick was committing himself to arrest Luther. That was in fact exactly what Miltitz said when he gave the Rose to Feilitzsch: now the prince will surely seize the friar. But the councilor didn't commit Frederick to anything, and Miltitz more or less pretended he was just joking—of course Frederick could have the Rose! What Miltitz really hoped, he added, was that the archbishop of Trier would still judge Luther: that man's judgment would be good enough for him, and Miltitz's plan of reconciliation might then come to pass.

It wasn't good enough for Rome though. In November the papal curia wrote Miltitz to say they weren't happy with Frederick's continued delays, which they blamed partly on Miltitz: he'd spent almost the whole past year in the empire and hadn't accomplished a thing. Pope Leo also kept pressuring Frederick directly, making sure that various letters went out to him, including one from Rafael Riario, who knew Frederick's deceased brother Ernest: yes, Luther had shown some promise and good ideas at first, the letter said, but now he had gone too far, and was clearly just being ambitious, always a favorite charge of anyone who didn't like critics. But maybe letters like Riario's struck a nerve, because by February 1520 Frederick was asking Luther to please keep quiet: he was sure that Rome was about to take real action. But Dr. Martin wouldn't promise anything, except to keep teaching and preaching the gospel, as he'd sworn to do. If the prince didn't want him to do either, then he would stop, but as long as he remained in his position he had no choice, even if it meant offending the pope. He'd already conceded and compromised as much as he could, he said, and had even written a letter of explanation and apology to every bishop in Saxony, just as Frederick had asked. But all he'd gotten from his efforts to be conciliatory were wounds, and so he was going to keep speaking out. "I stand alone," he said. "I have always been dragged into this affair, and now it is not right to withdraw as long as Eck keeps shouting. I am obliged to commend the cause to God and follow Him loyally, having committed my ship to the winds and waves." And don't forget, he reminded his prince again, "the Word of God can never advance without whirlwind, tumult, and danger," as the ancient Christian martyrs proved. Danger was in fact real for Dr. Martin, as he'd heard some months before from a friend in Halle: there was some doctor "who can make himself invisible at will and then kill someone" who had an order to kill Dr. Martin himself. And that was just one of the rumored attempts on his life.

Not content with badgering Frederick, Pope Leo also tried putting pressure on Dr. Martin again through his superiors in the Augustinian order, by writing to the new general of the order, Gabriel Venetus, that he simply had to get Luther to recant. Venetus in turn wrote Staupitz, recounting all the foundation-shaking damage Luther had done to the order's reputation, and how so many friars now followed his ideas, all of which could have been stopped if Staupitz had shown just a little more will. Their order wouldn't even exist without the pope, and they owed plenty to him, and so to have one of their own members denouncing the pope was unacceptable. If Staupitz wouldn't force Luther to stop his scurrilous writing—and everyone knew he could if he wanted, said Venetus—then maybe some of the precious privileges of the German Augustinian friaries would have to be reconsidered.

Surely pressure like this was why in May 1520 Staupitz resigned as vicar-general of the German Augustinians, and then some months later quit the order altogether to become a Benedictine monk—and in Salzburg, far away from Saxony. Dr. Martin felt abandoned by his old mentor. Staupitz had been quiet since the meeting with Cajetan at Augsburg, mostly to avoid getting the order into further trouble or putting himself in a position in which he'd have no choice but to punish his protégé. Although Staupitz and Dr. Martin had very similar ideas about justification, and indulgences, and the pope, they had very different views, or needs, about expressing them. Like Prince Frederick, Staupitz mostly stayed quiet on controversial subjects, which Dr. Martin sometimes took as indifference or even abandonment. He wanted to hear from Staupitz, especially since the *Anfechtungen* were back again in early 1520, with the usual questions filling his head: Who are you to question Aristotle, or Thomas, or Bonaventure, or many holy pontiffs? Dr. Martin even dreamed that Staupitz had left him for good and he woke up crying because of it. Staupitz finally wrote in May 1520 to offer his affection, but Staupitz wouldn't break from the pope or the religious life he loved, as he sensed Brother Martin seemed prepared to do.

Finally Pope Leo decided to put all the pressure he could on Luther, and Frederick, by having a commission draft a bull that would threaten Luther with excommunication. The commission, headed by none other than Cardinal Cajetan (for theology) and Cardinal Pietro Accolti (for canon law), had a draft of the bull ready by late January. But even then its members still wanted to try reconciling with Luther, since that would be far less noisy and messy than excommunication: all he had to do was compromise a little, and they would work with him. Any hope of reconciliation was crushed, though, when Leo invited someone to join the commission who wanted nothing to do with compromise: namely, Johann Eck.

All of Eck's letters to Rome, his insistence that only he truly knew how bad Luther was, and probably even his *Three Books on the Primacy of Peter,* had indeed gotten the attention of Pope Leo. Eck gladly accepted the invitation to join the commission, and arrived in Rome by April—and not exactly to the delight of his fellow commissioners. Cardinal Cajetan supposedly muttered, "Who let in that beast?" showing as much partisanship toward this German as he'd shown toward the Germans Miltitz and Luther, and as much as Eck and Luther often showed toward Italians. But Eck was unfazed and jumped right into his work: there should be no talk of reconciliation with Luther, he insisted, but only condemnation and excommunication. Eck even took the commission's first draft of the bull and added 41 specific errors to it, all taken directly from Luther's writings, as indisputable and specific proof of his heresy, as if to say to Prince Frederick, you keep asking for evidence and here it clearly is. Some of these, explained the bull, were obviously heretical, some were misleading, some were just wrong, but all were harmful. And it surely meant something that the 41 listed were even more numerous than the 30 that had gotten Jan Hus killed.

It was no surprise that the enthusiastic Eck was the member of the commission who ended up taking it personally to the Castello della Magliana, for the pope to have a look at, no doubt during the hunt.

THE DREADED BULL

Like any bull, this one had to be discussed in the college of cardinals before it was issued, and that discussion took place on May 21, 23, 26, and June 1 of 1520. Pope Leo came back from La Magliana for the first meeting, but that was enough for him, and he went back to his lodge the next day.

Besides Cajetan and Eck, Prierias took part in the meetings too, as did General Gabriel Venetus of the Augustinians. Eck was still the only German, and he was more determined than anybody to condemn Luther harshly, without any

BVLLA
Decimi Leonis, contra errores Martini
Lutheri, & fequacium.

deaurato, circumamicta varietatibus ;

Aftitit Bulla a dextris eius, in veftitu

Vide lector, opereprecium eft. Adficie*
ris . Cognofces qualis paftor
fit Leo.

Exsurge Domine.

further hearing. There was some arguing on that point, partly out of resentment toward the outsider Eck, and partly because the canon lawyers among them thought it was only fair for Luther to have a hearing: even the obviously guilty Adam had gotten a chance to defend himself, they said! But the theologians on the commission were unanimous in insisting that Luther be condemned. The cardinals finally compromised: Luther would be summoned to Rome instead of merely arrested, but he would get no hearing. And the excommunication wouldn't happen immediately, but he would get 60 days, from the time he received the bull, to recant.

The final draft of the bull, called *Exsurge Domine,* reached 30 whole pages when it was printed. It started with Psalm 74, which every vintner and farmer in Italy understood: "Rise up, O God, plead your cause," because "foxes have arisen" and the "wild boar from the forest" too, and everybody knew what both of those beasts did to vineyards and fields. It called on Peter to rise up too, and carry out the pastoral office he'd been charged with, in Matthew 16. And it called on Dr. Martin's favorite apostle Paul to arise as well, and also all the saints and the whole church, to rise up against lying teachers like Martin Luther who had bitter contention in their hearts and who boasted and lied, wrongfully attacking the holy pontiffs. Luther put aside the "true interpretation of Holy Scripture," the bull claimed, because he was "blinded in mind by the father of lies" and thought himself wise in his own eyes. He interpreted "these same Scriptures otherwise than the Holy Spirit demands," inspired only by his "own sense of ambition" and desire for "the world's glory," so that he no longer preached the gospel of Christ but the gospel of himself instead—or worse, the gospel of the Devil! The pope could hardly believe his ears when he'd first heard Luther's errors, because so many of them had been condemned in the past and as a theologian Luther surely knew that, but there they were, given new life by a few frivolous souls in the illustrious German nation, which the pope had always held "in the bosom of our affection" because it had always been so reliable in putting down heresy. If the Germans had done the same this time, then the whole church wouldn't have had to suffer such errors. The pope himself would suffer them no longer.

What a long list of errors they were too, a veritable syllabus of errors, taken straight from the writings of Martin Luther. Such as: that sin always remained even in the absolved and justified sinner. That in every good work even an apparently just man sinned, because of pride. That some teachings of Jan Hus were most Christian. That those who believed indulgences actually worked had been seduced. That the treasures of the church were not the merits of Christ and of the saints. And so on, regarding the sacraments, excommunication, the power of the keys, the authority of popes and councils, the burning of heretics, free will, purgatory, and more—but not a word about Luther's view of justification by faith, which still didn't rise to heresy. The claim that all 41 points were wrong didn't come with any explicit proofs from the Bible, which worried Eck, because he knew what Luther would say about that. And so Eck urged the commission to add such proofs, because they certainly existed. But the others felt they didn't need to prove anything to a heretic and so just asserted the pope's and the church's authority, which was what the whole argument was about after all.

After the list of errors came the conclusions and instructions. "No one of sound mind is ignorant how destructive, pernicious, scandalous, and seductive to pious and simple minds these various errors are," or how "destructive they are of the vigor of ecclesiastical discipline, namely obedience." Obedience was the "font and origin of all virtues," and without it, everything would fall apart. These teachings of Luther are "against the doctrine and tradition of the Catholic Church, and against the true interpretation of the sacred Scriptures received from the Church." Luther says that the Church that is guided by the Holy Spirit "is in error and has always erred," and that of course cannot be. All the faithful and all ecclesiastical institutions must reject these errors, or be excommunicated. All universities must reject them, or have their papal privilege revoked. And all people possessing the writings containing these errors must stop reading them, and even burn them.

The pope had given Luther every chance to repent, continued the bull, but he'd refused to come to Rome, and then he'd made things worse by appealing to a council, which he didn't believe in anyway. The pope could therefore only ask himself, "O good God, what have we overlooked or not done? What fatherly charity have we omitted that we might call him back from such errors?" The pope's men spoke with Luther in various hearings and wrote letters, and offered safe conduct and expenses for him to come to Rome, and if he had, then "we are certain he would have changed in heart, and he would have recognized his errors." But he refused to this day to listen, and so they had every right and reason to treat him now as a certifiably notorious heretic and thus excommunicate him on the spot. Instead they were treating him mercifully, and would embrace him, like the prodigal son, if he returned. All he had to do was stop preaching immediately and, within 60 days of the posting of this bull in his diocese, come to Rome and recant, or at least send a certified written recantation. Otherwise he and all of his followers would be declared notorious heretics. Any Christian who encountered him then—especially those in religious orders—should seize him and send him to Rome. And any place lodging him more than three days would be placed under the interdict, meaning the sacraments couldn't be administered there.

The bull was dated June 15, 1520, and first posted in Rome on July 24, on the door of St. Peter's basilica. The pope never signed it, and neither did the cardinals, which made Eck worry it wouldn't be seen as authentic, as did the multicolored ribbon in place of the usual hemp one. But surely people wouldn't doubt its authenticity when they saw which authoritative figures had been assigned to spread it around the empire: Eck himself and Girolamo Aleandro, the new nuncio assigned to Emperor Charles's court specifically for the Luther case. While in German lands, Eck and Aleandro were also to arrange public burnings of Luther's books, and to urge German princes (i.e., Frederick) to seize Luther when the 60 days were up.

The bull reached assorted parts of Saxony in late September and early October, by which time Pope Leo was already dreaming about the November hunt, and the real sort of wild boar, instead of the troublemaking monkish sort.

9

Little Flea

Cologne, the Church of the Franciscans. November 4, 1520. The Feast of St. Joannicus of Mount Olympus, Who Defied the Emperor.

rederick Wettin had always tried to avoid at least the appearance of playing favorites among his many castles, and so it wouldn't have been surprising if he did the same among the churches in his lands too. But nobody who knew him would've been surprised at all to see what sort of church he was worshiping in today, in faraway Cologne.

His endless curiosity and his boundless enthusiasm for relics had surely moved him to visit many of Cologne's plentiful churches during his past few weeks in that city, like strong-towered St. Severin's, or flat-roofed St. Pantaleon's, or ancient St. Andreas's, or tall and delicate St. Anthony's, or clover-choired St. Martin's, or the still-unfinished but already heaven-scratching *Dom*, or relic-overflowing St. Ursula's with pieces of 11,000 martyred virgins. But for his devotions Frederick was in the church of the Franciscans. Of course. Practically all of his ducal predecessors in Saxony had been buried in the Franciscan church in Wittenberg, and his longtime confessor was a Franciscan too. This church in Cologne was a lovely one besides—it had to be, given all the churchly competition in town—with its long Gothic nave that Franciscans so loved, and the tomb of one of the order's (if not Dr. Martin's) great heroes, the scholastic theologian Duns Scotus.

No, the only thing surprising about Frederick sitting inside this Franciscan church in Cologne was the Cologne part, and that Frederick had been in that city during these past few weeks instead of in Aachen for the coronation of the new emperor. He never missed big imperial events like that—not the Diets that happened every few years, and absolutely not the even-rarer coronation. And he'd fully intended to go to this one too. Even though traveling was unbearable for him now, thanks to his gout and all his stones from too much fine dining and all his achy badly healed bones from too much jousting, Frederick had climbed doggedly into a coach and set out for Aachen a month or so before. He didn't like going by coach, since it was twice as slow as a horse, and made him feel feeble, and was still bumpy even when his men rode constantly ahead to try to smooth out mostly unsmoothable roads, but he simply couldn't ride a horse anymore. Sometimes the bumping in the coach was so bad he had to be carried in a litter, but that was even slower than a coach, and what kind of jostling might you have to suffer anyway if one of the litter-carriers stumbled, or you had to move to scratch yourself? Still, not even the thought of all that jostling, or the latest attack of gout that had hit him along the way to Aachen, could have kept Frederick of Saxony from getting to the coronation on time. No, the only thing that could have done that was the plague.

In fact, the plague was raging in Aachen at the very moment Frederick had hoped to arrive there, and he didn't want to be anywhere near it—especially in his weakened state, and especially when he knew that so many of his male forebears had died right around his age (56), from either disease or hunting. And so he'd decided reluctantly to stop in Cologne, 50 miles short of Aachen, and send somebody who was healthier and less indispensable than he was to represent him at the coronation.

Even though he'd missed the big ceremony on October 23, Frederick knew that most everyone who was anyone—including the new emperor, Charles—would come straight over to Cologne afterward anyway, to finish their business and feasting and jousting far away from plague-ravaged Aachen. And so far Frederick had been able to see who he'd wanted to see, but there were two people he didn't want to see at all and had therefore been avoiding like, well, the plague: the papal nuncios Girolamo Aleandro and Marino Caracciolo, who wanted to bother him some more about Dr. Martin.

Surely that was at least partly why Frederick was in the Franciscan church today—not just admiring its beauty or the stirring words and music or just calming his soul, but practicing his favorite princely methods of avoiding and stalling. The nuncios had been pestering him for a meeting ever since they arrived in Cologne the week before, and Frederick had been able to give them the slip by saying he had important business with the emperor. Or by going to church—a lot.

But then suddenly somebody at least figuratively tapped him on the shoulder and handed him a batch of documents. Who tapped princes, even figuratively? And handed over, during Mass, serious documents bearing the seals of two nuncios?

Obviously Caracciolo and Aleandro knew about Frederick's fondness for Franciscan churches, and they were going to get their message to him whether he liked it or not.

THE BULL GOES NORTH

Rome had, of course, pestered Prince Frederick about Dr. Martin for more than two years now.

But since June of this year, 1520, the prince had had more reason than ever to fear that actual and substantial steps were about to be taken against his dear professor, who had almost single-handedly made Frederick's even dearer university so famous and full. And there was also more reason to fear that Rome might take steps against Frederick as well.

Sure enough, in early July 1520 one of Archbishop Albrecht's men in Rome sent Frederick a letter saying that a bull against Luther was on its way to Saxony, and hinting that it was as much about Frederick as Luther: arrest or expel him now, or risk tainting your family name, it warned. Urban de Serralonga also wrote Frederick to say that Rome more or less saw the prince as Luther's enabler, and if he didn't expel the little friar now or get him to recant then the prince would be in as much trouble as Luther. And you can stop insisting, continued Serralonga, that you'll only act against Luther once he gets a fair hearing: he has been invited to Rome more than once to have one, and because he refuses to come, a learned tribunal full of the highest churchmen has given him that hearing *in absentia*— and their judgment is on its way to Saxony right now in the form of a bull.

Frederick soon had an unfriendly letter from Pope Leo as well. "Beloved son," it began, "we rejoice that you have never shown any favor to that son of iniquity, Martin Luther." But Leo also made clear that he had seen right through Frederick's supposed neutrality, and that it was time to openly choose sides. Luther defended Bohemians and Turks, wrote Leo, and didn't want heretics executed anymore, and rejected the writings of learned doctors and ecumenical councils and the decrees of popes. In fact he wouldn't listen to anybody except himself, which made him even worse than heretics who'd gone before him. That was

Albrecht Dürer, *Frederick the Wise*.

why Leo had called together "good brethren" who had composed a bull under the guidance of the Holy Spirit, a bull that gave Frederick the usual two choices: arrest Luther if he won't recant, or bring him back to sanity.

No wonder that by August 15 Frederick was worrying that "they will drive the friar from me." He had Spalatin ask the lawyer Hieronymus Schurff to tell him frankly what the choices would be if not just Dr. Martin but also the university, the city, and, yes, the prince were all excommunicated. He also had Spalatin pass along the news about the bull's imminent arrival to Dr. Martin, and ask the friar's advice on how to respond to it. Dr. Martin suggested taking an indirect route: either the prince should claim not to have jurisdiction over this theological matter, or he should tell the pope that Luther would be more dangerous outside Saxony than inside. And maybe the prince could add that if the pope acted heavy-handedly against Dr. Martin—that is, without any real proof from scripture—then something twice as bad as the old revolt in Bohemia might happen in German lands. As usual Dr. Martin was better at theology than politics, and Frederick ignored those suggestions.

He and his advisers did consider, briefly, another suggestion of Dr. Martin's: try Cardinal Carvajal, the supporter of church councils, who'd opposed the bull this past summer in Rome, surely because it had ignored Luther's appeal to such a council. But finally Frederick decided on a more political approach: he would speak with the new emperor, Charles, himself, at the coronation in October 1520. Frederick also asked Dr. Martin to write the emperor, to ask for protection from Rome and to have his case transferred to German soil. Dr. Martin did so by late August, calling himself "a little flea" who ordinarily wouldn't dare to address someone as mighty as the emperor. But he had tried humility, and mediation, and explanation with other important people, and it hadn't worked. In fact, so many important people were now angry at him that he had no choice but to write for help.

Whether Charles read that letter or not, it didn't do a thing to stop the bull, because the two men carrying it northward left Rome in September. The 40-year-old special nuncio Aleandro was to carry the bull to the emperor in the Netherlands (where Charles had just arrived) and then to west German lands. Johann Eck was to take it to north, center, east, and south.

Agostino Veneziano, *Girolamo Aleandro*.

Aleandro was a good choice to send to Charles, because he had experience as both a diplomat and academic and was at home in all sorts of rarefied air—teacher of Greek in Paris, librarian of the Vatican, friend of Erasmus, and so on. He reached Antwerp on September 26 and within two days had exactly what he'd hoped for: a decree from Charles proclaiming the bull in the Netherlands, and ordering all of Luther's books there to be burned. The first fire was lit on October 8 in Leuven, which seemed a safe place to start, since the university had already condemned Luther. Surprisingly though, some of the theology professors grumbled, because they weren't sure how authentic the bull was, thanks to its unusual ribbons and missing signature—just what Eck had been afraid of. But the burning happened anyway, and within a few days preachers all over town were denouncing Luther, and also blaming their sometime colleague Erasmus for putting ideas into Luther's head. Erasmus was stunned by the burnings and the charges against him and denounced Aleandro, but it didn't stop the fires. The nuncio started planning even more of them, now in German lands too, for after the coronation on the 23rd.

Eck had a harder time than Aleandro announcing the bull in his part of the German woods and plains. He would later claim that he'd never really wanted to take the thing northward from Rome, but maybe he came to that insight only after all the unpleasant receptions he suffered from his fellow Germans. He decided to start in Saxony so that the bull reached Luther as soon as possible, and things went well enough at first: the Saxon bishops of Meissen, Merseburg, and Brandenburg all favored the bull and allowed it to be posted in their cathedral cities by late September, but those cities lay in Ducal Saxony, outside Frederick's Electoral Saxony, and even in the former far from everyone was happy with the bull. And then there was the problem of how Eck was ever in the world going to get the bull into Wittenberg.

He decided to go post the bull in Leipzig while he thought about it, because he was sure that the locals there and especially Duke George would be glad to see him again, after his great triumph of the year before. But to his astonishment most people weren't happy to see him at all, as long as he was bringing in something as foreign as that bull. The university told him he couldn't publish it, a few pamphleteers condemned it, and several locals even sent Eck nasty letters. Only the Dominicans, who let him stay in their friary, were friendly, and so was good old Duke George, who sent over a golden chalice filled with gulden to thank him for his good work. Even though George ordered the town council to publish the bull in Leipzig, it was so unpopular that Eck had to sneak out of town after dark on October 3 to avoid trouble. He headed home right away to Ingolstadt, nervously handing off the bull in cities along the way, collecting more threats, and suffering so much general unpleasantness that when he finally reached Ingolstadt he went quickly to the cathedral and put up a votive wax tablet to thank God he'd survived.

Eck never took the bull personally into Electoral Saxony, much less Wittenberg, but instead paid a few members of Leipzig's militia to do it for him, after he was far away. But that went badly as well. The rector of the University of Erfurt refused to post it, while the students there called it a "bulloon" and threw every copy into the river. The people of Zeist almost rioted. The bishop of Naumburg said he wouldn't post it until Frederick was back from the coronation and he could talk with him about it. And in Wittenberg itself the Leipzig militiamen handed the bull to some unsuspecting burgher, telling him to take it to the rector of the university, Peter Burkhard, then ran off. The rector accepted the bull into his unsuspecting hands on October 10, and was so furious about how he'd gotten it that he also refused to post it. Still, the papal court considered it officially delivered to Dr. Martin now: the 60-day grace period had begun.

The rector probably did show it to Dr. Martin that very October 10. He certainly sent it on ahead to Frederick's brother Johann, in Coburg, who was ruling

Saxony while Frederick was away at the coronation. While passing through Coburg on his way home, Dr. Eck also sent over a copy to Johann, rather than come in person (he didn't have the right clothes, he said). Johann forwarded one of the copies to Frederick in Cologne, who realized that the great and dreadful day had finally come: Rome had taken action at last, which would force him to take action as well, on one side or the other.

Other great and dreadful news followed: because of the bull, 150 students soon left the University of Wittenberg, more than one-fourth of the student population. If they stayed, they said, and Luther didn't recant or the prince didn't arrest or expel him, then they would be under the ban too, according to the bull. Still, with Frederick, great and dreadful days were never as final as they might seem. He wasn't going to give in yet, or quickly. He had Spalatin print *Exsurge Domine* right away, partly so Rome couldn't say he'd opposed it, but mostly because he knew most people in Saxony would be mad about it and get behind Dr. Martin even more than they were. And Frederick's advisers, including Hieronymus Schurff, were telling him on the very day of the coronation not to hand Dr. Martin over just yet but instead to stall some more, so that he could try talking the emperor into postponing the date of excommunication, which now officially stood at December 10.

Since stalling and postponing were Frederick's specialties, he was only too glad to do so.

FULL BOAR

Dr. Martin himself had been expecting action from Rome since early in 1520, and so when Spalatin told him around July that a bull was on its way he was hardly surprised.

No, the only surprise was that the thought of such a bull didn't bother him anymore, not the way it would have before, say, the Leipzig disputation. Now, even if he were excommunicated, he would still feel thoroughly Christian. He wrote back to Spalatin, "I despise the fury and favor of Rome; I will never be reconciled to them nor commune with them. Let them condemn and burn my books" all they wanted, because he would burn theirs right back. "The humility I've shown so far all in vain shall have an end," he promised.

And he wasn't kidding. Starting in the spring of 1520, when he sensed something was coming, he stopped mincing words about the pope, and for the first time publicly attacked him, in print. His enemies had always wanted to draw him out on the subject, and he'd long refused, to protect himself. They'd also, he complained, tried to reduce all theology to a single point: "Disagree with [the pope], and you're a heretic! Agree, and you're a true believer!" Now Dr. Martin would finally say in print what he really thought about the pope, and in German, too. It would mean more trouble for him, but it would also make him more popular than ever before.

His first such tract appeared in the spring, even before he knew the bull was coming: *On the Papacy in Rome Against the Most Celebrated Romanist in Leipzig*, a man named Augustine Alfeld, who Luther quickly dubbed the Alfeldian Ass. The work was longish at 50 pages and repeated many of the things he'd said at Leipzig, but the main thing was that it was printed, in German, and willing to mention the moral failings of the popes, which many people complained about, instead of just the doctrinal ones that Luther usually discussed. The proof that the papacy wasn't divine was completely clear, he said: everything truly divine was "disobeyed in Rome down to the last iota" while the pope was completely obeyed. If you needed more proof than that, then look at how Rome fleeced the Germans, like (of all people) poor Archbishop Albrecht of Mainz having to pay 30,000 gulden for each of his eight or so episcopal robes. "One blows the noses of us German fools and says afterward that it is divine order."

But even harsher and longer and more popular was a tract Dr. Martin finished in late June and published in early August called *To the Christian Nobility of the German Nation* (1520), which would be one of his biggest sellers ever, even though it was over 100 pages long. The title said it all, you soon realized: since the clergy and especially the pope were doing such a rotten job of leading the church, it was up to German nobles, and especially the new emperor, "our noble Charles," to lead it instead. Sure, nobles were as fallible as anybody, but Brother Martin wasn't looking for perfect leaders, or even a perfect church, only for who was most likely to improve things. Councils had had their chance to lead the church but were always thwarted by underhanded men with ties to the pope. The clergy, including monks and friars, would have loved leading, because like the old proverb said, "A *Mönch* must be in it, whatever the world is doing," but they'd proven themselves unworthy of the task. That left it to the great nobles, whom Paul had said were ordained by God too.

They certainly, wrote Dr. Martin, wouldn't do any worse than the popes, who had caused so much trouble to the church. He enumerated those troubles now, especially the financial ones, in exceeding detail. The cardinals had already sucked Italy dry and now they were going after Germany too, and some said 300,000 gulden a year went from German lands to Rome for ecclesiastical taxes, the crusade tax, and indulgences: "the pope eats the fruit, the Germans play with the peels." Dr. Martin didn't want revolt or violence against the pope, or some war of German independence from him, as some people were calling for. Instead he wanted Germans to show their greatness by humbly accepting God's Roman chastisement and repenting—and taking charge of their own church.

Now he set out his vision for that church, starting with the pope. Yes, there should be a pope, but he should be a different kind of pope than what the church had known: he should mostly study the Bible, and mediate disputes, and give up his temporal power. He should stop stupid ceremonies, like having people kiss his feet, should wear a simple bishop's miter instead of the silly triple crown, should shrink the college of cardinals, and should stop encouraging pilgrimages to Rome. The religious orders should stop multiplying, and stop begging, and stop preaching and hearing confession among laypeople, so laypeople would have better bonds with their pastors. The clergy should be allowed to marry, and stop saying private masses for the dead since those were mostly about making money. Laypeople should stop all their superstitious pilgrimages and supposed miracles and chasing after saints, which took them away from their families, and should remember that good works weren't for salvation but for a good society, and should quit indulgences and brotherhoods and extravagant dress and gluttony and drunkenness and foreign spices and usury and brothels. Universities should get rid of Aristotle and canon law once and for all, and study the Bible, not commentaries on the Bible. And more.

Some of these ideas had been advocated by German reformers before Brother Martin, as in the work called *The Reformation of the Emperor Sigismund,* from 1439. But it wasn't nearly as popular as the *Christian Nobility,* which printers were now furiously putting out. The first giant edition of 4,000 copies sold out in a week, a second edition followed right away, and ten more came soon after that. Many nobles liked it, as Brother Martin might have expected, including the knights Ulrich von Hutten and Franz von Sickingen, who'd never paid much attention to his writings on justification or indulgences but absolutely loved what he had to say about the pope, and even saw Brother Martin (to his considerable discomfort) as their new champion of violent German independence from Rome. Prince Frederick tried keeping his usual impassive face when the

Luther as Friar in *The Babylonian Captivity.*

Christian Nobility appeared, but the fat piece of game he sent Dr. Martin afterward, as a reward, had to be taken as some sort of approval. Spalatin and Link worried the book would make it hard for Dr. Martin to reconcile with Rome now, and his enemies thought the same—in fact the book brought out not only more supporters than ever, but more enemies too, who kept insisting it would lead to revolution.

Dr. Martin was just getting warmed up, though, because even harsher against the pope than the *Christian Nobility* had been was a book he published on October 6 with an even more aggressive title: *Prelude to the Babylonian Captivity of the Church.* This one openly called the pope the Antichrist, and this time not so much because of his moral failings but because of how wrongly he had interpreted and abused the sacraments of the church, which kept believers every bit as captive as the Children of Israel had been in ancient Babylonia.

Brother Martin had started writing on the sacraments back in 1519, ironically because George Spalatin was as usual trying to steer him away from controversial things and toward more pastoral writing. But it didn't work out as Spalatin hoped: anything with Brother Martin's name on the cover now had an excellent chance of becoming controversial no matter what the subject, and anything he wrote on the sacraments was going to end up being about the pope, just like indulgences always did. Sure enough, the three supposedly innocent books he first put out on the subject created another storm of criticism, with one critic finding 154 errors in just one of the books! The *Babylonian Captivity* was Brother Martin's response to that storm. It repeated but refined some of the things he'd written in his earlier books on the subject, and added the bonus feature of making the pope the absolute center of attention now, instead of just a side show.

Just as indulgences were "a knavish trick of the Roman sycophants" meant to give the pope some great (figurative) hunting, so were the sacraments too, insisted the *Babylonian Captivity*: they were wrongly used, and wrongly taught. To begin with, there should be only three sacraments (maybe even only two), not seven. Because anybody who'd read Augustine knew that a sacrament was defined by having both a sign and a meaning (or promise), and only two current sacraments—baptism and the Eucharist—had both of those. Penance missed a sign, but for now Dr. Martin was willing to consider it a sacrament. Just as importantly, he now added a third element to the definition of a sacrament: the faith you had in its promise. It was faith, and not the priest's authority, that made a sacrament work.

In baptism, the *sign* was simple: the old you was thrust into the water and a new you was lifted out of it (and he wished that people really were thrust in and immersed, to make it a full sign). The *meaning* was simple too: dying and rising from death, both physical and spiritual. But Luther argued that what gave baptism its power wasn't the water, or the priest's sprinkling, but faith in the promise of rising again, physically and spiritually, over and over again in your life, whenever you repented. That was why penance wasn't necessarily a separate sacrament: it was simply a return to baptism. For centuries, baptism had been seen as a one-and-done ritual never thought of again, while all the attention in religious life was on penance—exactly how indulgences got so popular. Now Dr. Martin was saying that baptism was central, and that the believer's faith mattered more than the authority of the priest did.

He said even more about the Eucharist. Laypeople should be able to take the cup as well as the wafer, so that this sacrament's sign was whole too. God was present in the wafer and wine, but they didn't literally turn into Christ's flesh and blood. The meaning of the Eucharist wasn't some sacrifice the priest offered to God in order to get God's favor, but instead a gift from God that He gladly gave to us. The Eucharist wasn't some never-let-you-down good work that guaranteed you good fortune but a promise of forgiveness. It didn't matter how many times you took the sign (the wafer), but that you had faith in the promise of eternal life. You didn't have to be pure to take the Eucharist, you didn't have to go to confession first, you didn't even need to take the wafer or wine: you just needed faith, like Augustine said, "Believe and you have eaten."

The rest of the *Babylonian Captivity* discussed the other four traditional sacraments briefly (confirmation, marriage, ordination, extreme unction), because he'd concluded that they, even more than penance, weren't really separate sacraments. It was all stunning, in its claims about how the sacraments worked, and also about the limited role of the sacrament-dispensing clergy, including of course the chief dispenser of all, the pope. Like Brother Martin's other criticisms of the pope during 1520, this one sold fantastically too, especially when it was translated into German. Brother Martin wasn't tired of Catholicism, just the Roman sort of it, and many Germans seemed to agree with him.

But, again, many others were still against such brazen ideas. Duke George banned the *Babylonian Captivity* right away in Ducal Saxony, because it was too Bohemian and antipapal for him, and Aleandro said it was completely blasphemous. Even some of Dr. Martin's supporters now turned on him for saying that the clergy should marry. And at least 31 furious printed responses emerged, an exceedingly high total even for Dr. Martin. Erasmus glumly concluded that it had made the rift between Luther and Rome unfixable.

Just four days after the *Babylonian Captivity* was published, Dr. Martin finally saw *Exsurge Domine*. The content and fishy appearance made Dr. Martin sure that he smelled Eck behind it. The bull was "lies and godlessness and Eckish in every aspect," and until he saw the lead, and wax, and ribbons, and signature, and seal, he refused to accept the bull as genuine.

Dr. Martin surely hated how the bull compared him to the wild boar of the forest who trampled the vineyard of the Lord, because when he'd lectured several years before on Psalm 80, where the metaphor of the wild boar came from, he'd compared the beast to the Turks, and Herod, and the Romans, because all of them were outside the church and trying fiercely to ruin it. A wild boar was proud, and ungodly, and self-righteous, and heretical, and eccentric, and cared for no one but himself. No, that wasn't him at all, he thought (even if he was a sinner). But Dr. Martin would have surely accepted, as a badge of honor, the sort of fearlessness a boar had, so fearless in fact it wasn't afraid to attack popes or to trample down and root up the pope's very man-made vineyard in order to save the true vineyard of the Lord nearby. And why couldn't a boar be God's instrument of grace? If Balaam's Ass could be, and if the *cloaca* tower could be full of God's grace, then a usually unruly boar could be too. Dr. Martin also would have loved the idea of being hunted like a boar by the hunt-loving pope, and fearlessly charging back at him.

He wrote to Spalatin the next day, October 11, with relief, saying "the bull is finally here. . . . Already I am much freer, certain at last that the pope is the Antichrist." He hoped that Prince Frederick would just ignore the bull, and that Rome would get too busy to take action (probably a vain wish when you were calling the pope the Antichrist). Or maybe the prince could talk the new emperor into issuing an edict that no one in the empire should be condemned who hadn't been clearly refuted from scripture—the latest in a long line of politically impossible ideas from the friar. But then he withdrew the suggestion himself: he shouldn't place his trust in any prince, he realized, but only God Himself. And his books weren't great, he knew, but they shouldn't be burned without a fair hearing, which he still didn't think he'd received, despite what Rome said.

That same October 11, Dr. Martin heard from the never-vanishing and always-scheming Karel von Miltitz, who wanted to meet. In late August, Miltitz had gone to the annual meeting of the German Augustinians to urge them to talk sense into their brother, Martin Luther. Most reminded Miltitz that technically Brother Martin wasn't actually their brother anymore, since he'd been released from his vow of obedience. But at least his old friends Johann Staupitz and Wenceslas Link agreed on September 6 to go to Wittenberg and try to persuade Brother Martin to write a polite letter to the pope, which should say that none of his writings had been meant personally but only against the office of the papacy. Dr. Martin seemed agreeable to that idea when those friends came by. But then Miltitz learned that the bull was already on its way from Rome, which put a damper on his plan. He was furious that Eck hadn't consulted him about it, and he wrote desperately to Frederick in Cologne to ask for funds to travel to Rome so he could bribe a few young cardinals to try to reverse the bull, because, he said, that was how things were done there. But nothing came of it. Still, Miltitz wanted to try again to reconcile Luther with the pope.

He and Brother Martin met the next day, October 12, at Lichtenberg on the Elbe, in Saxony, between Wittenberg and Leipzig. The nervous Dr. Martin took along four soldiers, a nobleman, Philip Melanchthon, and another friar, for support. Miltitz wanted to know whether Dr. Martin still hoped to be heard by the archbishop of Trier, and Dr. Martin told of his plan to appeal once again to a council. But the main topic was Miltitz's idea that Dr. Martin should not only write a private letter of apology to the pope but also publish it, so that everyone would see he didn't have anything against Leo the man and that this whole sad affair was caused by wicked Johann Eck. Dr. Martin could support a plan like that, because he actually believed it. He'd written politely to Leo before, but he agreed now to write a public letter, and to date it September 6, the day Miltitz had first presented the plan to Staupitz and Link. That way, the pope wouldn't think he was writing just because the bull had arrived.

Dr. Martin didn't have much confidence in Miltitz; he'd heard from various quarters that the man wasn't well-respected in Rome, and so it wasn't clear whether the pope would go along with any plan he hatched, or any letter Dr. Martin might write. As usual, he could trust only in God. But surely he found at least some earthly hope in all the support he was getting from so many people, and from Prince Frederick too. And he still hoped as well for at least a little support from the man who was about to get crowned on the head in Aachen.

THE EMPIRE'S NEW MAN

Frederick hadn't been at the coronation, of course, but he could easily imagine how it had gone: he'd seen one in 1486, and he was famous for his knowledge of protocol and ceremony, and his delegates to the event had surely reported every single detail to his eager ears.

At the Palatine chapel in Aachen, where the coronation had been held—plague or no plague—since Charlemagne, the elector-archbishop of Cologne, in charge because Aachen lay within his bishopric, would have seen to it that everything was ready, especially the imperial robe, crown, sword, orb, and scepter that had been proudly brought over for the occasion by the citizens of Nuremberg, where they were always stored. Even though Charles was just being crowned king here (the emperor part would happen only in 1530, in Rome), the imperial finery would remind everybody, including the pope, what office he'd really been elected to—and it would have all been laid out for everyone to see, as would, for this particular ceremony, some of the treasure of the Aztecs that had just arrived in April from Charles's conquistadoring soldiers in the New World.

The day before the ceremony, in a field outside of town, 400 of Charles's armored men on horse and 300 on foot would have gotten themselves into fighting formation, with Charles in the middle, and would have been greeted there by the electors who were present, all surrounded by their finely clothed entourages too.

The next morning, Charles would have walked to the church in his archduke-of-Austria robes, and be met by the electors again. The elector-archbishop of Cologne would have begun with the prayer, "Almighty, eternal God," and while the choir sang, "Behold I send my messenger," Charles and the other electors would have proceeded up the aisle. Even though he was only 20, Charles would have looked

majestic and unapproachable—in fact
so majestic that, like other chosen kings,
he wouldn't have bothered to answer for
himself when the crucial questions were
fired at him, but instead would have had
his friend the archbishop of Salzburg,
Matthäus Lang, speak for him. The
elector-archbishop of Cologne would
then have prayed, "God, who knows the
human race" and "Almighty eternal God
of heaven and earth" to begin the coronation itself.

At the crucial point, the magnificent
Charles would have lain prostrate before
the altar, to show his humility to God at
least, then would have come the Litany of
the Saints and the all-important six ques-

Bernaert van Orley, *Portrait of Charles V*,
1519.

tions he had to swear to, including the first, "Will you defend the holy faith?" the
second, "Will you defend the holy church?" and of course the last, "Will you show
submission to the pope?" each of which his spokesman would have answered, with
deadly seriousness, "I will," while Charles placed two fingers on the altar. Charles
would have also been deadly serious when the elector-archbishop anointed his
head, and chest, and shoulders with the sacred oil, in the name of the Father and
the Son and Holy Spirit, and then his palms too, and just as Samuel anointed
David to be king so Charles would be the "blessed and established king in this
kingdom over this people, whom the Lord, your God, has given you to rule and
govern." How the new emperor chose to understand all these words would of
course have very serious consequences for Dr. Martin Luther.

Finally would have come the removal of his old robes and the vesting of the
complicated and many-layered new imperial robes, including the priestlike stole
over Charles's breast, to remind everybody that he was equal to any clergyman,
then the granting of the sword and imperial ring, and finally the setting on his
head of the imperial crown by all three elector-archbishops. To make sure he
really understood what he was doing, Charles would have then taken the oath
of coronation all over again, then he would have finally been enthroned, after
which the elector-archbishop Albrecht of Mainz would have offered a short

sermon, and the elector-archbishop of Cologne would have turned to the crowd and asked whether they, representing the entire German people, would be obedient to this prince and lord, "after the command of the apostle," to which the proper response was *Fiat, Fiat, Fiat,* Let it be done. It all would have ended with the usual *Te Deum Laudamus,* We praise thee, O God.

It was surely a fabulous ceremony, and Frederick would have loved it. He would have also loved that Charles had sworn to observe the Electoral Covenant, a document that Frederick had helped negotiate for months, specifying what Charles could and could not do as emperor, and ensuring that he had to confirm the rights, sovereignty, liberties, and privileges of the territorial princes (such as Frederick), could appoint only native-born Germans to imperial offices, and had to establish a royal court in the Holy Roman Empire somewhere—in other words, the electors wanted Charles to become German, which he had never been (of his 32 most recent forebears, only one line was German), and to realize that even though this prestigious office had cost him a million gulden and every prince in Europe seemed to want it, his actual power over the empire's 10 million or so German-speaking inhabitants was really very limited.

The banquet afterward for all the great was surely fabulous too, including wine-gurgling fountains decorated with an eagle and two lions, and a nice gift of relics that Frederick would have envied. When everyone was satisfied, the leftover food would have been thrown to the gaping people of Aachen, from whom the banqueters hoped not to catch the plague, and from whom they fled as fast as they could in the next day or two, mostly to Cologne, where Frederick of Saxony, of course, awaited them.

Charles arrived in Cologne on October 28 or 29, and Frederick arranged to meet with him as soon as possible. They did so in the sacristy of the cathedral on October 31. It wasn't clear what the two great princes discussed, or even whether Frederick thought it best to discuss Dr. Martin's great matter explicitly, or to proceed, as he usually did, more obliquely by simply establishing good relations in the hope that this would lead to the desired result. According to Erasmus, who spoke with Frederick soon afterward, the emperor and prince did talk about Luther, and Charles agreed that he shouldn't be condemned any further without a fair hearing—meaning, presumably, on German soil. It was also possible that Frederick now handed over the letter he'd asked Dr. Martin to write to Charles, the one in which Dr. Martin called himself a little flea, just in case the emperor hadn't gotten it last summer; they weren't entirely sure of that, since the emperor hadn't responded.

The two men then parted. They weren't just great princes, of course, but first-cousins thrice-removed. That was a mouthful, though, and so Charles just called Frederick "beloved uncle."

FREDERICK'S LATEST ANSWER

Whatever good will was built up in that private meeting in the cathedral of Cologne between emperor and elector, the nuncios tried to undo it with the blasted sheaf of documents they sneakily passed to Frederick in the Franciscan church a few days later.

Frederick left the Franciscan church, papers in hand, surely perturbed.

Aleandro believed that Frederick was a decent Catholic, but that most people in his entourage were blatant supporters of Luther. And the nuncio had been thoroughly alarmed, while traveling through the cities of the Rhineland before and after the coronation, at just how much popular support there was for Luther. All of which explained why Aleandro thought it was so important to get Frederick on his side.

When Frederick (or more likely a secretary) opened the sheaf of documents, he saw that the nuncios and pope weren't nearly as interested as the emperor had seemed in trying to find some sort of peaceful solution with Dr. Martin. Instead the papers contained all the usual themes, which Frederick now knew by heart: praise for his ancient princely family in serving the church and the pope, his obligation to do the same, the danger that Luther posed to all of Christendom—worse than the danger of Hus!—and that steps had to be taken now or the empire and Christendom would be in trouble. Luther had to be arrested if he didn't recant, and his books had to be burned. No more hearings were necessary, because Luther had already been judged *in absentia* in Rome, and the emperor and other German princes were sure to agree with that judgment.

The documents so troubled Frederick that he quickly arranged a meeting with Erasmus, Charles's former tutor, who had also come to Cologne after the coronation. Frederick wanted to hear from somebody who was outside of his own circle and who wasn't an enemy of Dr. Martin. He wasn't sure exactly how Erasmus felt about the friar, because Erasmus was Frederick's sort of man: famously non-forthcoming with his opinions. But Frederick surely knew that Erasmus didn't love either Dr. Martin's divisive tone or the harsh tone of the bull, and was as interested as Frederick in finding some sort of peaceful settlement, so that Christianity (and good letters) wouldn't be torn apart.

When the two men met the next day, November 5, Frederick asked: had Dr. Martin really erred? After weighing his answer, Erasmus was more forthcoming than usual: "Yes, he has erred in two points: in attacking the crown of the pope and the bellies of the monks," because he'd said the pope wasn't divinely appointed, and priests and their many sacraments weren't as important as they'd supposed. Of course that didn't really answer Frederick's question. Obviously Dr. Martin had erred *politically* in saying such things, but what the ever-political Frederick wanted to know was whether he had erred theologically. Erasmus suggested that a tribunal should decide that question, and Frederick agreed: that had been his thought too. But Erasmus also recommended that Charles and other Christian princes should appoint the members of that tribunal. Like Frederick, Erasmus wanted it to include more scholars than bishops, and laypeople as well as clergy. If the tribunal exonerated Luther, the matter would be over. But if it condemned Luther, and he didn't recant, Frederick would have to arrest him.

When the meeting ended, Frederick was left thinking, "He is a strange fellow. One does not know what to make of him," which was as fine an example of the old proverb about the pot and the kettle as could have been imagined. Spalatin walked Erasmus back to his rooms, and while Spalatin waited Erasmus, in an uncharacteristic burst of excitement, wrote down 22 specific guidelines for the tribunal he envisioned, including some comments that blamed the pope for the whole situation. But Spalatin had barely made it back to his own rooms before Erasmus was at his door asking to have the document back. He didn't want anything that specific being traced to him, since so many people were blaming him for the Luther affair anyway. Maybe it was best for Erasmus to therefore stay out of things altogether. Spalatin handed the document over, but he'd already made a copy, and it was miraculously published in a few months, to Erasmus's most certain horror.

Frederick liked enough what Erasmus had said to him, especially about the tribunal, that he passed it along to the nuncios when he responded on November 6 to their sneakily delivered letters. He also said he wasn't just going to hand Dr. Martin over, not now or maybe even not on December 10, the day *Exsurge Domine* was set to expire, and that the Dr.'s writings shouldn't yet be burned, because they still hadn't been refuted to Frederick's satisfaction, despite what *Exsurge Domine* claimed. Frederick also wanted a serious, thorough tribunal, not some quick-and-dirty condemnation. And how could the nuncios demand that Luther be arrested now when such a tribunal might still find him innocent? That would ruin Frederick's reputation. The friar deserved the chance to defend himself before an acceptable tribunal.

The nuncios were not even close to happy with that response, needless to say. They made the usual claim that Luther had already had his chance for a hearing in Rome. And they also didn't want the archbishop of Trier, Frederick's good friend, or any other German churchman to head up the tribunal, and they certainly didn't want any layman to sit on it, because only the pope had authority to decide matters of faith and doctrine. Still, the nuncios didn't want to spill Luther's blood: they just wanted his offensive books burned, and for the next Diet to put Luther under the imperial ban, if he didn't recant. Then nobody, not even Frederick, could give him ecclesiastical or temporal protection without consequences for themselves too.

Frederick left Cologne the very next day, November 7, bouncing painfully home, which was brave because he would have to bounce south again to the next Diet in less than two months. Even though he missed the coronation, at least this trip hadn't been in vain. He'd had a pleasant meeting with Charles, even if Aleandro had fumed about it and also complained that all the enemies of Rome had been gathered together in Cologne. Soon after leaving that city, Frederick wrote a letter to Charles asking explicitly what might have not been clear in their personal meeting—namely, that perhaps the hearing they had discussed for Dr. Martin could occur during the very next Diet, to be held soon in the great imperial city of Worms.

Wittenberg, Outside the Elster Gate, Again. December 10, 1520. The Feast of St. Mercurius, Who was Martyred by the Emperor.

Spalatin had supposed that Dr. Martin would keep things small, maybe lighting a few obnoxious books on fire in the pulpit during a sermon, or denouncing the books and then snuffing out all the torches in the church, the way the Romans used to treat obnoxious writings. But no, he had to have a big public ceremony, with a big roaring fire, and disturb the peace of the ever-cautious Spalatin yet again.

Philip Melanchthon spread the news about the fire, telling students to attend and posting a notice about it on the door of the city church. It would happen at 9 in the morning on the Monday after St. Nicholas's Day, he announced, just outside the Elster Gate and thus right near the Augustinian friary. That location wasn't just to make things convenient for Dr. Martin, it was also where the city's carrion pit was, and where the clothes of people who died in the nearby hospital had long been burned, meaning that if a big roaring fire was what you wanted, well, this was just the place to have it.

That morning Dr. Martin and especially his fellow theologian Johann Agricola were still hunting for copies of the books to be tossed in. Dr. Martin already had *Exsurge Domine*, and the various editions of papal decretals that made up canon law (from 1150, 1234, 1298, 1317, 1325, and 1484), plus the sin-obsessed confessor's manual by Angelus de Clavasio that (along with the Devil) had once caused Brother Martin so many spiritual problems, and plenty of books by living rivals like Eck and Emser. But he was still missing the works of dead rivals like Thomas Aquinas and Duns Scotus and other scholastic theologians.

Albrecht Dürer, *Philip Melanchthon*.

If he'd ever had copies of such things, he didn't anymore, and fellow professors who were asked to contribute their copies to the fire wrinkled their noses at the thought, as they weren't in the habit of burning expensive and still useful books, even if they didn't like their contents.

Still, they had the main things, and they would be enough for a good blaze. They would also be enough to make Dr. Martin's enemies even madder at him than they already were, but he didn't even care: they'd burned his books recently, so why shouldn't he return the favor? He didn't like striking out first, he'd always said, but when his enemies struck him then he liked to strike back in the same way, which in this case was with a big roaring fire. Plus it was an ancient Christian as well as Roman tradition to burn evil books, as in Acts 19. Plus the Holy Spirit was telling him to go ahead, because there was no longer any hope that his adversaries would listen to the truth he was telling them and only something like a fire would give them a chance to wake up.

If those weren't reasons enough, then Dr. Martin had about 30 others too, in the form of 30 laughable excerpts that he'd taken straight from the copies of canon law that were about to go up in flames. Like that the pope and his men weren't subject to God's commandments. Or that the pope wasn't subject to councils. Or that the text in 1 Peter which urged all people to obedience somehow didn't apply to the pope. Or that the pope was the sun of Christendom and princes only the moon. Or that even if the pope led multitudes to hell he couldn't be punished for it. Or that the salvation of all Christendom depended mostly on the pope. Or that no married person could ably serve God. Or that the pope's laws were equal to the gospels. And many more. Yes, the pope should certainly refute wrong when he saw it, but sometimes he refuted what was right, and unlike the gospels he preferred to refute with force, and force was

Luther Burns the Papal Bull.

unbecoming someone claiming to be the one and only true vicar of the Prince of Peace.

But even with a rock-solid group of reasons like this beneath him, and even though he'd been daringly saying that he no longer felt attached to Rome and didn't need the pope anymore, Brother Martin was still a little wobbly at the thought of the fire. He walked out the Elster gate with the armful of books he'd collected and joined the crowd, setting most of the books down near Agricola, who'd collected even more and probably also the necessary pile of wood. Now Agricola ritually lit the wood and threw in the first books to get the blaze going. Then it was Dr. Martin's turn. He wanted to throw in *Exsurge Domine* personally, and the way he remembered it, he trembled as he stepped out of the crowd, walked forward, and dropped it in, while paraphrasing part of Psalm 21, "Because you have confounded the truth of God, today the Lord confounds you. Into the fire with you!"

Today, December 10, was the day that his grace period granted by *Exsurge Domine* officially expired and supposedly excommunicated him, but he was excommunicating the pope and the curia right back, in front of a big crowd.

The items turned to smoke and ash, the flames died down, and the crowd wandered away, with Dr. Martin himself heading back through the Elster Gate to class, or to his tower.

THE FIRST BURNINGS

Since returning from Cologne in early November, Prince Frederick had continued to protect Dr. Martin from Rome, but even more than in the past they both had to wonder just how long that protection could last, since the dreaded day of December 10 was looming.

Even though Dr. Martin didn't care any more about being excommunicated, Frederick cared immensely, because it would force him to make the arrest or expulsion that Rome had long been nagging him to make. And so he'd kept doing what he could to delay the moment, mostly by still trying to arrange a German hearing for Brother Martin. Frederick still wanted that hearing to take place before an independent panel of judges, but because Aleandro had been insisting since the coronation that Luther should simply be condemned by the next Diet and not be heard at all, Frederick decided as usual to be pragmatic and suggest a compromise. What if Dr. Martin's German-soil hearing happened during the Diet itself, instead of as some separate event? And shouldn't it be a true hearing instead of just a summons to be condemned? That was the idea he sent to Charles's councilors in November 1520. The councilors liked the idea, and wrote back to Frederick on November 17 to say they would urge the emperor to follow it. Charles himself seemed to agree, writing personally on November 28 to his "Beloved Uncle Frederick" to say that he should bring Luther along to the upcoming Diet at Worms, set to start in January, so he could be questioned by competent judges and have no injustice done to him, as the customs of the empire required. Just make sure he didn't write anything else against the pope in the meantime, or do anything else provocative.

But when Aleandro kept on burning Luther's books in November, Frederick worried that Dr. Martin might get provocative indeed, as he was oh-so-wont-to-do when provoked himself. Why couldn't he just ignore the burnings? wondered Frederick. They weren't even going that well, as sentiment for Brother Martin, and against Rome, was only growing in German lands. In Cologne on November 11, for instance, the executioner wouldn't light a fire under the books because he hadn't been shown any imperial mandate telling him to, and he lit it the next day only when the elector-archbishop of

Cologne practically forced him to. The burning went even worse in Mainz, home to Archbishop Albrecht, on November 28: Albrecht was trying to be a zealous burner of Luther's books, because he'd just been awarded the latest Golden Rose from the pope, but once again a reluctant executioner wanted to know whether the books had been legally condemned. When the crowd yelled "No!" the man refused to go on. And once again, the fire was lit only the next day, when Albrecht talked a gravedigger into doing it, but no crowd came to watch, because most people were busy chasing Aleandro with stones, and threatening his life: luckily for him a local abbot came to his rescue. Ulrich von Hutten, that rare knight who was also a man of letters, threatened Aleandro with bodily harm because of the burnings, then wrote an unexpectedly sensitive poem to mourn them, called "Lament over the Lutheran Conflagration at Mainz." Again, Hutten hadn't paid much attention to Luther's doctrine, only to Luther's attacks on the pope, but that was all the doctrine Hutten needed: "Shall the divine Word, the divine doctrine for which Luther stands, vanish? Shall the pope be honored and what is good be suppressed? A Leo has become a shepherd. To a servant of God they do violence." It all thoroughly alarmed Aleandro.

But Dr. Martin wasn't popular with everybody, especially after the *Babylonian Captivity.* Four of his friends had once been such great supporters of him that Eck had even added their names to *Exsurge Domine,* as Luther's coconspirators, but now three of those four were about to recant their "Lutheran" beliefs in the hands of Eck himself. The theologian Wolfgang Capito, who'd once egged printers on to publish Dr. Martin's works, was now saying he spread only conflict and really ought to reconcile with the pope. Dr. Martin's fellow Augustinian, Crotus Rubianus, was saying the same thing in Erfurt, while Aloisius Marlianus there even preached explicitly against Luther on November 6. And although Staupitz was encouraging whenever Dr. Martin heard from him in distant Salzburg, he was still rarely heard from.

And the more Dr. Martin wrote, the more numerous his enemies became, and the bigger the fire they could make of his books.

MAN OF MANY, MANY WORDS

In fact Dr. Martin had been writing more books than ever.

Even if some friends abandoned him and new enemies attacked him, he could always count on his "fast hand and rapid memory," that allowed him to write so much, and on his good friends the printers, who sent his writings into the world. There were more than 60 printers in German lands, most of them in big Cologne, Strasbourg, Basel, and Augsburg, but some in little Wittenberg too. And many of them put out at least a few of his books.

Before 1518 he'd published just two titles, which hardly anybody had noticed, but then came the wondrous spread of the 95 theses, the even more wondrous spread of the *Sermon on Indulgences and Grace,* the 15 or so other titles of 1518, and over 20 titles each year in 1519 and 1520, three-quarters of them now available in German, and almost half of them eight pages long or less. By the end of 1520 he'd authored more works (around 60) and had more editions printed of those works than anybody else in the history of the empire.

Yes, Brother Martin was the printers' good friend, and the one most responsible for their sudden burst of business, even if they couldn't have told you all the specifics.

Between 1500 and 1530, German-language printers would put out around 10,000 editions of the sort of little pamphlet favored by Dr. Martin.

Around 7,500 of those would appear between 1520 and 1526 alone, and a full 20 percent of them were from Dr. Martin—11 times more than from the next most popular author, Andreas Karlstadt.

Those 7,500 or so pamphlet editions were good for 6.6 million copies, which was 55 times higher than the total number of all things ever published in German lands before that time (thus ever since Johannes Gutenberg invented movable type around 1450).

German presses put out 40 German-language works a year around 1500, then 150 in 1518, then 570 in 1520, with Dr. Martin writing a big chunk of those himself, precisely because unlike so many of his rivals he wasn't "ashamed in the slightest" to write to the uneducated. In fact it seemed to him that if churchmen had all written to them sooner, "Christendom would have reaped no small advantage and would have been more benefitted by this than by those heavy, weighty tomes" and by the sorts of questions usually argued about at universities.

Printers outside the empire liked Dr. Martin too: one in Paris wrote in November 1520 that Luther's books sold faster than anybody else's. But they were most popular in German lands. When Johann Froben of Basel published Luther's collected works at the end of 1518 and reported that they sold better than anything he'd ever done, Froben's other best-selling author, Erasmus, fumed. Froben was *his* printer, and Erasmus demanded that he stop printing Luther if he wanted to keep Erasmus. Anywhere Dr. Martin's books were printed, there was soon too much work in the shop. The delays this caused in Wittenberg were why he persuaded more printers to come there, or why he sometimes shipped his writing to printers in Leipzig or elsewhere. But wherever one of his tracts started, printers elsewhere soon picked it up, with the usual path running from Wittenberg to Leipzig to Augsburg to Basel to Strasbourg and then beyond, which helped explain how people all over the empire knew the name Luther by the end of 1520.

And printers weren't just putting out his big controversial titles either, like the *Christian Nobility* and the *Babylonian Captivity,* because those weren't necessarily what everybody wanted from him. Some people preferred the more pastoral works that Prince Frederick and Spalatin were always trying to get him to write, and not just to distract him either but because they thought he was so unusually good at them. And Dr. Martin liked writing such works as well: one of his main purposes as an author and preacher and confessor was to ease heavy consciences, since he understood so well himself what it was like to walk around with one of those.

And so in these troubled years of 1519 and 1520 he wrote not just controversial things but also his eight-page *Meditation on Christ's Passion,* to give people some direction with their devotions on Good Friday, and his *Exposition of the Lord's Prayer for Simple Laymen,* which at 50 or 60 pages wasn't all that simple but still tried to remind people they were praying to their father, not their judge, and to hallow God's name with their lives, not their words, and that "forgive us our sins" was the most powerful indulgence letter ever. His short *On Rogationtide Prayer and Procession* condemned processions as excuses to get drunk and urged people to pray not just for good fields and health but faith in God's promise of forgiveness. *A Sermon on Preparing to Die* was on a favorite old subject, but it unusually urged people to stop thinking about how terrifying hell and sin and death were and to keep their minds instead on Christ, while *Fourteen Consolations,* written for Frederick when he came home sick after the emperor's coronation, tried to get people to combat life's troubles not by asking the help of the 14 favorite saints but by considering 14 helpful concepts instead—like Word, faith, peace, divine guidance, communion with fellow believers, and more. *A Discussion on How Confession Should be Made* wanted people to trust God's Word of mercy instead of the thoroughness of their confession or the authority of the priest. The *Brief Form of the Ten Commandments,* and *Brief Form of the Creed,* and *Brief Form of the Lord's*

Prayer all offered practical and simple approaches to each. The longer *Treatise on Good Works,* which he thought one of the best things he'd written, refuted all those who said he wanted to abolish good works: he was all for works, he explained, and should even be called the doctor of good works, but he wanted people to understand them rightly—good works grew out of faith and didn't save you, and if you understood that, then you were likely to do even more works than if you thought they did save you. And his practical *Sermon on the Estate of Marriage* was typical in saying that sex was sinful and marriage was a hospital to contain lust, but novel in saying that married love was the highest sort of human relationship, and that bringing children up properly was worth more than a pilgrimage or a mass. And there were plenty more than these, most of them as uncontroversial as Frederick and Spalatin hoped, but still tainted enough with the name Luther for enemies to throw them into fires.

Maybe the most remarkable thing about these little pastoral books meant to soothe wasn't just their clarity but that Brother Martin wrote them in the middle of his most unsoothing troubles with Rome, and while writing as well the unsoothing books that came out of those troubles, like the *Babylonian Captivity.* In November 1520, he wrote two more such books, just after the emperor's coronation and just before the big bonfire near the Elster Gate.

The first was his response to *Exsurge Domine,* which in Latin he called *Against the Execrable Bull of the Antichrist,* although in the German version he left out "Execrable" to be more polite before the masses. He was sure, he wrote, that the bull was the "progeny of that man of lies, dissimulation, errors, and heresy, that monster Johann Eck," rather than the pope himself, because it had Eck's "style and spittle" all over it. Plus it was all wrong: every single one of the 41 points it condemned were in fact absolutely crucial for salvation. And until somebody proved from scripture that they were wrong, Brother Martin wouldn't retract a single one. "Doesn't your whorish forehead blush that your inane smoke is withstanding the lightning of the divine Word?" he asked the bull's author(s). Oh where were you now, "most excellent Charles the Emperor," and where were the bishops and doctors, who should all be condemning this sort of thing? If they wouldn't condemn it, well then he would do so himself, by his authority as a baptized child of God. And as a "co-heir with Christ" he would stand every bit as much as Peter on the rock that the gates of hell could not overcome (i.e., faith) and tell Rome to repent.

The second unsoothing tract of November was the letter of apology Miltitz had urged Brother Martin to write to Pope Leo, which by now had grown into an additional 50-page book called *The Freedom of a Christian*. Dr. Martin wanted the letter and book published together, but some enterprising printers decided to put them out separately, and increase their sales.

And what an apologetic thing the letter seemed to be, just as Miltitz had asked. Oh, some were bound to question how sorry Brother Martin really was about his recent attacks on the pope. But those attacks, he now explained, weren't against Leo himself: they were against the office he held, and all the monsters around it. Dr. Martin had actually long admired Leo the man, and even looked to him, "my beloved father," for inspiration during these past few years, because he, Dr. Martin, had had to wage war against his own set of monsters: if Leo could keep up his good personal reputation in the midst of such creatures, then why couldn't he? Yes, Brother Martin despised the pope's "sycophants," but "I have never alienated myself from Your Blessedness" personally, contrary to what many were now saying. In fact whenever he talked about Leo the man, he spoke only good and honorable words because "your reputation and the fame of your blameless life, celebrated as they are throughout the world," couldn't be denied by anybody. Leo was a true sheep among wolves, or better yet a Daniel in Babylon, because the Roman curia was Babylon and Sodom rolled into one, since it despised church councils, feared reform, and wouldn't fix itself. Yet even when he attacked those wolves, Dr. Martin didn't mean to attack their morals any more than Leo's, because every one of us was a sinner, including himself. He was so conscious, he said, slightly mixing his scriptural metaphors, of the beam in his own eye that he could never "be the first one to cast a stone at the adulteress." No, he had "no quarrel with any man concerning his morals but only concerning the word of truth," and it was the untruth being taught by the papal court that caused him to snap at it sometimes—sure, maybe too sharply, but it was all meant well. Still, no one in Rome appreciated it, especially not that newest servant of Satan there, Johann Eck, who had provoked all this arguing to begin with because of one little word Dr. Martin had let slip regarding the authority of the pope. Eck was Leo's real enemy, said Dr. Martin, full of lies, and tricks, and wiles. But if his own attacks of late had seemed personal to Leo, like when he'd called the pope the Antichrist, then Dr. Martin hoped that Leo would accept his apologies. He apologized too if he was stepping over his bounds now, but previous churchmen had also dared to warn popes. And so he hoped that Leo would accept his letter, and the accompanying tract, as a peace offering, meant to explain himself and his theology once and for all. "If men do not perceive that I am your friend and your most humble subject in this matter, there is One who understands and judges (John 8)."

The tract itself, *The Freedom of a Christian,* explained more thoroughly than anything Brother Martin had written so far what the life of a Christian should look like, and of course it all had to do with justification by faith, laid out now in yet another new way. The main themes came right at the start, in two seemingly contradictory statements of exactly the sort Dr. Martin loved: "A Christian is a perfectly free lord of all, subject to none. A Christian is a perfectly dutiful servant of all, subject to all."

The lord theme made this tract Dr. Martin's most optimistic explanation of justification yet. A Christian was lord because he was justified by the faith in Christ that freed, and not by any law that constrained. This faith wasn't some reward for good deeds you'd done, but just a simple and passive trust in God's promise that He would justify you if you let Him. You did this by willingly entering the relationship Dr. Martin had already spelled out in his *Sermon on Two Kinds of Righteousness:* Christ the bridegroom gives you His righteousness, and you, a "poor little harlot," give Him your sins. Other writers had used this metaphor before, but new with Brother Martin was that Christ was doing this without demanding any prerequisites first. You didn't have to worry any longer about whether your works were good enough, you didn't have to worry about whether you were keeping the law perfectly, you didn't have to carry around your guilt, or feel constantly like you deserved punishment—no, you were lord over all those worries now. You had faith that God would save you, and you let God be God, and no longer thought that you were God and could save yourself. No, you assented, passively, and that made you, ironically, king, priest, and lord.

But what about the second theme: how was a Christian who was lord and free also a servant and bound? Ah, the servant part was what stopped you from going wild with your newfound freedom and lordship. Humans needed to be tamed, which was why there was the law. The law didn't save you, of course: it just made you aware of your sin, which made you look for God's righteousness, which was actually what saved you. And once you were filled with that righteousness, you couldn't help serving others; you also even started truly keeping the law, and practically spontaneously now instead of obligatorily, since Christ was actually doing the keeping rather than you, and you became a sort of Christ to others. But trying to save yourself by keeping the law yourself didn't make you turn toward others at all (unless it was to do good deeds that you thought would give you salvation), because you were so obsessed with your own salvation. A true Christian who lived by faith in Christ naturally turned to his neighbor, and just as Christ gave you His riches for nothing, so you started handing out His riches too, and serving. That was how a Christian who was lord over all was also the servant of all.

Dr. Martin had made many of these points in earlier tracts, but he said it again and more clearly now, partly to explain to Leo what exactly he meant with his theology, and partly because even those who liked his message still weren't getting what he was saying. Yet he didn't just repeat and rephrase things here: the part about Christians being lords and even a sort of Christ was brand new, a more daring statement than ever of the "priesthood of all believers" idea that he liked. Just like in 1518, this new daring in his writings came straight out of the very latest troubling events around him: being criticized more heavily than ever made him not only more confident than ever in his theology of justification, but made him put things more hopefully than ever before. Just like Christ was both divine and human, he said, so your justified soul now coexisted with Christ as divine and human as well.

But all the optimism in the world didn't mean that Leo was going to like Dr. Martin's view of things. It wasn't clear whether the pope ever got the *Freedom of a Christian,* or the letter that went with it. If he did, he surely would have been shocked that Dr. Martin was giving him advice or talking to him like an equal. And he would have been disappointed with Dr. Martin's view of justification, and that there was no sign of any recanting. But a lot of other people liked the tract, as it sold out fast and was reprinted.

It also gave Aleandro yet another item to toss into his November fires containing Luther's books, as if there weren't enough already.

MEN OF MANY, MANY SALES

Dr. Martin was puzzled more than once by the popularity of his books.

The only way he could explain it was, as usual, by God. For some reason, He had thrown Dr. Martin "into this game" of spreading the gospel not just by mouth but in print. And so he would go along with it, even if he sometimes didn't want to, and even if he had to fight the Devil all along the way.

But even Dr. Martin could have seen that there were some this-worldly forces helping out his sales, including his own very considerable efforts.

He didn't invent any clever new literary form in his books, or improve an old one, the way Erasmus did with his hilarious dialogues. In fact the forms Dr. Martin favored were pretty old-fashioned: straightforward commentaries and sermons, without even any rhymes or folk songs (yet). But he was fresh in other ways, starting with his ability to put controversial and complicated bits of theology into simple terms, even in German, and thus avoiding as much as possible the technical language of the scholastics and the fancy ornaments of the men of letters. He also dug right down into his readers' (and listeners') emotions and fears and hopes, which he knew well, because they were often his own emotions and fears and hopes, and it made his theology more personal than most theologians made theirs. So did his ability to entertain, and to be tender and emotional, instead of just formal and rational and detached. Sure, he had his weaknesses in writing, just like in preaching. Sometimes he fired over his audience's puzzled heads in his books and pamphlets too. Sometimes he was a little sharp, but he always figured that it was better to upset a few people than to upset God by not speaking the truth, and besides his supporters liked it when he was sharp to people they wanted him to be sharp with. Sometimes he exaggerated, a habit he brought over from all the disputations he'd done, but that helped him attract certain readers too. And he sometimes got repetitive in writing, partly because he plagiarized himself all the time and partly because he was a little too proud of his fast hand and rapid memory, which meant he almost never revised: especially in his long controversial pieces, he could have used some serious editing. Still, not everybody read every book of his to notice, and what he had to say was often novel enough that those who did notice forgave him anyway. And his short sermonlike pieces were stunningly concise and clear.

Brother Martin's authorly appeal also had something to do with how much care he put into the look of his books. That meant first of all insisting on good fonts, which was why he was thrilled when Melchior Lotter of Leipzig decided to have his son open a shop in Wittenberg in 1519 and bring all the latest fonts from around Europe with him. It also meant finding interesting designs for his covers, unlike the plain old no-nonsense no-interest designs of Johann Rhau-Grunenberg. Brother Martin kept using Rhau, out of loyalty, because the man had printed some risky things for him, but he looked for new design ideas from people like Frederick's court artist, Lucas Cranach, who lived down the street from the friary in Wittenberg and who soon created some cover pages that pretty soon almost every printer in German lands was copying—a decorative border all the way around the page, and a blank space in the middle for the title and for Dr. Martin's prominently featured name (not all authors' names were prominently featured).

Certainly Dr. Martin's books and pamphlets didn't appeal because of some rise in literacy among Germans, because that still stood at about 30 percent in towns and 5 percent overall. No, most people *heard* what he wrote. He became a household name by the end of 1520 not because masses of people read his tracts silently next to a candle at home, but because preachers read them aloud at church, and other people read them aloud at taverns or on a marketplace or street, and those listeners told still other listeners what they had heard. It was like the miracle of the loaves and fishes except with words, and it made the already impressive sales of his books more impressive still. Thus, a typical printing ran to about 1,000 copies, and so the 24 printings of the *Sermon on Indulgence and Grace* made it a huge seller—but even 24,000 copies represented just a tiny and literate part of the overall population, and by themselves they weren't enough to make Luther famous. No, what did that was the reading aloud, and the passing and telling along. Some of the biggest sharers of Brother Martin's books were his hundreds of fellow Augustinians, who mostly did their sharing from the hundreds of pulpits they had access to around the empire, and the pulpit and the right sort of preacher were still a lot more important to the vast majority of people than the newfangled press was. In fact any community that liked Brother Martin's sort of theology was going to bring in his sort of preacher before they ever bought up a gigantic batch of his pamphlets.

Of course that word-of-mouth spreading didn't explain *why* so many people were so interested in Dr. Martin's message. Some liked his pastoral works because they brought exactly the sort of spiritual comfort they were looking for from theology. But plenty liked his pastoral works and especially his more controversial works because they seemed to provide answers to the pressing political and social and economic problems they saw all around them—answers that Brother Martin himself never intended. People might then even put those answers into new and still more popular forms, like a play or song or hymn or even just a plain old rumor, and transform Brother Martin into a champion of causes he didn't really want to champion at all.

His *Christian Nobility,* for instance, sounded to certain German knights like a call for a violent war of independence from Rome, which they would be

only too happy to lead. The knights' common claim that the pope was trying
to increase his power in German lands wasn't actually true; he was far too busy
trying just to control what he already had in central Italy. But Germans did pay
ecclesiastical taxes to Rome, and bought Roman indulgences, and Maximilian
lost all sorts of German money on his wars in Italy, and it was easy to blame all of
those on the pope, the way such powerful imperial knights as Franz von Sickingen
and Ulrich von Hutten did. The knights had seen their social and political prestige slip away over the past decades, and they also resented the growing power of
ecclesiastical princes like Albrecht of Mainz, who seemed to be allies of Rome, and
who as far as the knights were concerned used their ecclesiastical courts to oppress
knights, such as by sending away the knights' concubines. In fact the decline of
the knights probably had more to do with the growing power of secular princes
like Frederick and Duke George, and of imperial cities like Augsburg and Worms,
and of the limits the imperial court had imposed on knights, than it did with any
schemes from Rome, but it was easy for knights to see a war against Rome as the
solution to all their problems. Such an idea had been around for decades by now
in German lands, but it got new life, to Dr. Martin's chagrin, with tracts like the
Christian Nobility and the *Freedom of a Christian*.

Other people in German lands heard the *Freedom of a Christian* in their own
peculiar way too. Some, but not most, territorial princes wouldn't have minded
being free from Rome, and taking charge of the church (and its lands) within
their territories. And some peasants might have certainly cared about the theological subtleties of the spiritual freedom that came from justification, but
more cared about freedom from their local landlords who were trying to bring
back old obligations that peasants thought they were done with, and freedom to
choose their own pastor or preacher, and freedom to hear the Mass in German
instead of Latin, and freedom to pay a lighter tithe, and freedom to hunt venison and fowl in the woods and to fish in streams, and freedom to cut wood and
use meadows when they needed to, and freedom to have fewer rules, and, yes,
freedom to send less money to Rome too.

The point was, when people read or heard the "freedom" of a Christian and
the "captivity" of the church, they easily read or heard them according to their
particular ear, and easily made them part of a bigger struggle between right and
wrong, between God and the Devil. Brother Martin believed religiously in the
apocalyptic struggle too, and the battle between God and the Devil, but he didn't
want to fight it in the same physical way certain peasants and townspeople and

knights seemed ready to, as in with swords and guns. Still, that sort of adapting of Brother Martin's messages to one's own particular concerns was exactly how Brother Martin became so popular, and how he became a household name in just a couple of years, whether he liked it or not.

In 1515 somebody with too much time on his hands made a list of the 100 most famous professors in Europe, and Dr. Martin's name hadn't even been close to appearing on it. But at the end of 1520 he was almost certainly at the very top of that list, and he was surely at the top of the list of the most famous reformers anyone could name too. To those who liked him, he was a holy man, which made him a lot more legitimate than being a professor did. And it wouldn't be long before the many images already circulating of him would include a dove flying over his head, just like there were doves over images of holy men like St. Ambrose, and St. Augustine, and St. Jerome, and St. Gregory the Great too, suggesting that, yes, the Holy Ghost was most certainly with Martin Luther.

Printers didn't puzzle over his popularity, though: they were just thrilled about it, and reaped all the profits. In fact, Brother Martin never took a single cent from all the many things he wrote, while a whole string of printers supported entire shops and families.

REQUIEM FOR A POPE

On the afternoon after Dr. Martin's bonfire, some 100 students of the University of Wittenberg organized another even louder and more rambunctious event.

Starting somewhere in town, they headed loudly down the street procession-style toward the Elster Gate, with a lot of song and trumpets and no doubt beer, and with many of the students riding on a float that featured a giant papal bull on the mast, like a sail. Some of them were dressed as charioteers, and at least one was dressed like the pope. Along the way, many in the noisy and growing crowd gathered firewood, because they were headed back to the spot where the bonfire had been that morning. They wanted to have another fire, surely to support their professor and not just to have an excuse to miss his or anybody else's class.

Once outside the Elster Gate again, they lit their fire and held a mock requiem for papal law, singing *Te Deum* and the old "angry song" *O Poor Judas*. The student dressed like the pope then took off his triple crown and threw it into the fire. A few sourfaces who were watching the event so they could tell the bishop, in Brandenburg, about it, reported everything they saw, because the bishop wouldn't like this any more than he'd liked Brother Martin's own book burning that same morning.

Dr. Martin may not have liked the afternoon event either, but the more he thought about his morning bonfire the more he liked it. He soon told George Spalatin that it was probably the best thing he'd ever done. He spoke about it in class too, the very day after, and in German so everyone would be sure to understand: the events of yesterday were but a trifle, he said. Books were nothing, and now the pope could see how easy it was to burn them. The real question was where students stood on the content of the books he'd burned, and there he was ominously clear: they had to run from the pope as fast as they could, or they wouldn't be saved. It was that simple. His students were the future clergy of the church, and future leaders of society too—they had to do the right thing, even if it was dangerous. As it was for him.

Prince Frederick and George Spalatin understood that danger perfectly well, which was one reason they didn't like either one of the fires. Another reason was that Charles had just promised Frederick, in his letter of November 28, that Dr. Martin would be given a hearing and treated fairly at the upcoming Diet—as long as he didn't do anything provocative. What chances would he have of being invited now, after something as provocative as his bonfire? Especially as rumors about it kept spreading and growing. Some people were soon saying the fire was a lot bigger than it actually was, and that there'd been horsemen and infantry all around to keep Luther safe, as if Prince Frederick had approved it all! Giles of Viterbo, the former general of the Augustinians, denounced the fire in very learned fashion: the pope's position, and papal law, were holy, insisted Viterbo, based not just on scholastic opinion but the Bible and the church fathers! Rejecting them, burning them, as Luther had, made you a heretic. And so it was the emperor's duty, he insisted, to take action.

Around the time of the bonfire, Spalatin had asked Dr. Martin what he would do if the emperor summoned him to the Diet (there could be no thought of an invitation anymore). He would go, he said, because he was sure any summons from the emperor would be from God: if God wanted to use the emperor to chastise him, and not save him, then his life was a small one anyway, and God surely had his reasons for doing so. That was another risk of speaking gospel truth: that you'd bring not glory to yourself, but trouble. Still, he wouldn't abandon the gospel because of it, even if Charles threatened him. Instead he'd remember the second psalm: when the great were conspiring against you, just trust in the Lord. Sure, if he had to die he would rather that it be at the hands of the pope and the Roman curia, not of Charles, so that Charles wouldn't have his new reign stained so early with the blood of an innocent: everybody knew how badly that had gone a century ago for the Emperor Sigismund, whose empire had suffered so greatly after he'd wrongly put to death the condemned Jan Hus. Still, he wouldn't run away from any summons from Charles, if it ever came.

And by no means, he said to Spalatin, would he ever recant.

11
God Help Me

Worms, Near the Mainz Gate. April 16, 1521. The Feast of St. Turibius of Astorga, Who Persecuted Heretics.

Even though he'd been met by cheering crowds at every town along the way, each one must have seemed like a miracle, all the way up to the last and biggest crowd of all, maybe 2,000 people, now waiting for him in Worms. This time trumpeters were waiting too, high on the tower of the cathedral, clear up in the heavens, ready to blast the good news that he was here.

Dr. Martin and his party drew close to the Mainz gate, at the north end of Worms, by around 10 a.m., meaning they had probably stayed the night before in the little town of Oppenheim, about 15 miles north, then set off that morning soon after sunrise at 6:30. That had given some eager messenger enough time to ride ahead to Worms to announce that the party would be arriving within hours, which was how 2,000 people came to be waiting on the streets that morning, and how a bunch of trumpeters would have known to get themselves up on the tower.

As the party passed through the Mainz gate, the reception was bigger and louder than when Dr. Martin had entered Leipzig for the disputation two years before. Then, the crowd had been a little hostile, and a wagon had humiliatingly collapsed. But now there were cheering and trumpets and jubilation and absolute sturdiness. Some people hadn't expected him to show up at all, he knew, but he'd been determined to get to Worms even, he said, if there were as many devils waiting for him as there were tiles on the roofs. Today there wouldn't have been much room on those roofs for any devils, because people were up there instead, trying to get a glimpse of the famous Luther as he rode in.

Worms 1610.

He'd never had a reception like this before, and he was surely glad for it, as long as it was a sign that people were being moved by the gospel instead of something else. Sure, a few in the crowd might well have been cheering his theology of justification by faith alone, but probably not as many as Dr. Martin would have liked. Even though his *Freedom of a Christian* was still selling fast, people still weren't understanding its message of justification the way he wanted, which was why this very month he'd written yet another tract on the subject explaining in yet another way how it worked and what it ought to mean in their lives. But he'd be patient with them, because it was hard even for him to have faith sometimes, and so if most people were cheering him because they saw him as their champion against the pope, or even as some holy man who would save Germany, he would just keep teaching them what he really stood for, and hope that their very passing enthusiasm for him would someday lead to a very lasting understanding of the gospel. He kept telling people he was no saint, or hero, but they kept calling him one anyway.

First in the party through the gate was the big imperial herald, Kaspar von Sturm, up on his high horse and with an image of the imperial eagle on his

Luther Entering Worms.

cloak. He had carried the summons from Worms a month before all the way to Wittenberg, and after handing it over to Dr. Martin had turned around a few days later and ridden back with him.

Next came Dr. Martin himself in a strong, two-wheeled wagon that the town council of Wittenberg had rented from the local goldsmith Christian Döring, the partner of Lucas Cranach, so Brother Martin could be sure to arrive in time, and have a little comfort and company on the long trip. Seated with him were his fellow theologian Nicholas von Amsdorf, his fellow Augustinian Johannes Petzensteiner, and his noble student Peter Swaven, who could provide some extra protection. Despite being able to sit during this latest long journey of his, instead of as usual having to walk, Dr. Martin looked worn, and his tonsure a little ragged.

Behind the wagon came another friend, Justus Jonas, on a horse some Saxon nobleman had arranged for him.

One rumor said that eight armed horsemen also accompanied the party right up to the gate, but another rumor said it was a hundred, led by the imperial knight Franz von Sickingen, who'd guarded Frankfurt during the recent election of the emperor but who now wanted to make sure that Luther's imperial safe conduct was worth the parchment it was written on.

Dr. Martin was greeted by a couple of Prince Frederick's ever-present councilors, who said they would lead him to his quarters. He wouldn't be staying with the prince, whose entourage already spilled beyond his rooms and who had to keep up his image of neutrality toward Dr. Martin anyway. Instead he would stay at the monastery of the Knights of Rhodes—the Hospitalers—farther down Kämmerer Lane. When the wagon stopped at his destination, Dr. Martin stepped out, and a priest came out of the crowd to hug him and touch his habit three times, making Dr. Martin's enemies smirk that reports of miracles were sure to follow.

The councilors showed him to his room, which he would be sharing with them, and maybe the bed too, if the usual arrangements in guest-lodgings of the time were any clue. For a friar used to having a whole cell (and bed) to himself, it couldn't have been a very relaxing arrangement in what was an already unrelaxing situation: after all, he'd come all this way to Worms not for some hero's welcome but because he'd been summoned to the imperial Diet to answer for his alleged crimes against the church.

INVITED AND NOT

When Dr. Martin held his big bonfire in December 1520, *Exsurge Domine* and numerous volumes of canon law weren't the only things that went up in smoke.

So did his invitation from the emperor to come to the Diet for the long-anticipated hearing. Charles had made that invitation back in November partly out of respect for Frederick, but also because his imperial oath said he would "under no circumstances permit anyone, whether of high estate or low, elector, prince, or otherwise, to be placed under ban and double ban for any reason without a hearing." But imperial and canon law also said that incorrigible heretics didn't deserve hearings, and when December 10 came along and Dr. Martin still hadn't recanted but instead burned the bull that demanded his recantation, Aleandro insisted to everybody that it only proved what an incorrigible heretic Luther obviously obviously was. "One who has been condemned by the pope, the cardinals, and prelates should be heard only in prison," not at a Diet, Aleandro told Charles's council on December 14. Besides, the Diet was made up mostly of laypeople, and laypeople had no right to judge matters of faith: all they could do was carry out the judgment of the church. Aleandro also urged Charles to send a delegation to Prince Frederick to demand that Luther recant the 41 errors condemned by *Exsurge Domine*, and if he wouldn't recant then Frederick should burn Luther's books and throw him in prison until the emperor decided what to do with him. Aleandro was so frustrated with Frederick by now that he was variously calling him the Saxon Fox, the Basilisk, the Despicable Saxon, and the Fat Groundhog with the Eyes of a Dog.

Charles probably wouldn't have used those names for his "beloved uncle," but after he got word of the bonfire in Wittenberg he agreed with Aleandro about Luther. On December 20, he wrote Frederick and canceled his invitation for Luther to come to Worms and be heard. Since the 60-day grace period of the bull had expired on December 10, he had to presume Luther was now excommunicated, and since any city giving shelter to an excommunicant could be placed under the interdict by the pope, Charles didn't want Worms to suffer, he said. But Frederick beat the emperor to the punch: even before receiving Charles's letter, he sent one the other way saying that in the very bright light of all the recent burnings, maybe it was best for Dr. Martin not to go to Worms after all.

That was where things stood on the day the Diet was supposed to start: January 6, 1521, Epiphany, or Three Kings Day. It was scheduled then to remind everyone of the three crowns Charles now wore, as king of Spain, Naples, and the Germans (he was merely count and duke many times over in the Netherlands and Austria). Frederick heroically subjected himself one more time to the horrors of bouncing carriages and potholed roads—though here in winter he might have ridden in some areas on smoother runners instead—and arrived in Worms just in time, on January 5. But for various reasons the opening of the Diet was delayed until January 28, which gave Frederick time to raise the matter of Dr. Martin again with the emperor.

Soon after arriving, he asked for another audience with Charles. The two men didn't have the same once-close relationship Frederick had shared with Maximilian, despite all the "beloved uncle" talk. But Charles still had to respect Frederick, and was even indebted to him, since Frederick had seen to it that Charles was elected unanimously as emperor back in 1519, even when Frederick himself might have won. Plus the two "cousins" were practically in-laws now too, since Charles had promised his sister to Frederick's nephew and heir, Johann Frederick. All this gave Charles some incentive to make sure that Frederick, and his subjects, were treated fairly. By the end of their meeting, Charles had decided that Luther should again be invited to Worms for a hearing. Frederick sent a letter to Dr. Martin in Wittenberg with the good news, and had his men start talks with the emperor's men on exactly how that hearing should go.

Frederick's chancellor, Gregor Brück, met at least four times with the emperor's confessor, the Franciscan Jean Glapion, during the next couple of weeks. Glapion wanted to meet with Frederick personally, but the prince was as usual careful not to appear to be Dr. Martin's advocate, and so sent Brück instead. Only in private would Frederick give any clue how he felt about his famous subject: "Would to God that I could help Martin right and proper," he wrote to his brother Johann back in Saxony, presumably meaning instead of just doing his usual stonewalling. Still, Frederick gave a somewhat visible hint of his sentiments by sending his brother Johann and various towns copies of Dr. Martin's books, as if to approve them. And since he did almost nothing to rein in Johann's and Johann Frederick's blatant support of Dr. Martin, people suspected that Frederick wasn't neutral at all, even if he was keeping up appearances.

Glapion stunned Brück in the first couple of meetings by saying that he actually agreed with some of Luther's early ideas, and admired Luther's gifts, and didn't think all 41 errors in *Exsurge Domine* needed condemning. He even doubted that Dr. Martin had actually written the *Babylonian Captivity*, but if he really had, then it would help very much if he would say he'd lost his mind for a moment. By the third meeting Glapion was even agreeing with Frederick that the hearing at Worms should be run by scholars, instead of churchmen.

Brück and the other Saxons were thrilled by all this, but they were also suspicious, especially when they heard the conditions Glapion had in mind, such as that if Luther really had written the *Babylonian Captivity,* then it would have to be totally retracted before there could be any talk of a court of scholars, and that the hearing would have to be in private instead of before the whole Diet. A shifting target like that made it hard for Brück, and Frederick, to tell how sincere Glapion really was. Maybe if Glapion would do something to quiet down all the bishops and cardinals who'd started attacking Brother Martin as soon as they got to Worms (especially Archbishop Albrecht of Mainz), they might believe him. And was Glapion really expecting Dr. Martin to stop writing while he waited for his hearing? Because Frederick knew that wouldn't happen. By the last meeting between Brück and Glapion, there was still no agreement on how the hearing should go or whether there would even be one. And on January 27, the day before the Diet was to begin, the Venetian ambassador was saying in his ambassadorial way that somebody had told him that Charles had told somebody else that Luther shouldn't even be on the agenda.

Thus by the time the Diet started, Brother Martin was apparently being uninvited again, despite Charles's recent agreement with Frederick. Maybe Aleandro had again gotten primary hold of Charles's youthful ear by then. Or maybe Charles was alarmed by all the popular support for Luther in Worms and simply refused to buckle under it. Most likely, Charles by the end of January had read the letter of the 18th from Rome letting him know that an official bull of excommunication, affirming the conditional excommunication of *Exsurge Domine,* had been approved by the pope on January 3. As Aleandro had been saying until he was out of breath, excommunicated people weren't invited and heard, they were summoned and condemned—and maybe not even summoned. And in the empire, excommunicated people were supposed to automatically be placed under the imperial ban as well.

Here, just before the Diet began, was when Charles reportedly tore up the letter Luther had written to him last August.

THE EMPEROR'S BALANCING ACT

Like every other Diet, the one at Worms shook up the host city for months.

The greatest of the great in town always put on at least one huge event, to polish their reputations, and Frederick of Saxony was one of the best at doing so—which wasn't surprising, since he'd learned from the best in German lands, Maximilian, who'd learned from the best in Europe, the Italians. The point of these "representations" was to give tangible form to the abstract qualities the great wanted to have associated with their name. The electoral outfit Frederick paraded around in at the Diet, for instance, including red doublet, red stockings, red robe with big white collar, and red velvet hat with ermine lining, said everything about his status. But he wanted to say something as well about his courage, piety, intelligence, loyalty, and generosity, so he also sponsored lively theater, elaborate dinners, loud music, and grand entries, and crowned poet laureates, and handed out coins and books featuring his very electoral self. At his first Diet, in 1487, Frederick rode into town with several hundred horsemen wearing his colors, and carrying flags and banners with his coat of arms, while his trumpeters with their odd-shaped horns and impossible notes played just the right triumphant music. He also hosted a twenty-course meal that featured almost the entire animal kingdom, even more music from his trumpeters, and gambling tables that were busy long after dark.

And of course Frederick always sponsored jousts, which he liked as much as Pope Leo liked the hunt. Frederick was too gouty to joust himself anymore and so he'd taken up woodworking instead, but he still loved to watch and comment on technique, horses, weapons, saddles, and armor, so much that almost half the letters he traded with his brother Johann said something about jousting. Foreign observers at Worms thought there was too much jousting there, but Frederick and most other German nobles didn't care: up went grandstands, and the coats of arms of combatants, and tents and corrals at the edge of town for all the armor and horses. And to Frederick's most assured delight one of the stars of the action at Worms was none other than his nephew, Johann Frederick, who was thrown just a few times and who pranced around on a horse with a saddle blanket that said, "My luck runs on stilts." Johann Frederick's future brother-in-law, the Emperor Charles, even paid the ultimate compliment by asking the star for some reading materials on jousting.

But of course when there was time, the three estates at the Diet met separately and together to treat political matters too. The agenda included the same old subjects of public peace, and the imperial supreme court and police, and trade and tolls, and the Turks, but also some new ones, like whether the Diet would help pay for Charles's upcoming crowning in Rome, and for the 24,000 troops he wanted for his looming war with France. But as usual a couple of matters really stood out: (1) who would run the empire when the emperor was away from it, which was likely to be often, given all his other lands? and (2) what was the emperor finally going to do about the *Gravamina,* the list of "Complaints of the German Nation Against the Holy See in Rome," which by now had swelled to more than 40 pages? Not just the crowds cheering Martin Luther but also the great nobles and towns of the estates had grievances against the pope too.

Nowhere on the busy Gothic-lettered agenda was the name of Martin Luther, but that didn't mean he was forgotten. The estates knew very well about his troubles, and most of their members could even grunt approval of his ideas that happened to go along with their *Gravamina,* especially the ideas that criticized the pope. But what most princes and nobles at the Diet (and they mattered most) didn't like was Luther's seemingly total overhaul of the church's teachings and rituals. The *Gravamina* were about frictions with the pope, not about theology and religious customs, which most princes and nobles wanted to keep just as they were. In fact, if the emperor wanted to punish Luther for heresy, most of them were ready to go along. But the key phrase was "go along"—they wanted their say in any punishment.

It was Charles's very first Diet, and it was already clear what a delicate balance he would have to find. To get the fat subsidy he wanted the estates to provide for him to travel to Rome for his coronation as emperor, and to get the other subsidy for the 24,000 soldiers he needed to fight against France, Charles would have to push the pope about the *Gravamina* that the estates were so adamant about. But Charles couldn't push the pope too hard precisely because he needed the pope to crown him emperor—plus as emperor he would get some very nice material benefits from the pope, as in a percentage of all church income in the empire, and he didn't want to lose those either.

The shadow of Martin Luther made the balancing even trickier than usual. Even though most princes and nobles were ready to punish Luther, Charles knew he couldn't do so on his own, in private, or punish too severely either, as they would consider both a violation of their rights and refuse to give Charles what he wanted. Luther would therefore have to show up on the agenda at some point.

On January 29, only the second day of the Diet, there were already rumors that Charles was preparing a mandate against Luther that he would present to the estates for their approval. On Ash Wednesday (February 13), Aleandro spent most of the speech he was finally allowed to make urging the estates to approve the forthcoming mandate, so that the heretic Luther would be under both the church's ban and the imperial ban, and have nowhere to hide. Aleandro made it all as alarming as possible: Luther was responsible for all the trouble in the land, he was the resurrection from hell of the Bohemian Jan Hus, he rejected ceremonies and monastic vows, he denied transubstantiation, he appealed to councils even while he rejected their authority, he appealed to scripture then threw out the parts he didn't like, he challenged the pope's authority to make laws, he denied saints and free will and indulgences, he was "a heretic and an obstinate heretic" which by the way made him a "revolutionary" too, because as they all knew heresy always led to revolution, which was maybe the greatest sin of all. Luther and his books had to be banned forever from the empire and the church, said Aleandro.

It was a big speech about a person still not even officially on the agenda. And it made a big impression too, including on Prince Frederick and his advisors, and

Ulrich von Hutten.

even on the distant towns of Merseburg and Meissen, in Saxony, where Luther's books were soon burned. Maybe Aleandro made small tactical mistakes in his speech by offering too many yawn-provoking examples to support his points, and by taking time to refute all the rumors (spread by Erasmus and Hutten) that he, Aleandro, was a Jew, which was an insult he couldn't let pass. But Aleandro's real mistake was holding back the news that Luther had actually already been excommunicated, in the papal bull of January 3, and that he actually had a copy of that bull in his soft courtly hands. If Aleandro had mentioned that bull in his speech, and shown it to the estates, he might have won them over right then and there, and they might have readily approved the mandate when Charles presented it two days later.

But Aleandro didn't show or tell the bull, because he had a slight problem with it, and his name was Ulrich von Hutten. Hutten had sworn to take revenge on the person of Aleandro if Luther were condemned, but even worse for Aleandro was that the January 3 bull excommunicated not just Luther, but Hutten too. That would give the knight even more incentive to go after Aleandro. No, the nuncio didn't really want to publish the bull at the moment. Instead he sent it back to Rome for revisions: please remove Hutten's name. Then he would publish the revised version after he was safely back in Rome. But as far as the Diet knew, Luther's status in the church and empire was still up for discussion.

This became clear right after Charles, on February 15, presented the promised mandate. It said mostly what Aleandro had said: that Luther was a Bohemian; that he didn't need a hearing since he'd already been condemned (in *Exsurge Domine*); that the estates should accept that condemnation as final, just as the emperor had, and thus regard Luther as already excommunicated; that Luther and his supporters should be arrested if they didn't recant; and so on. Five of the seven electors agreed with the mandate, when they met to discuss it (although the ailing and usually calm Frederick got so mad speaking against it that he reportedly had to be separated from his rival, the elector of Brandenburg). But in the meeting of princes and nobles, most said they couldn't go along with putting anyone under the ban who hadn't been officially excommunicated. Yes, *Exsurge Domine* had expired on December 10 and it promised that excommunication would follow, but a new bull positively declaring excommunication still hadn't come. Maybe Luther deserved a hearing after all.

Surely somewhere in the back corridors of the Diet, the bull-withholding Aleandro felt like ritually shedding his robes, since he had the proof of Luther's excommunication right in his pocket, but didn't have enough nerve to show it.

On February 19, in a joint meeting of all three estates on the mandate, the members presented yet another concern: what would common people do if an unexcommunicated Luther were condemned without a hearing, which everybody knew he was entitled to by imperial law?

Aleandro could hardly even understand why Charles needed to consult the estates about a ban, so the idea that they all needed to take popular opinion into consideration too was completely inconceivable. Oh, opinion was strong, he knew that. He'd seen all the Luther-supporting crowds when he'd come down the Rhine Valley from Antwerp to Cologne, and then from Cologne to Worms too, and now most of all right here in Worms itself. Nine-tenths of Germans were yelling "Luther!" he wrote to Rome, and the other tenth "Death to the Roman Curia!" And despite Aleandro's bonfires and condemnations in other places, Luther's pamphlets and books were everywhere in Worms, as were the writings of others who openly ridiculed the pope. Some of these other writings included images of Luther as a humble friar with haloes and doves over his head, which some people were even kissing like they were holy objects! One showed Luther and Hutten together, Luther holding a book and Hutten a sword, over a caption that said "Champions of Christian Liberty." Another showed Luther, Hutten, and Hus all together—the unholy trinity. A parody of the Apostles' Creed said about the pope that "under his power truth suffered, was crucified, died, and buried," and "I believe in the canon law, in the Romish church, in the destruction of faith and of the communion of saints, in indulgences . . . in the resurrection of the flesh in an Epicurean life, given to us by the Holy Father, the pope, Amen." A whole wagon couldn't hold all the scandalous writings for sale, lamented Aleandro, who was even afraid to go out on the street because of all the Germans who "put their hands to their swords and gnash their teeth at me." But not even

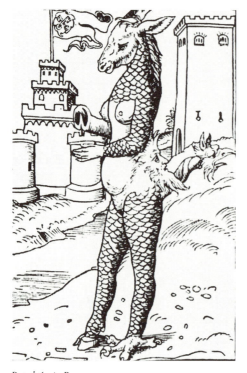

Papal Ass in Rome.

threats like that meant that popular opinion should be listened to: it was the job of the estates to lead, not to follow! Aleandro also hoped that Charles would have the focus he needed to push his mandate through, because he was distracted by so many other things going on outside the Diet, like his feud with the nobles of Hungary, and the revolt going on in Spain, and arranging the marriage and inheritance of his brother Ferdinand, so that Ferdinand would be his ally instead of his rival.

Just as Aleandro feared, during that February 19 meeting, the estates didn't approve the mandate exactly as it was written but wanted a compromise instead: Luther should come to the Diet, and if he recanted his offensive teachings on things like indulgences and the sacraments and other favorite practices of theirs, then he could be heard on the teachings that they liked, such as the overreaching authority of the pope in German lands. But if he wouldn't recant, then the estates would support the emperor's mandate completely, and in return the emperor would take up their *Gravamina* with the pope. Either way, the estates would win.

This wasn't the outcome Aleandro or Charles had hoped for, but at least Charles seemed willing to go along. He would summon (not invite) Luther to Worms, he said, to give him a chance to recant, and if he recanted then there could be a limited hearing for him. Plus the emperor would discuss the *Gravamina* seriously with the estates, just as they'd so long wanted. On March 1 Charles even asked the estates (1) when and where should Luther be summoned (it didn't have to be Worms, where the crowds were so threatening), and (2) should his books be burned right away, or after his recantation? The estates, surely led by Frederick, wanted Luther summoned to Worms itself, and to have an imperial safe conduct. On March 6, Charles presented his revised mandate: Luther could come to Worms with the requested safe conduct, and his books wouldn't be burned (yet). But all of his books were to be confiscated, and the mandate made it sound like he was already condemned. Still, condemnation was in the eye of the beholder: Frederick didn't like the confiscation or the prejudicial tone, but Aleandro thought the safe conduct and the no-book-burning gave the impression that Luther wasn't condemned and that his books weren't all that dangerous. Whatever one thought of this final version of the mandate, it was finally printed on March 17 or 18, and was sent around the empire starting on March 26 or 27.

The summons to appear at Worms probably went out to Dr. Martin the same day that Charles presented his revised mandate to the estates, on March 6. Its opening words maddened Aleandro as much as parts of the mandate did: "Our noble, dear, and esteemed Martin Luther" it began—that wasn't how you addressed a condemned heretic! The summons also said that the emperor and Diet wanted Luther to come to Worms "to answer with regard to your books and teachings." The "to answer" couldn't have pleased Aleandro either, because it made it sound like Luther would be questioned instead of condemned—which was exactly how Dr. Martin would read it too. Finally, the summons gave him 21 days from the time of receipt to get to Worms.

Prince Frederick wasn't sure whether Dr. Martin would actually answer the summons, especially once he laid eyes on the mandate and saw that his books were to be confiscated and that he was already more or less condemned. Chancellor Brück even warned in the pessimistic voice of the experienced lawyer that given the tone of the mandate he wondered whether the emperor might feel he could ignore the safe conduct he'd promised Dr. Martin, because everybody knew what had happened a century before in a similar situation: despite an imperial safe conduct from the Emperor Sigismund, Jan Hus had ended up at the stake anyway, on the grounds that you didn't have to keep your word to a heretic. It all made Brück shudder, and his advice to Brother Martin was simple: don't set a single foot outside of Saxony. But it was also true that the princes who supported Brother Martin probably wouldn't let anything happen to him either, and so ultimately Brück left the decision to him.

BAD FRIDAY

Long before he heard that bit of legal advice, Dr. Martin had of course already made up his mind that if he were summoned to Worms, he would go, even if it meant a little fire.

But it was unclear for months whether the invitation, and then summons, would ever come. Between December 1520 and March 1521, the pendulum swung back and forth—now he was going, now he wasn't.

During all that uncertainty, Dr. Martin's usual lecturing and preaching and writing helped him keep his mind on other things. At Frederick's request, he wrote a tract called *Ground and Reason for all the Articles [or Theses] Wrongly Condemned by the Roman Bull,* explaining why *Exsurge Domine* was so wrong. But Frederick certainly didn't ask him to write the highly flammable *Why the Books of the Pope and His Disciples Were Burned by Doctor Martin Luther,* which Brother Martin put out in late December, or the endless tracts he kept trading with Hieronymus Emser, like *To the Goat in Leipzig,* or *An Addition to Goat Emser,* or the *Answer to the Hyperchristian, Hyperspiritual, and Hyperlearned Book by Goat Emser in Leipzig.*

Brother Martin also wrote still more pastoral works, including *Comfort When Facing Grave Temptations, A Sermon on the Worthy Reception of the Sacrament,* and *A Sermon on the Three Kinds of Good Life for the Instruction of Consciences,* this last being his latest attempt to explain justification by faith. In fact by early 1521 Dr. Martin had written so many tracts that he had to write another explaining what Christians should do if confessors started refusing to grant them absolution for reading any of them. The *Instruction for Penitents Concerning the Forbidden Books of Dr. M. Luther* provided a series of snappy things to say to such confessors, like: "My dear sir, I have come to confession not to be trapped but to be absolved." Or, "You are much too insignificant to settle the issue here," as many learned men were still debating the issues. Or, "My dear sir, you are a father-confessor, not an officer. I am obliged to confess what my conscience prompts me to confess. It is not your duty to force me to confess; neither is it your duty to probe the secrets of my heart," which were for God alone. And if the confessor brought up the condemnations of *Exsurge Domine,* the penitent should say that a lot of pious people didn't think much of it at all, "for the pope's opinion is wont to vacillate. He institutes something or other one day and rescinds it the next." If none of these responses worked, and the priest still didn't want to grant absolution, then the penitent shouldn't worry: you could do without altar, priest, and church, because the Word of God itself would absolve you.

But even though he kept busy and was the object of much attention, Dr. Martin also felt somewhat alone in early 1521, as more friends abandoned him—even Staupitz seemed to completely disappear. In truth his old mentor was still quietly supporting him. When Cardinal Lang of Salzburg demanded in January 1521 that Staupitz repudiate the 41 errors condemned in *Exsurge Domine*, Staupitz said he couldn't repudiate anything he hadn't stated himself. But that private act wasn't enough for Dr. Martin: he was afraid Staupitz was still defending the pope in public and forgetting everything he had taught Dr. Martin about mercy. He wanted Staupitz to speak out in public! "You are too humble, as I am too arrogant," he wrote his old mentor. But his mentor feared for him: "Martinus has begun something dangerous," he wrote.

Dr. Martin was energized again, though, by March 19, when he finally got news from Worms that he would probably be summoned after all. He also got a list of the teachings that had caused offense, including the 41 noted in *Exsurge Domine*, but a lot more too, because he'd written so much since then. At least he knew he was going now, and what to prepare for. Against the claim that his brand of Christian freedom would upset the political order, for instance, he jotted down numerous reasons why that was false. Against the charge that he was just like Hus, he wrote down sarcastically that no he wasn't: he was actually a much bigger heretic than Hus ever was, meaning of course that neither one of them was truly a heretic at all. And he also made a note to say again that he still supported the church, just not the Roman version of it. He condensed all his notes into a series of theses and sent them off to Worms. Spalatin had them by March 24. Surely the secretary wasn't thrilled by the "bigger-heretic" comment, but he saw already that Brother Martin wasn't coming to Worms to recant.

For all his resolve, though, Dr. Martin must have lost at least a little breath when he saw big Kaspar von Sturm coming toward him in Wittenberg on Friday, March 29. Did it happen on the street? In his classroom? At the friary? Wherever it was, the awful moment had finally arrived. He took the summons, read it, saw that he had 21 days to get to Worms, and said he would make himself ready.

Getting the summons on Good Friday surely didn't help relieve the dread he was feeling: just like Christ, he was about to go to his death, he thought. Oh, he was still determined to go, but he was still battling his *Anfechtungen* too, especially the ones telling him that he should just cave in and recant the true gospel once he was in front of the emperor, because it would be so much easier than standing firm.

The university gave him leave to go and 20 gulden for expenses, and a few friends were willing to accompany him on the journey, although not Melanchthon, who was too popular to be gone that long. The small party left Wittenberg for Worms just a few days later, probably Tuesday, April 2.

Going southwest, they rode through Leipzig, then Naumburg, then Weimar, where Dr. Martin got some more expense money from Duke Johann but also the news about the imperial mandate and the confiscation of his books. The news was bad enough that the herald Sturm asked Dr. Martin whether he wanted to keep going. Yes he did, he said, which was when he made his crack about devils and tiles. Then it was on to Erfurt, Gotha, and Eisenach, and in every single place (except Leipzig, where he again got only a token gift of wine), there were cheering crowds, which helped him understand how Jesus must have felt riding into Jerusalem. Some 40 or even 60 horsemen escorted him into Erfurt, where local worthies gave speeches praising him for daring to tame Roman arrogance with the sword of holy scripture, and where so many people came to hear him preach in the Augustinian church that the balcony threatened to collapse, causing some people to break windows and jump out. Dr. Martin assured them it was a trick of the Devil to get them not to listen, because they most certainly needed to listen. They still didn't get it: good works couldn't save them. He had learned that lesson himself, in this very friary: he'd supposed that worshiping God and being free of sin meant becoming a priest or a friar, and doing such endless good works as singing the psalter, and reciting the rosary, and saying countless prayers and masses, and kneeling before the altar, and hearing confession. But even if you did all these, you'd still have so much envy in your heart that if you could choke your neighbor and get away with it, you would, which he knew because he'd felt that way himself. Worshiping God meant taking His grace into your miserable little heart. The friars there in the crowd wouldn't like hearing this, he knew, but he had to say it.

He also preached in Gotha and Eisenach, but in Eisenach, where he'd been a teenaged student, he felt sick and subjected himself to the still-favorite cureall of bleeding. The trip was hard after that, in fact he was sick the rest of the way and then through the entire Diet too, mostly with an upset stomach, which surely had something to do with the anxiety that was bound to accompany the thought—"you are about to die." By April 14 the party was out of Saxony and in Frankfurt, where Dr. Martin recovered enough to play the lute, and to write Spalatin that the confiscation of his books was surely an attempt to frighten him away from the Diet, but "Christ lives, and we shall enter Worms in spite of all the gates of hell and the powers in the air."

On April 15, they were just 15 miles short of Worms, in Oppenheim, when an unexpected bit of drama intruded. Suddenly there appeared Martin Bucer, one of the rare Dominicans who admired Brother Martin, ever since seeing the disputation at Heidelberg in 1518. Bucer was now the court chaplain of Franz von Sickingen, the dread imperial knight who had become a Luther-sympathizer. His master, Bucer explained, had been advised by none other than the emperor's own confessor, Jean Glapion, that it wasn't safe for Dr. Martin to continue on to Worms; if he did, he would be burned at the stake, no question. Instead he should come to Sickingen's castle at Ebernburg (Boar Fortress), 25 miles due west, where he could speak with Glapion alone and together they would find a solution to this argument with the pope.

What in the world was Dr. Martin to make of this? He had every reason to trust Bucer, and Sickingen. But Glapion? He didn't know the man at all. And didn't Glapion's overlord, the emperor, want to burn Dr. Martin's professorly self? Why would the emperor then send Glapion with such a warning? Why couldn't he and Glapion just talk in Worms? Was the imperial safe conduct that flimsy? Brother Martin made his decision by counting: it had been 17 days since he'd gotten the summons in Wittenberg, meaning he had four more days to get to Worms. If he sidetracked to Ebernburg for, say, two days, he could still make it in time. But it would be close, and what if he got even sicker along the way? Then he might not make it to Worms at all. No, he couldn't risk it, he decided. He had to go on.

The decision to do so would have been even easier if Dr. Martin had known that taking a detour from the expected route would render his safe conduct invalid. Was that what Glapion was trying to do, and thus make it easier to burn him? The Saxon councilors in Worms hadn't exactly trusted Glapion when negotiating with him, and now Dr. Martin didn't either. Glapion was furious when he rejected the invitation, but Dr. Martin's friends were convinced that it was all a trick meant to trap him: Sickingen and Bucer, both admirers of Dr. Martin, were just the unwitting agents of it.

The traveling party stayed the night of April 15 in Oppenheim, instead of detouring through Ebernburg, then set out for Worms the next morning. On April 16, the third day after Misericordias Domini Sunday (which was the third Sunday after Easter), they rode in to cheering crowds. And trumpets.

A VERY WARM MEETING

Aleandro wasn't happy at all about the crowds.

He tried to dismiss all the enthusiasm for Luther as some sort of mad passion. And he also worried that the *Gravamina*-loving Diet wasn't going to simply order Luther to recant the long list of errors it had compiled against him, but would instead say he had to recant only those errors that offended dogma: those that offended the pope they would probably let him talk about to his heretical-heart's content, and agree with him.

The emperor wasn't thrilled about the crowds either. He and his men wanted Luther to come into town quietly, and stay at the emperor's palace so he couldn't spiritually infect anybody, but Charles didn't really want to keep him under house arrest either. He also must have realized that there was no way in the world the people of Worms would have ever let Luther enter unnoticed.

In fact, almost as soon as he arrived not only were the masses gawking but a long line of the great came calling too, to get and give advice and even, like the masses, to just stare at him. Yes, most princes and great nobles were decid-edly against him, but a sizeable minority absolutely were not. Some of his stately visitors warned that a few bishops were trying to tell Charles that Luther's safe conduct could be violated without a second thought, but the visitors added that the rest of the Diet—even those against Luther—would be furious if that hap-pened. The most distressed distinguished visitor was probably Philip of Hesse, who needed urgently to know whether Dr. Martin had been serious in the *Babylonian Captivity* about allowing a woman with an impotent husband to take another one instead. This wasn't exactly the moment for such a personal matter, replied Dr. Martin, but he would one day respond to that question and be ever so sorry that he did.

Someone who didn't visit was Jean Glapion, even though Dr. Martin wrote him almost immediately upon arriving to say that he was ready to talk. Glapion responded that it was pointless, but as usual he tantalized: if Dr. Martin would re-cant the 41 errors in *Exsurge Domine*, then maybe they could discuss some of his more recent objectionable teachings, like on the sacraments. But Dr. Martin as usual said that he wouldn't recant anything that hadn't been proven wrong by scripture.

It was a long first day and night in Worms, especially since Dr. Martin still wasn't entirely well. And he got no more rest the next day, April 17, because first thing in the morning he was asked to hear the confession of an ailing Saxon knight, and not long after that the imperial marshal, Ulrich von Pappenheim, came knocking to say that Brother Martin was to appear before the Diet that very afternoon at 4. At that hour, the marshal came back with Kaspar von Sturm, to walk him over to the bishop's palace, where the joint meetings of the estates were being held, right next to the cathedral.

People were still lining the streets, hoping to see Brother Martin, which was why Pappenheim and Sturm led him on a detour, through the back garden of the Hospitalers, then the lodgings of the elector of the Palatinate, then several side streets. There were people along this route too but they were out on ordinary business and so when they suddenly saw Martin Luther walk past they were stunned. The biggest crowd was gathered near the bishop's palace, where guards were blocking the main door because the hall inside was already full. Dr. Martin and the emperor's two men probably went in through a back door.

A few steps farther and they were suddenly walking into the crowded hall, full of hundreds of members of the Diet plus however many onlookers had squeezed in. Dr. Martin's enemies said he was "laughing" and proud, but his friends said he just had a "joyful countenance," as he swung his head from side to side, taking it all in. One fellow wrote that Luther was "robust in physique and face, with not especially good eyes, and lively features which he frivolously changed." Anyone else who described him mentioned his eyes too, like the Polish ambassador who said they were "piercing and twinkle almost uncannily, the way one sometimes sees in a person possessed." Cajetan said, "His eyes are as deep as a lake," and a student described his eyes as "deep, black, blinking, and glittering like a star." Coming near the front of the assembly, Brother Martin recognized his acquaintance Conrad Peutinger from Augsburg and said hello, but Pappenheim told him not to speak unless spoken to. Prince Frederick was surely near the front too, and like most others there was probably seeing Luther for the very first time. Dr. Martin was dressed in his big-belted Augustinian habit, his tonsure was newly shaved, and as usual it was bigger than most tonsures, probably because he was used to it rather than because he was still trying to impress God by doing everything more strictly than everybody else.

Not more than 20 feet away sat the emperor himself, too great to stand like most others—Charles, the luckiest man alive. Charles, son of Philip the Fair and Mad Joanna, king of Castile and Aragon and so on and so on up to 72 different titles, including of course king of the Romans. Charles, whose motto was *Plus Ultra*, or Further Beyond, in defiance of the ancient warning "No Further" supposedly posted at the Straits of Gibraltar, because *his* lands would go as far as he wanted, farther even than the lands of his namesake Charlemagne. Charles, who wasn't quite as grand in person as in theory, with his thin but well-formed body of merely average height, and eyes that the Venetian ambassador said "bulged and stared" like they didn't really belong to him but had been pasted on, and a lower jaw that jutted out past his upper and drooped and even drooled when he was in thought, which another observer said made him look like an idiot. Charles, who was at least serious, and conscientious, and thoughtful, and loyal, and moderately talented, and entirely confident of his position but not necessarily of his person, as here at 21 he still couldn't settle on a wife, though he'd been engaged twice and had already fathered a couple of children. And finally, Charles, the devout Catholic, "the greatest protector and upholder of the Universal Church," who, like all princes, including Frederick of Saxony, saw absolutely no contradiction between his devotion and his fathering two children outside of wedlock.

However youthful the emperor was, however slightly out of place with his Flemish haircut and shaved face, it would have been hard even for Dr. Martin not to have been impressed. Of course the emperor wouldn't himself address Dr. Martin, and not only because he didn't have any German or fluent enough Latin but because he was the emperor: just like at his coronation, people spoke for him. In this case, his spokesman was a man named, coincidentally, Johann von der Eck(en), or Eck: he was the official, or chief judge, at the court of the archbishop of Trier, but he had virtually the same name as Dr. Martin's old rival. The choice of this Eck was a surprise for Frederick's councilors, who'd expected Glapion to do the questioning. Maybe the emperor and his men gave the job to Eck because they wanted to haunt Luther with the shadow of another Eck, but more likely it was because this Eck was also thoroughly German (Glapion was French), was an experienced prosecutor and judge, and had shown how eager he was to obey both pope and emperor, even gladly taking orders from Aleandro as to what questions he should ask of Luther. Since Eck was staying with Aleandro in Worms, the two had been able to prepare together.

Dr. Martin had long hoped to settle his troubles by having a hearing before the archbishop of Trier, and Eck was the judge of that archbishop's ecclesiastical court, so if you squinted you could maybe say that in a way Dr. Martin was finally getting his wish. But the setting of the Diet was a lot more intimidating than a simple hearing would have been. And the archbishop of Trier was just sitting there staring, and not all that sympathetically either. And most importantly, Dr. Martin was about to learn that this wasn't even really a hearing at all.

Aleandro, and Glapion, and Eck were determined not to let Luther explain himself at the Diet, but to answer just yes or no or "I recant." And that was exactly how Eck proceeded. He spoke first in Latin, so that the emperor and other non-German-speakers could follow, then repeated everything in

Luther before the Emperor and Empire.

German, for the sake of non-Latin-speakers. "His imperial majesty has summoned you here, Martin Luther, for two reasons," Eck began: first, for him to acknowledge whether the many books on the table were his, and second, to say whether he wanted to retract anything in them.

Dr. Martin was stunned. That was it? Just like at Augsburg with Cajetan? Only recant or deny? Not explain? And unlike at Augsburg, this time hundreds of people waited for his answer. While he pulled himself together, his friend and legal advisor Hieronymus Schurff, standing nearby, shouted, "Let the books be given a name," and so the titles of the 30 or so books were read aloud, to be sure they were all Dr. Martin's. When the reading was done, Dr. Martin answered first in German, then in Latin, the opposite of Eck, apparently since he had a different primary audience in mind. "Yes, the books are mine," he said softly. Some thought he also said, "and there are more too." His enemies, especially, who were sure he couldn't be very bright, couldn't believe he'd written so many. As for whether he would recant? Since the question "concerned faith, the salvation of souls, and the divine Word," it would be "rash and dangerous" for him to say anything on the spot, he said: he might say too much or too little, or even come under Christ's judgment in Matthew 10, "Whoever denies me before others, I also will deny before my Father in heaven." And so he humbly beseeched "your imperial majesty for time to think." Sounds of surprise went up. Was he losing his nerve? Being slippery? Most likely, Dr. Martin was still a little stunned.

Eck thought it was slipperyness, and so did Dr. Martin's critics. But Eck dutifully walked over to consult the emperor and the great princes, then returned: yes, Dr. Martin could have some time, even though he should have been able to see from the summons "why you have been summoned, and therefore don't deserve a longer time for consideration." But so he couldn't complain that he'd been treated hastily or unfairly, his imperial majesty out of his "innate clemency" was giving Luther one day to think about his answer. Eck warned him as he did so to keep in mind the unity of the holy, catholic, and apostolic church, and the peace of Christendom, and not to trust his own opinions, or to twist sacred texts, or to bring in foreign doctrines that would overturn the Christian religion and arouse and confuse the world. Think how many people you've already seduced and sent to hell, said Eck! Try coming to your senses, because if Luther did then his imperial majesty would promise "the hope of pardon and grace, and also that he would obtain these favors easily for him from the most holy Father." And by the way, Luther was to make his answer orally, not, as at Augsburg, in writing.

But like at Augsburg, he was at least going to get a chance to speak after all.

Even though Aleandro wasn't present during this meeting, he could report to Rome (surely thanks to Eck) that Luther wasn't as proud in leaving the hall as in entering it, and that asking for a delay actually hurt his reputation. Someone else reported that even Frederick was fed up with Luther now, saying to the archbishop of Trier that "the wicked *Mönch*" had ruined everything. Maybe Frederick did say that, but if he did he would soon change his mind. Others reported that as Luther left the hall all sorts of people were encouraging him: be brave, be manly, don't fear those who can kill the body but not the soul (Matthew 10), you'll be given what to say in that very hour (Luke 12), and the predictably messianic "blessed is the womb that bore you" (Luke 11). The encouragement continued after the herald Sturm took Dr. Martin back to his room, as another long line of the great came to see him, especially nobles who assured him he didn't have to worry about his life: they would protect him, and if they couldn't then they would start a revolt. Dr. Martin wrote a few lines to the Viennese man of letters Johannes Cuspinian, saying that "with Christ's help" he would "not in all eternity recant the least particle." But he had to think about how to phrase things. If people would just leave him alone for a while.

To get his thoughts together, he started writing out a draft of what he wanted to say, even though he wouldn't be allowed to read it.

AN EVEN WARMER MEETING

Just as promised, Kaspar von Sturm was back at Brother Martin's lodgings the next afternoon, Friday, April 18, at 4.

There'd been more visitors that morning, including Conrad Peutinger, who reported that Dr. Martin was in a good mood while they chatted about Peutinger's wife and children. But he'd been able to prepare his answer, and now it was time to head back into the street. Again they were full of people, and again Sturm led him another way, until they arrived safely at the palace.

This time Dr. Martin didn't go right in, as the Diet was busy with other matters, but instead he stood for two hours in a crowded anteroom full of people straining to hear and see what was going on inside. The standing and straining and crushing were exhausting, but finally he entered, this time into a bigger hall than last time, to accommodate the even bigger crowd. A few supporters again offered encouraging words and put friendly hands on his back and shoulders. It was late enough in the day that torches had to be lit all around, even though the sun wouldn't go down for several more hours.

Eck repeated in his best schoolmasterly way that the friar had really had no right to ask for extra time, since "the obligation of faith is so certain for all that anybody, whenever he is asked, should be able to give his certain and constant reasons, not least of all you, so great and so learned a professor of theology," he added sarcastically. He repeated his two questions: were these his books, and did he want to retract anything?

Dr. Martin was ready this time, and spoke loudly, surely at least out to the 80 feet a good preacher should be able to project. As ordered, he had brought no notes, and there was no official scribe to write things down, but he and a few others wrote out his comments afterward.

He began by asking for forgiveness if he used the wrong titles or gestures in addressing the Diet, as he hadn't ever lived at court but only in "the cells of *Mönche*." He also reminded them that his whole purpose, in all his speaking and writing, was to honor God and instruct the faithful.

As to the first question: yes, again, the books were his, unless somebody had published an unauthorized version of something, which had happened before.

As to the second, that was more complicated: "I ask you to observe that my books are not all of the same kind," he began, then in good scholastic fashion he divided them into three.

First were books on faith and morals that no one, or even the papal bull, could possibly object to.

Second were those against "the papacy and the affairs of the papists" who with their teachings and "very wicked examples" had "laid waste the Christian world." He couldn't retract those either, because that would deepen the wounds of those in this "illustrious German nation" whose consciences had suffered "unbelievable tyranny." Even canon law admitted that "papal laws and doctrines contrary to the gospel or the opinions of the fathers are to be regarded as erroneous and reprehensible," and if he retracted what he'd said about such errors then even more errors would follow and people would suffer more. "Good God, what sort of tool of evil and tyranny I then would be!"

And third were those books he'd written against individuals who had defended Roman "tyranny." Here Dr. Martin seemed to waver: for these works he would partially apologize, he said. "I confess that I have been more harsh against them than befits my religious vows and my profession." He'd never pretended to be a saint, which was why when he did get harsh with people it was always against their teachings, not their conduct—after all, his own conduct was imperfect too. And he didn't try justifying his harshness, as he had at other times, when he'd said that even Paul had harshly called his enemies dogs, babblers, servants of Satan, and worse, so why shouldn't he? No, Dr. Martin simply apologized. But he couldn't and wouldn't apologize for the contents of these books either, or he'd be going along with Roman tyranny again.

In short, he knew that he was human and could err, as he had with his tone. If he'd erred with his content too, then he would gladly be corrected and even throw the offending books into the fire himself. After all, if Christ was willing to listen to anyone who could point out errors in his teachings ("If I have spoken wrongly, testify to the wrong," John 18), then "how much more ought I, scum that I am." But he was still waiting for someone to show him how he was wrong.

As for all the "excitement and dissensions" he'd aroused, well, he wouldn't apologize for that either. In fact, it was "clearly the most joyful aspect of all" for him, because it was a sign the gospel was doing its usual upsetting work. He even worried that if "this most noble youth, Prince Charles (in whom after God is our great hope)," should try to bring peace by silencing the gospel, then even more trouble would result, as Dr. Martin could show with endless examples from the Bible, involving Pharaoh, the king of Babylon, and the kings of Israel. No, better to let the Word spread, and upend for a while, because eventually it would cause things to turn out right.

In the end, he didn't presume to offer advice "to your high and mighty understandings; but I owe this testimony of a loving heart to my native Germany. I conclude with recommending myself to your sacred majesty and your highnesses, humbly entreating you not to suffer my enemies to indulge their hatred against me under your sanction. I have said what I had to say."

His speech finished, Dr. Martin was asked to repeat it in Latin, for the sake of the emperor especially. It was unusually hot for April, and the crowded room and torches and stress of speaking and the two hours he'd had to wait made things worse. He was exhausted and "bathed in sweat," and the Saxon councilor Frederick von Thun advised against repeating his speech, maybe fearing he wouldn't be able to say it exactly as he'd given it in German. But after hesitating, and taking a few breaths, Dr. Martin repeated it anyway.

When he was done, Eck rose again to say that he still hadn't answered the question. So he would ask it again: do you retract your writings or not?

And Dr. Martin spoke again. "Your Imperial Majesty and Your Lordships demand a simple answer," so here it was: unless he was convinced by the testimony of holy scripture—and not popes or councils alone, since they had erred—then he couldn't retract anything. "I cannot and will not recant," because his conscience was captive to God's Holy Word alone, and "acting against one's conscience is neither safe nor sound. God help me. Amen."

Later writers would add a defiant "Here I stand" before "God help me," but nobody recorded those words at the time. Nobody recorded that any deafening cheer or electric silence went up either, especially since he had had to rather anticlimactically repeat this simple answer in Latin too. Still, it was dramatic enough: even with the emperor and a roomful of great nobles and churchmen expecting him to give in, this Augustinian friar said his conscience wouldn't let him.

It was nothing new to appeal to conscience. But conscience didn't mean his own personal opinion, or even the voice of God inside, as it would one day mean. No, to Brother Martin, and others too, it meant the battleground where God and the Devil fought, and in his case his conscience had been conquered by

God's Holy Word. The Devil had been forced to flee. That was why he couldn't recant. He was sure he had God's Word right.

The discussion wasn't over. Eck jumped up to refute Luther and his conscience, condemning how harshly he'd spoken against the pope and praising the emperor's patience in listening: Luther was lucky to be heard "before so kind an emperor, who listened to you for some time with more moderation than you showed in your speech." Then he ridiculed the distinctions Luther made among his books; if he had simply recanted the ones that contained errors, then "no doubt his imperial majesty, in his innate clemency," would have allowed the rest to stand. But by retracting nothing Luther was just keeping alive heresies that had already been condemned, and "in this you are completely mad." Most of all Eck attacked Luther's insistence that he would be judged only by scripture: if the church had to justify with scripture every last condemnation it made, the arguing would never stop, and everyone would want a scriptural reason for everything, at least in the way they understood scripture. Besides, this was exactly what all other heretics before Luther wanted too—to have holy scripture "understood according to your judgment and the workings of your mind" instead of the teachings of the church. Did he really want to use scripture, in his wrongheaded way, to condemn rituals like the sacraments and practices like indulgences, "which our fathers held with absolute faith, on behalf of which they would have endured all sorts of punishment, all torments, and for which at last they would rather have endured a thousand deaths than to have fallen away from in any way at all?" He needed to stop saying that he was the only one who understood the Bible, and to stop thinking that his judgment of it was better than that of so many distinguished doctors, and to stop expecting discussion about "things which according to the faith you are bound to believe as certain and clear." He would skip over the rest of what Dr. Martin said, since it was getting late, and say just this: if he would recant, the emperor would intercede with the pope for a pardon. But if he wouldn't, the emperor would protect the church and the papacy and wipe out the memory of all Luther's books, the good ones as well as the bad, just as was done with the Arians and Montanists and Photinians and Nestorians and other heretics. All of them had had some good Catholic teachings amid their erroneous ones, but for the sake of the faithful their works had to be wiped out completely, "for no doctrine is more effective in deceiving than that which mixes a few false teachings with many that are true."

So, once and for all, Eck asked, do you wish to recant? Yes or no?

Of course Dr. Martin couldn't restrict himself to just one word, even though everyone in the hall was weary, and hot, and restless. Instead he pleaded with the emperor not to force him to deny his conscience. He could only repeat what he'd said for years now: unless they could prove to him that he was wrong, he wouldn't retreat an inch.

By now they had gone on for more than two hours, and it was getting dark, and people were starting to move toward the doors, but Eck wasn't quite done. He said sharply that Luther could not possibly show that councils had ever erred.

But Dr. Martin said he could do so anytime.

"Lay aside your conscience," Eck replied, "lay it aside because it is in error; and it will be safe and proper for you to recant." Luther would never be able to prove that councils had erred, said Eck, at least not in matters of faith, but again Dr. Martin shouted back that he certainly could. Finally somebody called a recess.

Some said that Brother Martin left the hall sweating, but also raising his clasped hands over his head in triumph, while his usual guards escorted him out. Others said that he was followed and insulted all the way to his rooms by a small crowd gesturing at him and jeering and making loud noises. Back in his room, he found a mug of Eimbeck beer waiting on the table. He guzzled it down, and uttered a quiet word of thanks for Duke Eric of Brunswick, who he learned had so thoughtfully left it.

ONE LAST TRY

Reactions to Brother Martin's speech came fast.

That same night, the supposedly disgruntled Frederick the Wise wasn't disgruntled at all, but said to Spalatin that "Father Martinus spoke well before the Lord Emperor, all the princes, and the estates," especially in the Latin version, even though "He's much too bold for me." Still, Frederick sounded as insistent as Brother Martin now in saying that any refuting of his claims had to come from scripture.

Dr. Martin was immediately overwhelmed again with fawning visitors, this time including great princes and counts and prelates, and maybe even Prince Frederick himself, so many that his "little room" couldn't contain them all. Ulrich von Hutten praised him from a distance when he heard about his defiance, but still worried that the nuncio "Caiaphas" was working with the emperor "Pilate" and the "wooden-shoe monk" Glapion to have Luther crucified. A Luther supporter posted early in the dark morning a sign on Worms's town hall that read *Bundschuh, Bundschuh, Bundschuh* (a laced farmer's boot), the symbol and battle cry of rebellious peasants, which was guaranteed to terrify some of the great. Archbishop Albrecht, who was mentioned on the sign, rushed frantically over to the emperor's rooms, but Glapion and another councilor laughed at him, even though their names were mentioned too. Maybe the two men were a little more bothered by signs saying that 400 nobles and 8,000 horses and infantry were ready to attack if even one hair on Luther's head were harmed, or by another sign that quoted Ecclesiastes 10, "Woe to the land whose king is a child," mostly because that sign was snuck right into the emperor's own quarters.

Among Luther's foes, Aleandro heard that six members of the college of electors, including Frederick, were ready to condemn Luther. The Frederick part wasn't true, but it was true that Duke George, in the college of princes, now disliked Luther even more than before, if that was possible, and forbade any of his subjects from attending Wittenberg University. The reactions to Luther's speech that mattered most, though, were those of Charles and the collective estates.

On the morning of April 19, the very next day, the emperor and nuncios gathered with the estates to discuss how to proceed. Charles began by having read out, first in his native French then in German, his own handwritten opinion of what ought to be done. He noted his magnificent heritage from the "most Christian emperors of the noble German nation," the kings of Spain, the archdukes of Austria, and the dukes of Burgundy, who had all been faithful sons of the church and defenders of the Catholic faith and its rituals, decrees, ordinances, and holy customs, which heritage he was obligated to continue. It was impossible, he said, that "a single friar" should be right and over a thousand years of Christianity wrong. He would stake kingdom and friends, body and blood, life and soul, to defend the church against upstarts like Luther. He insisted that not only he himself but all the estates too would be "forever disgraced" if they allowed even the suspicion of heresy to survive in the empire. He would send Luther back home safely, to keep his promise, but as soon as the friar was back home Charles would proceed against him as a notorious heretic, and he expected the estates to do the same, conducting themselves "as good Christians as you have promised it to me." Charles was fed up: he would never again seriously think about reconciling with Luther.

The three estates met together that same afternoon to discuss their response to Charles's statement, with Elector Joachim of Brandenburg reminding everyone they had promised to go along with condemning Luther if he wouldn't recant, and he obviously hadn't. But some were ready to support Luther, and a lot of others were afraid of the violence that might result if they condemned somebody as popular as he was. The next day, April 20, the estates agreed to present another plan to Charles, pushed by of all people Archbishop Albrecht and his brother Joachim: they wanted to try one more time to reconcile Luther with the church, so they wouldn't have to condemn him, and undoubtedly start some violence. Luther had said he was willing to be instructed, so why not try exactly that, with a new set of instructors? Charles and Aleandro didn't love the idea, but on April 21 the emperor gave the estates three days to get Luther to recant. The estates therefore quickly named a committee to try, led by the archbishop of Trier, and sent word to Dr. Martin that he was to come to the archbishop's rooms on the morning of April 24 to talk things over some more.

While he waited over the next two days, Dr. Martin received more visitors, wondered about his fate, and surely thought about what he might say now. At the appointed time, Kaspar von Sturm came by yet again to walk him over to the appointed place. But this time the four friends who'd come with Dr. Martin to Worms went along too, since it wasn't clear what kind of meeting it would be.

Waiting in the archbishop's room were nine people, including old foes of Dr. Martin, like the elector Joachim and Duke George, but also mild supporters, like Conrad Peutinger of Augsburg and Hieronymus Veh, the chancellor of the territory of Baden. Veh, a man of letters, did most of the talking. They were there, he said, not to argue anymore with Dr. Martin, but out of the pure charity that they (except maybe Duke George) felt for him. That, and the unity of the church, was why they'd asked the emperor for the chance to speak to him again.

But the conversation didn't go much differently from the one that had happened before the whole Diet almost a week before. Veh tried to get Dr. Martin to see why his criticism of church councils was so harmful, and causing so much unrest. And he repeated that if Dr. Martin would recant some of his writings, then at least others would be saved. But Dr. Martin wouldn't budge: he wouldn't recant what he'd said about councils or anything else, because he was teaching the word of God, not of man. They could therefore have his blood and life before he'd recant. Eck and Johann Cochlaeus, an expert in the Bible and a former supporter of Brother Martin, then tried reasoning with him, pointing out that heresy almost always originated in somebody's private interpretation of scripture. Dr. Martin and then Schurff responded by explaining why their interpretations weren't merely private. Finally, Cochlaeus took Brother Martin by the hands and pleaded with him to restore unity to the church by recanting, but still no luck. That same night Cochlaeus even came by Dr. Martin's rooms, to urge him not to leave Worms yet but to stay and have a public disputation with him, to settle this once and for all. When Brother Martin refused, his faithful brother-friar Petzensteiner jumped in and challenged Cochlaeus instead; Justus Jonas jumped in and got angry with Cochlaeus; and Luther's noble friend Rudolf von Watzdorf jumped in and wanted to fight the man. Brother Martin separated everybody, then brought Cochlaeus into his bedroom to talk some more, but the conversation ended with Cochlaeus promising to write against Dr. Martin and Dr. Martin promising to write back, which everyone was sure he would do, especially since Cochlaeus meant "snail" and would give Dr. Martin yet another name to poke fun at.

The talks on April 25, the last day allowed by Charles, went no better. This time Peutinger and Veh visited Dr. Martin for three hours, asking him whether he would be willing to let the emperor and estates (rather than the pope) judge his books. Dr. Martin again said he would be glad for that, as long as the writings were judged from scripture. After lunch, the men came back and asked as well whether he was willing to submit his books to some future council of the church? Again he said that he would, with the same condition. Peutinger and Veh ecstatically reported to the archbishop of Trier that Luther was ready to submit his works to a council, or the estates! And if they judged those books to be in error, then he would submit! But before running to tell the good news to the emperor, the skeptical archbishop decided that he'd better confirm this with Brother Martin himself—and sure enough, that wasn't quite what he'd said: Peutinger and Veh had left out the "judged from scripture" part. The archbishop now called Spalatin into the meeting, to try to get Brother Martin to budge, but to no avail. Finally the discouraged archbishop asked if there was anything that could be done. Probably not, said Dr. Martin, except what Gamaliel said in Acts: if this work was from men, it would come to nothing, but if from God, it would last. With that, the archbishop kindly dismissed him.

The committee had done its best, but now had to report their failure to the estates, and the emperor. Johann Eck was soon calling on Dr. Martin to say that "Since you have not chosen to listen to the counsels of his majesty and of the estates of the empire, and to confess your errors," the emperor was now going to act against him. Luther would get his safe conduct, giving him 21 days to get back to Wittenberg, but he wasn't to preach along the way or incite any disorders. Dr. Martin thanked Eck, and asked him to thank the emperor, his ministers, and the estates for their "warm audience" and the safe conduct. He would comply with all of their wishes as long as those wishes didn't contradict the Word of God—by which he meant he certainly was going to preach on the way home.

After a nice meal the next morning, April 26, organized by his friends, Dr. Martin started the long trip back to Wittenberg, accompanied by the same companions who'd come with him to Worms, plus Hieronymus Schurff and, for a while, about 20 horsemen provided by Franz von Sickingen too. But there was no Kaspar von Sturm. Had they snuck ahead without him? Or was he delayed? Whatever the case, Sturm caught up with them at Oppenheim, to ensure their safety, and of course to keep an eye on Brother Martin.

FLIGHT

Luckily Brother Martin still had Prince Frederick of Saxony on his side.

The prince had already written his brother Johann back in January that he wished he could help Dr. Martin "right and proper." Now that the talks were falling apart, and now that Frederick was convinced Dr. Martin hadn't been treated fairly, thus according to the laws of the empire, he decided it was high time to provide that help, in the form of a very concrete plan. He and his councilors had long discussed how they might protect Brother Martin in the event he was condemned, or was close to being condemned. The trick, of course, was to protect him in a way that wouldn't get the emperor and certain other princes mad enough to do something about it, as in attack Saxony. And the solution was vintage Frederick: rather than visibly protect Dr. Martin and cause a confrontation, he would simply drop him somewhere out of sight.

Dr. Martin had gotten wind of this plan even before leaving Worms. He wrote to Lucas Cranach on April 24 that "I shall submit to being 'imprisoned' and hidden away, though as yet I do not know where." He wasn't thrilled about it, but he would follow his prince's wishes.

With his safe conduct from the emperor, and 40 gulden from Frederick for expenses, Dr. Martin and his party headed north to Wittenberg on the 26th. Aleandro thought Luther would flee to Bohemia or Denmark, and there were again whispers that Charles might not honor the safe conduct and would have Luther captured along the way, which made the traveling party nervous. But they rode on through Frankfurt, and were in Friedberg, in Hesse, by April 29. There, Dr. Martin tried getting rid of the imperial herald Sturm by sending him to Worms to deliver some letters to Spalatin and the emperor, which said basically the same things he'd already said before. Surely Dr. Martin and his party didn't want Sturm to see what was about to happen, and they wanted to protect him too; as herald, Sturm was obligated to defend with his life the bearer of an imperial safe conduct, and if some friendly kidnappers should happen to come along, Sturm would almost certainly fight them, and lose.

Once the herald had left, the party rode on to Grünberg and Hersfeld, where Brother Martin was received like a hero, as he was in so many other towns along the way. Before leaving Hersfeld on May 2, he broke the terms of his safe conduct by preaching at the monastery there—at 5 in the morning to avoid too much notice. They reached Eisenach on May 3, where he preached again, then he met relatives in Möhra on May 3 and 4, where he preached yet again, in the open air this time because the chapel was too small. He sent Schurff and Jonas and Swaven ahead on May 4, saying he wanted to spend more time with his relatives, and surely he would be safe now that he was in Saxony. Now only Petzensteiner—the brother-friar required to be with him—and Amsdorf were still in the wagon.

The three men set off the next day, May 5, which was when the attack finally came, in a ravine near the castle of Altenstein. Petzensteiner jumped out of the wagon when he saw horsemen riding up. Amsdorf knew what was happening but pretended, for the sake of the driver, to be alarmed when the horsemen pointed crossbows at them—surely the driver would tell the story to others, so they had to make it good. Dr. Martin played along too, snatching up his New Testament and Hebrew Bible amid all the cursing and yelling, then running alongside the kidnappers until they were out of sight.

The kidnappers were of course Frederick's men: Hans von Berlepsch, from an old noble family and the castellan (or person in charge) at one of Frederick's least-used castles, the Wartburg; and Burckhard Hund von Wenckheim, of Altenstein castle. If Charles had sent out men to capture Dr. Martin, these two beat them to it. Once they were out of sight of the wagon's driver, they put Dr. Martin on a horse too, and rode off, taking various long detours in case anyone was following them and even to confuse his friends Amsdorf and Petzensteiner, who knew about the kidnapping but weren't to know where he'd been taken. Finally the little party of three arrived at Berlepsch's castle, the Wartburg, around 11 p.m., exhausted.

Only the knights, and Frederick and Spalatin, knew where Martin Luther now was.

12
No More Hours

A Castle in Western Saxony. February 24, 1522. The 22nd Birthday of Charles Habsburg, Emperor.

Brother Martin had meant to stay until Easter (April 20), as Prince Frederick had suggested, or even until the current Diet ended in Nuremberg. But he'd been at this castle for 10 months, and away from home for 11, and that was long enough, especially when home was where he was needed.

Sure, he was tired of pretending to be a knight, and of signing his letters "from Bohemia" in case they were intercepted, and of not being able to preach, and of having no real company, especially no scholars, around him. But mostly he wanted to go home because things weren't going the way they ought to be going in the church there, and he couldn't have that. Not there.

Wittenberg was just one little church of Christendom, of course, but it was his church, tied to his name and to the gospel he'd been teaching, and so the gospel had to be taught right there. Sure, he'd always said the gospel caused trouble, but the trouble going on in Wittenberg had nothing to do with the gospel, in fact was dead against it. He wanted to halt the trouble by going there and preaching God's True Word again, which was always the best way to drive out the Devil. He had come to this lonely castle and fought the Devil all alone all these months, so he wasn't afraid to fight him at home now too, in public.

A few months before, he'd heard reports of trouble in Wittenberg, but it seemed to be just ordinary trouble, the growing pains that always happened wherever the true gospel was planted. But the latest reports and the fact that the town council was now begging him to return and take charge of the local church made clear that this round of trouble was different. He had to go home now, even if it was dangerous, and even if Prince Frederick kept saying it still wasn't time.

And make no mistake, it was dangerous to go back, for him and for Prince Frederick too, because Dr. Martin was, after all, an outlaw. If he went openly back to Wittenberg, not only could some reward-seeking scoundrel lay hands on him, but the emperor and the ever-watching Duke George would have the proof they needed that Frederick was obviously (and not just possibly) sheltering a condemned heretic, giving them the excuse they needed to try taking Frederick's precious duchy away. But even with danger like that looming for him and his dear prince, Dr. Martin was determined to go home anyway.

He picked up his well-worn pen to break the news to Frederick, and to explain himself. He didn't say right out that he was coming home, but tried using instead a light and widely roundabout approach that played on Frederick's love of relics. The prince liked relics, wrote Brother Martin, and he was about to get a new one very soon, for absolutely free. And not just some little splinter-of-wood relic either, but "a whole cross, together with nails, spears, and scourges." And just like the real cross, this one would hurt but would ultimately be good for him, so just accept it. "Stretch out your arms confidently and let the nails go deep. Be glad and thankful."

Brother Martin knew that Frederick would get that he, Brother Martin, was himself the painful relic, even if most anyone else reading it would not. He signed the letter, "Martin Luther," and sealed it with the seal he'd used since 1517: a black cross set in a red heart, which was set in a white rose, which was set against a blue field, all of which were surrounded by a gold ring. The cross mortified and caused pain, but believing from the heart brought justification, spirits and angels (white), heavenly joy (blue), and eternal blessedness (the gold ring).

He dispatched the letter as usual through his host, then started getting ready.

AN EDICT FROM WORMS

When news spread that Brother Martin had disappeared on his way back from Worms, almost everyone was sure he'd been killed by one of his enemies, and maybe even by the agents of Charles himself.

Someone wrote a mournful hymn, and Albrecht Dürer wrote a mournful poem that asked, who will teach us the holy gospel now?

The news reached Worms by May 11 at the latest, six days after the disappearance. That people suspected Charles of taking or even harming Luther might have offended the emperor, given the sense of chivalry he'd built up from his love of knightly tales, and since he'd had nothing to do with the deed. Instead, the emperor had kept busy in Worms trying to convince the Diet to condemn Luther, and continued to do so even after the news of the disappearance arrived. Charles obviously didn't think the friar was dead at all.

On April 30, just days after Brother Martin had left Worms, Charles reminded the estates again of their promise to punish Luther if he didn't recant, and since he hadn't recanted, it was now time. On May 8, Charles presented them with a draft of an edict meant to do that punishing, an edict which he failed to mention was written by Aleandro, who didn't have even the smallest toe in any imperial office. Naturally the estates wanted some revisions to the edict, to Aleandro's never-ending distress, and Aleandro did change a few things, but he saw no need to submit it to the estates again and so he sent it to the printer. Only when the type was already being set, on May 12, did Aleandro learn from Charles's divinely named grand chancellor, Mercurino di Gattinara, that the estates had to approve the revisions too, bringing the press to a clanging stop.

By May 21, the estates still hadn't approved a revised version of the edict, but they were weary of their four months in Worms and voted to disband anyway. Prince Frederick left town as fast as he could, maybe to get ahead of another attack of gout, maybe to escape the strain of having to keep pretending he didn't know what had happened to Brother Martin, but almost certainly to avoid having to vote on Charles's edict. The elector of the Palatinate left too, and so did others, and by the time Charles's final Edict of Worms, as it was called, was presented to the Diet on May 25, only a rump of that body remained. Without any discussion, Elector Joachim of Brandenburg declared the edict approved. It was dated May 8, the day of the original draft, when almost everybody had still been in town, just in case somebody complained that the full Diet hadn't actually gone along.

At least Aleandro was there to watch Charles sign both the Latin and German versions on May 26. When he was done, Charles smiled and said that maybe the nuncio would be content now. Oh yes, said Aleandro, and the pope and "all Christendom" too. Sure, the way the edict was rushed through might raise a few eyebrows, and so might the fact that the January 3 bull of Luther's excommunication still hadn't been published (and wouldn't be until October). But there, in longlasting ink, was the official imperial verdict on Brother Martin: he was now officially called the "reviver of old and condemned heresies and inventor of new ones."

The edict reminded everyone of Charles's inherited duty to keep their religion pure and free from heresy. It recounted the efforts of the pope to kindly instruct Luther, and to assemble a palace full of prelates, theologians, and linguists to judge his books fairly, but even after all that Luther, "this man of wickedness," refused to renounce his "detestable and perverse" errors, which were well-enough known by now: destroying the seven sacraments, performing the Eucharist the way the "damned heretics of Bohemia" do, belittling confession, teaching that every Christian was part of the priesthood, provoking laypeople "to wash their hands in the blood of the priests," calling the pope infamous names, insisting there was no freedom of the will, rejecting purgatory and masses for the dead and indulgences, despising the saints, burning the decretals, speaking ill of sacred church councils, and praising heresies buried in hell a long time ago. He was more a devil than a man, but his religious habit had made it easy for him to deceive people.

The edict told the emperor's version of the events at Worms too: that Charles had hoped "good admonitions" might convert Luther and so he'd summoned him, that Luther had arrived only to ask for a delay that shouldn't have been granted, that he'd been promised an interview with the pope and the survival of his good books, that he'd instead made "evil words and gestures" and said he couldn't possibly change God's Word—as if he was ever asked to—and that several notable men who'd kindly tried to help him had had to conclude that "he was mad and possessed by some evil spirit." So Charles had sent him home to await punishment.

And the edict declared at last that Luther was now an "estranged member, rotten and cut off from the body of our Holy Mother Church," an "obstinate, schismatic heretic" who, once he was home, was not to be received, defended, sustained, or favored; instead he was to be "apprehended and punished as a notorious heretic," and "brought personally before us" again, and whoever helped capture him would be rewarded generously, while whoever aided him would have his goods confiscated, no matter how high his rank, and anyone who bought, sold, printed, kept, or read any book by Martin Luther would be severely punished. The edict was to be sent to every part of the empire, in the local language, and people were to be called with trumpets from the corners of every village to hear it.

But as official as it was, the edict of May 26 hadn't exactly had the effect that Charles, and Aleandro, had hoped it would. That was partly because Luther was nowhere to be found, but probably mostly because Charles soon left not only Worms but the empire altogether, for Italy, where he got busy fighting the king of France. And he would stay away for almost 10 years. Without Charles around to press the matter, German princes who didn't like the edict were just going to ignore it, and the man presumably protecting Luther too.

SORE ASS

As far as Dr. Martin was concerned, the edict was the Devil's work. But even though it had forced him into this castle so high that anyone traveling there couldn't help but wonder how he would ever reach the top, and how all the stone and brick and timber used to build the massive thing had ever possibly made it up, it was sometimes easy to almost forget about the edict, because he was in his own little world now.

Frederick had chosen this hiding place well, because of all his dozen or so castles the Wartburg was one of the most remote and least busy. Founded in 1067 as a *Warte,* or observation point, it was famous for hosting the legendary life-and-death contest of Minnesingers around 1206, and then was the home of St. Elizabeth of Thuringia for a while after that. It burned in 1320, but was rebuilt after 1450 by Frederick and his father, and now it was hardly ever used.

One of the newest parts of the castle was a two-story addition at the front that had rooms on the ground floor

The Wartburg.

for the castellan and a room and narrow bedroom on the upper floor for the
occasional knightly prisoner or guest,
like Brother Martin was supposed to be.
Hans von Berlepsch, the castellan, was-
n't really guarding Brother Martin as
much as he was seeing to his needs, and
making sure nobody knew he was there.
That was why the new guest was called
Knight George, and grew out his tonsure and hair, and wore leggings and a
doublet when he went outside, and was
always attended by two noble boys, like
any real knight was.

Lucas Cranach, *Knight George*.

Brother Martin was of course
glad for Prince Frederick's help and
attention, but this new world at the
Wartburg was completely disorienting. He wasn't sure how long he would stay,
or what he should do while there, or how much danger he was in. Just three
days after arriving, he wrote Melanchthon (through Spalatin, his only con-
nection to the outside world now) that he wished he would have spoken even
stronger at Worms, like Elijah had against the idolatrous priests, and that he
wanted "nothing more than to meet the furor of my enemies head on!" But
it didn't take long for his furor to shrivel up. Stuck in his room, and hardly
moving around, and eating new sorts of food, helped give his already sickly
body another painful affliction, constipation, his own God-given "relic of the
cross." "My ass is sore," was how he summed things up in one of his first letters, and his regular reports on his irregular bowels were a main feature of his
letters from then on. By July the soreness was bad enough that he was ready to
go to Erfurt and see a doctor, but the plague was raging there, so he stayed put.
Mercifully, Spalatin sent some medicine, possibly from the master apotheker
(as well as master painter) Lucas Cranach, and that helped. But by August 15
Brother Martin had "elimination" only "every fourth, sometimes even fifth
day," and then only with so much sweating and effort and soreness that he
almost passed out. At least in October he could write that "at last my behind
and my bowels have reconciled themselves to me." For the moment.

Surely some of his physical troubles were connected to his spiritual ones, and the biggest of those just had to be isolation. Only a few people were around the Wartburg at all, yet he was still supposed to keep to himself, for his safety and Frederick's: even Frederick's brother Duke Johann didn't know Brother Martin was at the castle until he happened to visit the place in September. Once Brother Martin went out to watch a hunt, but mostly he felt sorry for the animals chased by dogs, since he knew how they felt. And he had some nice theological chats with Hans the castellan, but very little contact with anyone else. Living almost like a real hermit went against the very social nature of Brother Martin the official hermit. He would later advise people with melancholy to go out and mingle, based on Ecclesiastes 4, "Woe to one who is alone." He was also sure that Christ was tempted in the wilderness because he was alone, and that Paul regained hope after his shipwreck because he saw his brothers. "Flee solitude!" Brother Martin would often urge, and that counsel had a lot to do with his stay at the Wartburg. "I had rather burn on live coals than rot here," he wrote, and he signed his letters mournfully, "In Solitude," and "In the Kingdom of the Birds."

The isolation was bad enough that it made him think he should just go preach somewhere despite the risk, even if Duke George found him and killed him. Or maybe he should go to Erfurt and become a craftsman. Sure, *Anfechtungen* never left a Christian completely, but they were worse here than usual, thanks to loneliness: "the former weakness of the spirit and faith persists," he wrote a friend. He was again feeling like he had to prove himself to God instead of trusting in God's grace, and was again hearing the Devil's nagging question: "Are you alone wise?" Yes, the Devil was after him more than ever in this godforsaken place: he now felt more sexual temptation than usual and heard poltergeistish sorts of noises too, like the Devil was pelting the walls with nuts or rolling casks down the stairs. Once a strange dog came into his room and he threw it out the breathtakingly high window, because he was sure it was a demon. Still, Dr. Martin refused to be afraid and he turned the Devil into a sort of comic character to be argued with. When he went to bed he said, " 'Devil, I must sleep. That's God's command, work by day, sleep by night. So go away.' If that doesn't work and he brings out a catalogue of sins, I say, 'Yes, old fellow, I know all about it. And I know some more you've overlooked. Here are a few extra. Put them down.' If he still won't quit and presses me hard and accuses me as a sinner, I scorn him and say, 'St. Satan, pray for me. Of course you have never done anything wrong in your life.' " Other times he didn't argue at all, because the Devil had 5,000 years of experience, so he would just loudly "fart" at him, even if Pope Gregory the Great had thought it "a mortal sin to break wind," or he would show the Devil "my ass," because that was where devils belonged. Mostly Brother Martin knew that his worst *Anfechtungen* came when he was alone, with no fellowship, singing, eating, drinking, or joking to soothe things.

His troubles weren't just caused by loneliness, though, or his new diet, but by the guilt he felt over how people were suffering for his message, or even using it wrongly. Already in May 1520, three canons in Erfurt were excommunicated because they'd hosted Brother Martin on his way down to Worms, but even more disturbing was that many students and craftsmen and peasants around Erfurt then revolted in protest. Brother Martin hated violence, especially when people justified it with the gospel. And some of his followers were doing exactly what his accusers at Worms had complained about: interpreting the freedom of a Christian to mean freedom from all manmade authority and all laws not found in scripture. Others were taking freedom to mean the freedom to force the church to get in line with scripture, right now. If people would only understand justification by faith, he sighed, then they'd see that he was talking about freedom from sin and from the burden of law, and thus the freedom to love your neighbor spontaneously.

He tried to combat his troubles, and the erring, by writing, starting with letters—especially to his flock in Wittenberg. Even though he thought his letters were nothing more than pieces of "*cloaca* paper," Philip Melanchthon and Nicholas von Amsdorf, who Brother Martin considered the spiritual leaders of the town now, appreciated them. They would get along fine without him, he said, so please no more of this "Wittenberg has lost its shepherd!" Yes, he wanted to go back to Wittenberg, but he could just as well go to Erfurt or Cologne when he was done hiding, because Wittenberg had enough shepherds. And stop moaning about your weaknesses, he told them: of course you sin and are weak! Like Staupitz used to remind him, real grace cured real sins, not piddly ones, and the real sins they were most certainly guilty of should have only made them believe even more in grace than before! And don't be so timid before Prince Frederick and Spalatin: respect them, but "not one-half "of what he'd accomplished" would have been accomplished had I obeyed the court's counsel." They were human too, and if you wanted to gain something, you had to venture. Yes, he sounded very daring from up in the castle.

But Dr. Martin didn't just write letters at the Wartburg, he wrote books too, piles of them, to add to the pile that lay on the table at Worms, because books were his only pulpit now. Sure, like every writer, he knew he could have written twice as much as he did if he hadn't been plagued by demons, and doubts, and sickness, and everyday cares, and had spent all of his time putting pen to paper instead of dilly-dallying around or looking out his narrow little window onto the vast valley below in order to put off as long as possible the soul-sucking task of writing. But what he did get out was still astonishing, even if Johann Rhau-Grunenberg was slow as ever at printing it. And of course the new books let everyone know he was still alive.

Plenty of his pastoral writings from early 1521 were published only after he got to the Wartburg, like his six-page *Sermon on the Worthy Reception of the Sacrament,* which reminded people that their trust in the promise of grace was what made them worthy, not the act of taking the sacrament or all the confessing they might do beforehand. After arriving, the first things he wrote and sent off to Spalatin for printing were again for his "poor little flock" in Wittenberg: commentaries on Psalms 22, 36, and 68, and on the *Magnificat* too. At the end of the summer, at the request of Duke Johann, he wrote *A Sermon on the Ten Lepers,* to explain that confession should never be forced on anyone. He also wrote his longest-lasting pastoral work, his *Postil,* or collection of sermons, so called because of the phrase *post illa verba,* "after these words," meaning the words the priest read from the Gospels or epistles just before his sermon. The sermons weren't actual sermons, though, to be read word-for-word from the pulpit, because some of them were 173 pages long; they were more like theological foundations for sermons. Just as important was the little instruction book that came with the *Postil,* called *What to Look for in the Gospels,* which laid out how to approach scripture in general: look for the gospel not just in the Gospels but throughout the whole Bible, and look for the law not just in the Old Testament but the New as well; remember that the gospel wasn't a set of rules to be followed but the happy news that Christ promised to save you; and realize that Christ wasn't a good example you had to imitate but a gift pure and simple from God. If you did all that, then you'd know how to preach and be a gift to your neighbor. If you didn't, you'd end up preaching about rules and issuing decretals.

Naturally Brother Martin couldn't stop himself from writing controversial works at the Wartburg too, even though he was so far removed from the fray, because as Jerome had said, the enemies of the church had to be opposed. His biggest seller in the summer and fall of 1521 was his speech at Worms that he now wrote down, but he also worked on a long Latin book against Jacob Latomus, a theologian at the University of Leuven, who'd taken up Dr. Martin's challenge to refute him with proof from the Bible—except, said Dr. Martin, Latomus didn't actually use the Bible, but only the usual currently approved scholastic-theologian-inspired interpretation of it. Much shorter was his German *On Confession, Whether the Pope has the Power to Require it*, which answered that the papal law *requiring* people to confess could safely be regarded as "the shit in front of you in the street." His *Counterverdict Against the Parisian Theologians* made fun of how those theologians had condemned 104 excerpts from his writings just by classifying them under one of the already-known heresies, which was one of the sloppiest and most presumptuous things he'd ever seen. And his *Bull of the Supper-Devouring Most Holy Lord, the Pope*, commented bitingly on the pope's annual Maundy Thursday list of enemies of the church, which list Brother Martin had finally made in 1521.

One polemical tract he wrote at the Wartburg was aimed at his old rival, Albrecht of Mainz, who thought he might take advantage of Luther's disappearance to offer a brand-new papal indulgence to anyone who visited his relic-filled church in Halle. But Dr. Martin found out about it and wrote *Against the Idol at Halle*, sending it to Spalatin in November, for printing. But Spalatin said he would rather not: it was probably best for a fellow under the imperial ban not to attack a cardinal, and thus draw attention to himself and to Frederick. Dr. Martin was furious: if he wasn't afraid of attacking a pope, why would he be afraid of a cardinal? Publish it, he said, and quit worrying about moderation and peace, or he would send it to somebody else, with even nastier language. But he wouldn't need to after all: Dr. Martin had also written Albrecht to say that he'd sniffed out his little plan and was now giving him 14 days to stop, or he'd publish a new tract against it. Albrecht quickly wrote back to say he was a worthless sinner and would cancel the indulgence. Dr. Martin held onto the manuscript, just in case Albrecht slipped again.

Surely the work that made the biggest splash, though, was *The Judgment of Martin Luther on Monastic Vows*. He'd had doubts about those vows since 1519, when his many other duties made it hard for him to make up all the Hours of the Divine Office he'd missed in choir. He would try making them up in bunches, going even three days without food, because so many authorities said the Hours were *the* most important part of the religious life you'd vowed to follow, and you'd have to account to God for every single syllable missed. But binge-chanting gave him insomnia, and made him wonder just how important it really was. At the Wartburg he actually had time to catch up on his Hours, but it was easy to lose track of time here, and he'd already decided that vows were fine for children who did things out of obligation, while the gospel was for grownups who did things out of love. And so he stopped saying them altogether. In every sense there really were no more Hours now.

Also making him think twice about vows was all the arguing over celibacy suddenly going on. Dr. Martin had already told Goat Emser that forbidding priests to marry was straight from the Devil, as proved by 1 Timothy 4, and he'd said much the same thing in the *Christian Nobility*. In spring 1521, some priests around Wittenberg started taking Brother Martin seriously, and got married. Archbishop Albrecht wanted them arrested, but Prince Frederick told the professors at his university to study the subject first: Karlstadt and Melanchthon held disputations and concluded that both scripture and the early church allowed priests to marry, probably mostly because the flesh was just weak. After all, the office in Rome responsible for legitimizing births would between 1449 and 1553 consider almost 23,000 cases of children who'd been fathered by priests—about 275 a year. Although Dr. Martin truly pitied "the wretched boys and girls who are vexed with pollutions and burnings," he also thought there were better reasons than weak flesh to question celibacy, since you could use that to justify anything. He therefore wrote up a bunch of theses to sort out his thoughts, saying that you should never vow anything because you were forced to or because you hoped for a reward, because there you were just trying to save yourself again; but if you vowed voluntarily because you felt it was good for you or was a way to express God's gift that was inside you, then it was fine; and if you'd vowed involuntarily, then it might be fine for you to now marry. By November, some of Brother Martin's fellow Augustinians in Wittenberg started marrying too, causing the prior to pull out his remaining hair and to plead with Frederick to do something. Brother Martin felt responsible and had his new book on monastic vows ready on November 21, at over 100 pages long, and in Latin.

The book was as much an attempt to reconcile with his father as it was to instruct monks and friars, because it began by telling Brother Martin's own troubled story behind his vows. His father had been against his entering the religious life—and he had been absolutely right, said Brother Martin now. Oh, at the time his young self had been sure that by disobeying his earthly father and mother he was pleasing his heavenly father. But as early as his first Mass, when he'd tried to make up with his father by explaining that he'd been called to the religious life "by terrors from heaven," Hans had shaken his certainty by saying, let's hope it wasn't the Devil calling instead. And when Martin had chastised his father for being so angry, Hans shook him up even more by asking, "Haven't you heard that parents are to be obeyed?" And Hans was right again. He, young Martin, had entered selfishly, to do good works in order to be saved; he'd disobeyed his parents; and he'd taken vows that weren't required by Christ. Sure, sometimes you had to choose Christ over your parents, but only when your parents' word conflicted with His, and in this case it hadn't.

The *Judgment on Monastic Vows* rambled and repeated itself a little, as long things composed in 10 days were wont to do, but its main point was stunning: there was nothing wrong with vows (Psalm 76) if they were made freely, but monastic vows weren't in scripture, weren't voluntary, and didn't cover anything not already in your baptismal vows. Yes, Paul took a vow of celibacy, but he didn't make anyone else do so, and yes, Christ spoke of eunuchs for the kingdom of heaven but He didn't invite anyone to become one. Monastic vows even went against faith in Christ, because they were an effort to save yourself, even if the "street whore" theologians at the University of Paris said otherwise. They also often went against the commandment to honor your parents. And even though the religious life was a legitimate calling, it wasn't any better than any other.

When the new book was finally printed (Spalatin delayed it too, for fear of the controversy it would cause), it cleared out plenty of friaries and monasteries, which dismayed Brother Martin, because he wanted the leavers to be a little more reflective and soul-searching than they'd shown. His foes struck back: no one forced you into a monastery, and Isaiah 19 said, "Make vows to the Lord and perform them," and Christ said, "If you wish to be perfect, go, sell your possessions, and . . . follow me."

Oddly enough, Brother Martin still mostly felt like a friar himself, even though he'd been officially excommunicated in October 1521, and had been released from his vow of obedience years before, and now dressed like a knight, and no longer said his Hours, and now signed his letters just plain old "M. Luther" without adding "Augustinian" to the end. He wasn't at all running out to break his vow of celibacy like his enemies said he was dying to do, and he found it hard to break old habits, including wearing his actual habit, which he put back on when he left the Wartburg: "I, too, shall remain in this cowl and manner of life, if the world doesn't change," he said. Prince Frederick once sent him a piece of new cloth at the Wartburg for a new "hood or cowl," which Dr. Martin's friends were always begging him to get but after reading the new tract on monastic vows, Frederick joked that maybe Dr. Martin would use the cloth to make a stylish Spanish cloak instead.

There wasn't much chance of that.

A NEW TESTAMENT

But of all the many writings that emerged from the Wartburg, the most important was Brother Martin's New Testament.

He got the idea when he took a secret one-week trip to Wittenberg in early December 1521, to see for himself the troubles that were going on there. He didn't tell Spalatin, or the elector, that he was coming, but the castellan at the Wartburg let him go and even gave him a servant boy to make him look knightly along the way. After arriving, Brother Martin concluded that things weren't as bad as he'd feared: yes, there'd been some disturbances, and yes, he was furious at Spalatin for holding back yet another one of his fiery tracts from the printer, but mostly things were fine. Just one thing was missing, he thought, a thing that would actually help solve some of the troubles in town: a new translation of the New Testament. He decided to go back to the Wartburg and do it himself, since he'd finished all the other writing projects he'd planned.

The first Bible in German had been printed in 1466, and 17 other German versions had appeared since, but they were all translations from the Latin Vulgate rather than from the original Hebrew and Greek. After Erasmus published his new and improved Greek edition of the New Testament in 1516, a few scholars translated parts of it into German, but they were too literal for Dr. Martin's tastes: maybe he could do better himself, he thought.

Spalatin and Melanchthon got together what he needed when he went back to the Wartburg, including the latest edition of Erasmus's New Testament and the Greek dictionaries and lexicons that were starting to appear. By mid-December Brother Martin was hard at work. It took no time to see how big of a job it would be, and why most Bible translators (besides Erasmus) almost never put their own names on the cover: it wasn't just modesty but to avoid the criticism that was sure to follow. Dr. Martin's Greek wasn't as good as Melanchthon's, and he relied plenty on the Latin Vulgate that he knew inside and out, because his main goal wasn't so much to get the grammar right as to put the Word of God into memorable and understandable German.

To do that, you had to be good at listening, he said, especially to people at the market, and to mothers, and to children, and in fact his translation would be more oral than literary, a lot like his sermons and, even more than he knew, a lot like the earliest Gospels too. That oral quality came also from using plenty of synonyms, and metaphors, and pithy phrases, and beefy words, and uncomplicated sentences, and making up new German words like scapegoat (*Sündenbock*) and decoy (*Lockvogel*), and translating idiomatically instead of literally. For example, he rendered a passage in Matthew 12 that said literally, "Out of the abundance of the heart the mouth speaks," as "When the heart is full the mouth overflows." He didn't have any big theory of how to translate, except to translate what a passage meant to say instead of what it literally said, and to make things simple, and to pay attention to rhythm, which helped make his verses perfect for the hymns he would soon start writing.

Of course, an approach like that could make the language of the Bible a little rough or casual for some people, but to him language was a means to a higher end, which was of course to get people to believe in the promise of the Word that God would save them. Translating the Bible wasn't just about language, in other words, but theology, and like most Bible translators Brother Martin wasn't above tweaking a word or phrase to give it the meaning he thought it needed. And so he rendered the word "life" always as "eternal life," "mercy" as "grace," and "The Deliverer of Israel" as "The Savior," and "under the law" in Romans 3 as "in the law," and the "righteousness of God" as "the righteousness that avails before God," and "all have sinned" as "they are all of them sinners." Most daringly, when he came to the phrase, "We hold that a man is justified by faith," it became "by faith alone," but he also insisted that it was good German style to use "alone" to intensify meaning and thus wasn't just some arbitrary choice.

How he arranged the books of the New Testament (and later the Old) made a theological point too, because it showed which books he thought were most important—i.e., best at expressing what he considered to be the overall message of the entire Bible: the gospel of Christ. And so the books of Hebrews, James, Jude, and Revelation were all grouped low in the table of contents to mark them as secondary. They were still profitable, he said, and he even added 21 special woodcuts by Lucas Cranach to Revelation—one of which had the beast from the abyss wearing the papal triple crown—but they didn't contain much gospel. The books that contained the most were the Gospel of John, the Epistles of Paul (especially Romans, Galatians, and Ephesians), and 1 Peter. So when Dr. Martin and especially his followers started using the phrase *sola scriptura* (scripture alone), it didn't mean he relied solely on all scripture equally but on the best parts especially.

And much as he complained about all the commentaries on the Bible, he provided plenty of explanations in his to clarify the true meaning of crucial terms: sin was what you felt when you didn't believe in grace; grace was God's favor through the gift of the spirit; faith was the divine work inside you which made you feel reborn and allowed you to do good works; righteousness was the same as faith. Plus he wrote the prefaces of each book to emphasize that the gospel wasn't the same as the law.

It wasn't a plain, unvarnished Bible, in other words, but was shaped and molded the way other Bibles were.

Maybe his biggest accomplishment was doing all this translating in just 11 weeks, so that a draft was ready in late February 1522. He would put on the final touches with Melanchthon and Spalatin when he got back to Wittenberg. Eager to start on the Old Testament as soon as possible, he was already in January writing friends that he was brushing up on his Hebrew. But he would wait until he was back home to begin that part, because he needed even more help with it.

He would get his chance soon enough.

TROUBLE AT HOME

If Brother Martin ever had an ivory tower that floated up high above the cares of this world, then it was at the Wartburg.

But even then it was only sometimes, because of course he didn't really like being separated from the world, and also because he still kept his ear to the ground, like when Archbishop Albrecht tried to sneak through his new indulgence—and especially when the little troubles in little Wittenberg kept getting bigger and bigger.

For his first six or seven months away, the troubles seemed manageable, including those around the marriage of priests, but then the arguing over changes that some people wanted to see in worship got completely out of hand. The changes had started calmly enough, with Karlstadt holding a couple of disputations on allowing laypeople to take both the wafer and wine of the Eucharist, just like priests did, and just like Dr. Martin had urged in the *Babylonian Captivity*. But

Prince Frederick told Karlstadt to stop, because taking the sacrament in both kinds always conjured up images of Bohemia, and that always caused unrest. In September Melanchthon and a few others started quietly celebrating in both kinds, among themselves, and Dr. Martin wrote that he was all for it. He even said that when he finally got back to Wittenberg, he wanted to make some changes too, to make the ceremony more like it was in Jesus's time.

Things got a little noisier in October, thanks to Dr. Martin's replacement as preacher in the friary, Gabriel Zwilling, who gave a sermon not only urging lay-people to take the Eucharist in both kinds, but insisting that the friars should no longer say private masses: the Mass, just like Dr. Martin said, was an act of fellowship. The friars agreed. But the prior wasn't happy, and neither was Prince Frederick, who wanted any changes in worship to be orderly, and not to bring unwanted attention to Wittenberg, because heaven knew it didn't need it. He therefore formed a committee to make some recommendations everybody could agree on. But the committee couldn't itself agree: those from the university, in-cluding Melanchthon and Karlstadt, wanted a new-style evangelical Mass (in German, with communion in both kinds), but most of those from the All Saints chapter that ran the castle church wanted no change at all until a general church council decided things. Since the committee couldn't agree, Frederick just stopped all changes: a little town like Wittenberg couldn't toss out the customs of 1,000 years by itself, he said. And what would happen to all the endowments established for private masses? For now, he wanted nothing but a few more dis-putations at the university, to study the matter further.

As usual, the disputations didn't really solve much. In November 1521, friars started leaving the Augustinian friary—some to marry, some to have a different sort of Mass. Those who stayed stopped saying Mass altogether rather than say the old version. The arguing spread among laypeople now, too: on December 3 and 4, students and burghers with knives under their coats chased priests out of the Franciscan church and city church for saying the Mass old style, and took their missals too. And some leading burghers demanded that anybody should be allowed to preach during Mass, while other leading burghers were scandalized and called the troublemakers "ignorant Martinists." Everybody was blaming, or praising, Dr. Martin for the changes, even though he was far away.

Except that on December 4, he actually wasn't—that very night he arrived from the Wartburg for his one-week secret visit, wearing a beard and a red beret so that not even his mother would have recognized him, he said. He arrived too late that day to see the unrest in the churches, but what he heard didn't, again, really worry him. Of course students shouldn't attack friars—not even Franciscans—but you couldn't hold everybody back everywhere, and mistakes would happen when the gospel came to town, he said. He was happy enough with the situation that he went back to the Wartburg a week later.

But things got worse when he left. Prince Frederick was bothered enough by the events of December 4 to again ask his special committee to meet and agree upon a common order of worship, but again they failed. And so he frustratedly repeated his order: no more changes to the Mass! And anyone wanting to change anything had to come straight to him, not the town council, since he suspected they were the biggest agitators for change.

On December 22, just a week after Frederick's order, Andreas Karlstadt announced that he was going to celebrate a new-style evangelical Mass anyway, on January 1 in the castle church. The university church. Frederick's church. As archdeacon of the All Saints chapter Karlstadt had every right to say Mass there, but to defy Frederick like that was something else altogether. He knew, though, that the town council was on his side.

The uncertainty over who exactly was in charge of the church in Wittenberg was the crux of the problem: with Brother Martin gone, it wasn't clear. Melanchthon and Amsdorf were too professorly to take charge; Karlstadt was plenty energetic but still swallowing the Holy Ghost, feathers and all; the town council (24 prominent citizens) and the so-called Forty (10 from each quarter) were other serious forces, and were mostly following Karlstadt; the All Saints chapter was a force too, and was mostly against change; and so was Frederick, who was of course the most powerful force of all when he decided to be, but Frederick wasn't often in town. And so the remaining forces vied for at least the spiritual leadership of the town, and for the moment Karlstadt was getting the best of that struggle.

Andreas Karlstadt as Rector of the University of Basel.

Frederick was out of town as usual when Karlstadt made his announcement about the new-style January 1 Mass, but word reached him soon enough, and he asked Karlstadt to please refrain. But Karlstadt defied the prince again by moving the Mass up to Christmas Day. Maybe he did that because on Christmas Eve some vocal Karlstadt supporters in the city church yelled out, "the Plague and hellfire on all [traditional] priests!" and Karlstadt thought a good way to calm things down would be to give them the sort of Mass they wanted, as soon as possible. But whatever the reason, he went ahead on Christmas, and it was a huge success: 2,000 people attended, probably in two separate services, and took the Eucharist in both kinds, in their own hands, without having to fast or confess in advance, with everything done in German, and with Karlstadt wearing just ordinary clothing to officiate. It went pretty smoothly, and order seemed to be restored—all thanks to Karlstadt. He repeated the event on January 1, and Epiphany (January 6), with just as many people. Soon he was also preaching twice on Fridays, and not only in the castle church where he had an official position but also in the city church where he didn't. He was also growing out his hair, like an Old Testament prophet, and preaching that those who had been justified and filled with the spirit were actually obligated to not only do the Mass in the correct new way, but to fulfill every part of God's law in the Old as well as New Testament. On January 19 he even got married, to a 16-year-old bride.

The popular new-style masses were a huge scandal among the orthodox minority in town, especially when one communicant accidentally spilled some consecrated wine. The scandal only grew when the Augustinians from all of Saxony met in Wittenberg on January 6, so that each could consider whether he wanted to keep observing his vows, and almost all of those from the friary at Wittenberg decided they did not: they left the religious life. And they made sure before leaving to go to the friary church and destroy all the altars and images, because they and some others were now insisting that removing "idols" was also part of the new and true style of worship.

To the orthodox inside and outside of town, the world seemed to be falling apart in Wittenberg. Duke George, who wasn't just Frederick's rival but a member of the new imperial council set up at the Diet of Worms to be in charge when the emperor was away, took action. On January 20, he persuaded that council to issue a mandate prohibiting all innovations in worship in the empire and promising to enforce it through visitations by bishops.

Brother Martin was unsettled by all these events too, especially the new masses, when he heard about them at the Wartburg. For all his daring writing in the past few months, for all his urging of Melanchthon to be bold, for all his happiness at the trouble the gospel caused, he was a cautious creature when it came to changes in worship. Even before the mandate of the imperial council arrived in town, he wrote Spalatin on January 17 to say that although he wanted to finish his translation of the New Testament away from his usual worries, the arguing over worship in Wittenberg made him want to come home now. He didn't mind changes to the Mass, but *how* they were happening. They lacked love, and order, and care and patience for the weak, all of which told him that the Devil was behind it all—not exactly high praise for Karlstadt. The two men weren't close, and Dr. Martin never regarded Karlstadt as one of the spiritual leaders of the town—but there he was, seemingly in charge anyway.

Maybe feeling a little miffed that nobody was asking his advice in all this, Dr. Martin published a new tract called *A Sincere Admonition by Martin Luther to All Christians to Guard Against Insurrection and Rebellion.* Yes, he wanted to change the Mass, but if it happened by force or violence it would tarnish the whole gospel. The job of church leaders was to instruct hearts, not force change. The job of laypeople was to repent and be patient. Change to worship would come when hearts were changed. And please, he begged them all, stop calling yourself Lutherans (or Martinists): you're Christians. He, Martin, wasn't crucified for anybody but was "poor stinking maggot-fodder," just like they were.

His distress only worsened when he learned that on January 24, probably about the same day that the mandate from the imperial council arrived in Wittenberg, the town council defiantly passed a new church ordinance that put into law the new-style evangelical Mass of Karlstadt. All images were to be removed from the city church, believers were to take both elements into their own hands, the Mass was to be shorter and in German, and all the endowments for private masses were to be put into a chest for the poor. It was mostly Karlstadt's doing, but Amsdorf, Melanchthon, and Jonas all helped—and Karlstadt would have banned music too if they'd let him, because prayer was always better than the lascivious notes of an organ, he said.

Just a week later, a crowd of angry evangelically minded or possibly just trouble-seeking Wittenbergers followed the example of the departing Augustinian friars and smashed up the altars and images and pictures in the city church. Karlstadt kept insisting he wasn't behind it, but Prince Frederick blamed him, and had one of his councilors visit to tell him to tone down his preaching, and to stop preaching altogether in the city church, where he had no position. Frederick also blamed Karlstadt when students started to leave the University of Wittenberg once again, summoned home by their worried parents.

On February 13, Frederick had one of his own councilors meet with the town council too, and together they came to a compromise on the church ordinance, although annihilation might have been a better word, since almost nothing was left of the new ordinance except that the words of institution in the Lord's Supper ("Take, eat . . .") could be said in German, and that the elements could be given in both kinds. But it was still too much compromise for Frederick: there could be no change at all, he declared. It was causing too much disunity, and bringing too much attention from outsiders. The Diet of Nuremberg was coming up, and he didn't want to have to answer any more charges about protecting heretics. Spalatin added simply, "What a mess we are in."

Melanchthon thought so as well, even though he'd been in favor of the new church ordinance. Now he also blamed Karlstadt. Old ceremonies, and images, could be tolerated out of Christian freedom, said Melanchthon: they were "indifferent" to "spiritual righteousness." The university turned on Karlstadt too, especially when he started preaching that learning was worthless and all you really needed was direct illumination from God. Even the town council turned on Karlstadt, whose lead they had been following for weeks.

Karlstadt understandably felt abandoned, since he thought he was doing mostly what "my dear father Dr. Martin Luther" had wanted done. During February 1522, he quickly published two tracts in his own defense, but it was too late. Karlstadt thought there was a true way to worship, and Dr. Martin didn't: anything the Gospels didn't mention or were indifferent about (like images and music) could be left as they were, said Dr. Martin, until the people themselves decided what they wanted. Images weren't inherently bad (Moses had a brass serpent), only worshiping them was. Even venerating saints wasn't totally wrong.

Almost everybody who mattered now started clamoring for Dr. Martin to come home and fix things. Except of course Frederick, even when the town council politely asked him. Maybe after the Diet of Nuremberg, said the prince. On February 20, some of the leading members of the town council, including Lucas Cranach, went ahead and appealed to Dr. Martin directly anyway, asking him to come lead the church and take up his old post as city preacher. They all agreed that Karlstadt had been wrong, and thought that Dr. Martin would be able not only to restore peace, but bring about some changes in worship that the prince could accept.

Yes, it was time to go home, decided Dr. Martin, when he saw this. Melanchthon had been right back in the summer of 1521 after all: Wittenberg really didn't have a shepherd. Or at least, as far as Brother Martin was concerned, the right shepherd.

RETURN

Frederick wasn't fooled for a second by Dr. Martin's coy little letter.

He knew right away what a full-sized cross meant, and so he sent a message off immediately to the bailiff of Eisenach, Johann Oswald, not far from the Wartburg, telling him to go talk some sense into Dr. Martin, and to remind him that if he came home and into the open a new legal process would almost certainly be started against him. Oswald arrived at the Wartburg late on February 28 and delivered the message: rash action was never good, he repeated. Wait until the upcoming Diet was over, or both pope and emperor would now demand that Frederick hand Dr. Martin over, which would put both the prince and the Dr. in an impossible position.

Did Dr. Martin pause for a moment, to consider who would protect him if Frederick no longer could or would? At Augsburg, and the Diet of Worms, Frederick had stood behind him because Dr. Martin wasn't yet under the ban or excommunicated. But now that he was both, Frederick might not take the risk. Still, Frederick was plain old flesh too, and Dr. Martin couldn't even really trust in him. He was therefore going to trust in God first, and return, even though Frederick was against it. It was time to throw himself back into time, and the world, and do what he could to help heal his dear town of Wittenberg, which so many people were watching.

He set out from the Wartburg the next morning, Saturday, March 1, or possibly Sunday, March 2, on horse. Just like on his trip home in December, he was again dressed as a knight, but there was no noble servant boy with him this time, because he wasn't coming back. He probably stayed the first night in Erfurt, at his favorite tavern, the High Lily, where he got into an argument with a priest and almost gave himself away. A horrible storm then slowed him down and washed out some roads, so he had to stay at least one night in Jena too.

There he ended up at the Black Bear Inn, where on the night of March 4, Shrove Tuesday, he had dinner with a couple of Swiss students who were on their way to Wittenberg.

Curtain Down

On the Road from Jena. March 5, 1522. Ash Wednesday, When Everything is Sober.

The red-hooded knight was up early the next morning to leave, but before he could, the two traveling merchants, who'd by now heard the rumor that the knight was in fact Martin Luther, ran out to the stables to apologize for their bluntness at dinner the night before. The knight thanked them for their apology, but wouldn't confirm his identity, and when he climbed onto his saddle and rode off from the Black Bear Inn, the merchants were as mystified as the students.

He had about 100 miles to go to reach Wittenberg.

By leaving as early as he did, the knight probably made it across a nearby bridge that was about to wash away, but the students and merchants weren't so lucky. Leaving a little later, they either had to try a bridge up- or downstream, or wait for the water to recede a little. The next night, farther down the road, the students and merchants found themselves staying at the same inn again, where they also ate together again, although this time the merchants paid, in honor of their mysterious guest the night before, who, they by now were inclined to believe, really had been Martin Luther.

Surely the students were more thrilled to have met Dr. Martin, or Knight George, than he was them, but he was at least glad to see that some students were still coming from distant places to study at Wittenberg, since he knew many others were leaving the city, and not just because of Karlstadt's rants against learning or because their parents were calling them home but because of Dr. Martin's very own tract on monastic vows. Plenty of students paid for their university studies by joining religious orders, but now his new tract was making many wonder whether the religious life was worth as much as they and most others had thought. Who would still study theology? professors had to wonder. At least these Swiss boys wanted to.

Riding along now Brother Martin certainly had plenty to worry about besides how to attract students to Wittenberg, such as muddy roads, and rushing waters, and thieves, and avoiding Duke George, and finding good lodging the rest of the way, and especially what he was going to do about the troubles in town once he got home. His orthodox enemies were saying he'd gone too far and was to blame for the troubles going on not just in Wittenberg but all around the empire, in town and countryside. Yet his wild-eyed rival Karlstadt was still insisting that Dr. Martin was going too slow, and was all talk but no action. What a lot of nerve! He was the one, not Karlstadt, who'd been called before cardinal, Diet, and emperor, and things would change at the speed things needed to change.

Since the town council had asked him to be the city preacher of Wittenberg again, Brother Martin decided he would present his solution to the current troubles from the pulpit in St. Mary's, starting that very Sunday, Invocavit Sunday, the first Sunday in Lent, and then preach every day through the next Sunday too, eight days in a row. Lent was the perfect time to preach, because people were in the mood to actually listen and repent, which made it an even better time for him to return to town than, say, January, when he'd first thought of returning. Riding along he surely was mulling over ideas for what he would say.

Was it while riding along, rather than while sitting in his *cloaca* tower later, that he got the idea for the unexpected opening of his very first sermon? He wouldn't start it with something obvious, like "We have problems," but instead something that took them beyond their own little problems and made them seem small: "The summons of death comes to us all, and no one can die for another. Everyone must fight his own battle with death by himself, alone," he would start. "I will not be with you then, nor you with me." In other words, solving their troubles wasn't just up to him: every one of them had to help. "Everyone must himself know and be armed with the chief things which concern a Christian." Yes, that was how he'd start.

That evening he stopped at Borna, south of Leipzig, from where he could practically smell Duke George. Surely that nearness was why he stayed in the home of an actual knight, Michael von der Strassen, and why on this last part of his journey several other knights rode alongside him. But he was thinking even more about his own prince, Frederick, than about George, because that night he took time to write Frederick another letter, warning him again that he really was about to arrive, and explaining a little more than in his last letter why he'd ignored Frederick's message to stay put.

Yes, he'd gotten the prince's message, and he knew it was meant well: Frederick's wisdom was known far and wide, and he loved Frederick more than he loved any other earthly ruler. But Dr. Martin also meant well in wanting to help fix "that untoward movement introduced by our friends in Wittenberg to the great detriment of the gospel" and even to the detriment of Prince Frederick too, because look at how many people were shaking their heads at the city now.

The prince should have faith, because he should know well by now "that I received the gospel not from men but from heaven, through our Lord Jesus Christ," and that was what Dr. Martin meant to bring to Wittenberg. He had agreed to all the hearings and trials of the past few years not because he doubted the rightness of his message but because he'd wanted to persuade the people who attacked him, and instead of just denounce them, yet it hadn't done a bit of good: his overdone humility and timidity had only wounded the gospel, because he'd given the Devil an inch and the Devil had taken the proverbial mile. And he'd stayed out of sight for almost a whole year not because he was afraid of the Devil, or Duke George, who was "much less to be feared than a single devil," but because he wanted to be obedient to his prince. Still, now it was time to come home, even though it meant defying that prince.

Frederick shouldn't worry, though: he, Martin, wasn't looking for protection anymore and didn't want to get Frederick in trouble. No, Frederick didn't have to do a single thing for him, because "I am going to Wittenberg under a protection far higher than the elector's." In fact, if he knew that Frederick was going to try to protect him, "I would not go to Wittenberg at all," just to keep his prince out of trouble. Instead of protecting, Dr. Martin wanted Frederick to let the emperor's men, or Duke George's, come right in, if they suddenly showed up at the Saxon border, or the gates of Wittenberg, to arrest or to kill him. Respect their safe conducts, he wrote, and leave every gate open; that way Frederick couldn't be criticized by anybody. Frederick wouldn't be criticized by God either, because when a subject didn't obey his prince, as Brother Martin was doing now, then the prince couldn't be blamed if the subject were captured or put to death.

That was his message, written in haste. Remember that "I have to do with a very different man from Duke George. He knows me well, and I know *Him* pretty well." He signed it, and sealed it with his special rose with the white and blue and gold background, calling himself "your electoral highness's very humble servant, Martin Luther." He sent it off by a messenger—maybe one of the knights in his entourage?—who knew where Frederick was currently residing.

The next day, Thursday, March 6, Brother Martin left Borna, then that evening he rode into Wittenberg, dressed as a knight and accompanied by knights. He might have gone to stay with Nicholas von Amsdorf, since he'd already asked his friend about doing so, but he may also have gone back to his room in the friary, where he and Friar Bisgar and Prior Konrad were about the only ones left. Members of the town council knew where he was, and rushed over to ask him to preach as soon as possible. He agreed, then asked in return that Karlstadt's most recent writings, that had criticized him for being too timid, be destroyed. The councilors were happy to do so, and to show their gratitude for his return gave him some cloth for new clothing, just as Frederick recently had.

Brother Martin suddenly had more cloth than usual, and it had come faster and easier than all the times he'd had to pester Frederick's loyal but tightwadish treasurer, Deginhard Pfeffinger, who was "very good at spinning fine words, but these do not produce good cloth." He also needed a new habit more than usual, since he couldn't very well go into the pulpit on Sunday looking like a knight. Plus he wanted to show in deed what he planned to say in word: that you couldn't and shouldn't just change everything right away about the old religion. The old ways were rooted deeply in some people, and if you ripped them away then you might rip away their faith too. Even he had to go slow, and not just out of consideration for others but for himself, because the religious life was the life he'd known for so long now. He would stay in his shell, he said, until the world changed. And so he cut his knightly hair, and had the top of his head shaved again into his bigger-than-usual tonsure, and had his new habit prepared. He would appear to the people as he always had: as Brother Martin.

Frederick heard the next day about the arrival. He immediately wrote to Hieronymus Schurff to ask Dr. Martin to write a letter saying that he'd returned expressly against his prince's will, and only in order to help quiet all the troubles in town. Even Duke George would have to go along with a trouble-snuffing motive like that, Frederick was sure. Dr. Martin wrote that letter, and meant it: yes, he had to come to the aid of his flock, even if it meant disobeying his prince, because

(1) he wanted to keep them from rebelling, (2) they had begged him to return, and (3) he was himself partly to blame for the troubles: "the present commotion has its origin in me," he admitted. Of course he was thrilled that Wittenbergers had taken his gospel to heart, but they'd taken the fleshiest possible view of it, by focusing on external things, and they needed more instruction, in person. The Devil had wounded some of Brother Martin's sheep, who were "after all, my fold, entrusted to me by God." This wasn't any longer Martin Luther the prophet of change and trouble, but of peace. Purifiers like Girolamo Savonarola in Florence, and Hutten, and Sickingen, and even Karlstadt and the annoying Thomas Müntzer too, were all *Schwärmer,* or fanatics, who wanted to make the world perfect right now. But it wasn't how Brother Martin thought things should go.

On Saturday, March 8, Dr. Martin went to the home of Hieronymus Schurff, where his friends Philip Melanchthon, Justus Jonas, Nicholas Amsdorf, and Augustine Schurff had gathered, so they could hear what he'd been doing these past months and what he planned to do now. Suddenly they were interrupted by a knock: at the door were the two Swiss students Dr. Martin had encountered in Jena four days earlier. They'd just arrived in Wittenberg on foot and came straight there to present their letters of introduction to the Schurffs. Dr. Martin started laughing and said to the students, gesturing, "This is Philip Melanchthon I was telling you about." Melanchthon asked the students to tell about their journey, and they stayed for some time doing so. The evening, and the encounter in Jena, made such a lasting impression on one of the students, Johannes Kessler, that he wrote about it years later. He surely distorted, and forgot, and shaded what had happened, to suit his memory, and even biblicized or folklorized it, turning the story of a present hero into something resembling stories of past heroes, say, like the story of Emmaus, in which Jesus's disciples didn't recognize him either, or like similar stories about King Alfred and Richard Lionheart and Henry V of England. And was it too much coincidence or too much foreshadowing that the merchants in Kessler's account didn't have just any book with them at the Black Bear Inn but a book by Martin Luther? Actually, maybe not, because if the merchants did have a book in their bags, there was a pretty good chance (like one in five) that Dr. Martin had written it.

Brother Martin presumably went back to the friary that night, where he had his books, and it wasn't hard to imagine that he spent some time putting the last touches on at least his first sermon, which he would give the next day. It was a good day for the theme he had in mind too, because it would be March 8, the feast of St. Theophylact of Nicomedia, a resister of iconoclasm. And icon-oclasm, literal or figurative, was exactly what he meant to resist in his sermon. Wittenberg was not going to go down the road of violent and sudden rebellion and change, he was determined. Yes, there would be change in all the externals he'd written and taught about—the Mass, images, the Eucharist, fasting, con-fession, private masses—but those would come only *after* there was change in the hearts of his flock. When that change happened, then they could work to-gether as well to answer even knottier questions, like how should marriage cases be handled now? And should monastic vows disappear? What should happen to monks and nuns who didn't want to quit their vows or their life? What should they do with the almost-abandoned Augustinian friary? And how obedient should they all be to civic authorities? Dr. Martin certainly wanted his flock to be obedient, but he'd defied the emperor by not recanting, and Frederick by returning, and he'd encouraged Melanchthon to defy them too. And Frederick himself had defied the emperor by hiding Martin Luther. What would happen if the emperor or Duke George's imperial council decided to seize Luther and Frederick kept resisting? No one knew for sure, but Dr. Martin wanted to get his flock humble, and he especially wanted them to make any changes slowly. The main thing now was to preach the Word, and let it grow some roots. He'd done that for years, of course, but it would start over in earnest tomorrow and prob-ably take the rest of his life, or at least until Christ returned again to reform the church at last, which Dr. Martin was sure would be very soon.

He would tell his flock tomorrow what he'd already written in his tracts, but not all of them had seen or heard those tracts yet—that change had to be done rightly, with perfect peace and love instead of so much worry about some sup-posedly perfect way to worship. They had to think harder about what was essen-tial and what was allowable: faith was essential, but various forms of worship could be allowable, as long as the Bible didn't forbid them, and they didn't hurt faith, and they weren't enforced by law. Old forms of worship would collapse on their own when hearts wanted them to. For now, Brother Martin wasn't going to change much at all, he decided. He wouldn't require confession, or even com-munion at Easter, but just recommend them. He wouldn't force people to take both elements of the Lord's Supper, or even to take the host in their own hands, because many consciences couldn't bear it when they'd been told for so long that such things were wrong. And even when changes like that finally happened, well they still had to be optional for people, and not required of all.

What the people of Wittenberg needed most was patience, because "endurance produces character, and character produces hope, and hope does not disappoint" (Romans 5). And instead of insisting on your rights, "dear friends," see "what may be useful and helpful" to your brother. Some had stronger faith than others, even stronger faith than he did. But what they ought to worry about wasn't their own strength, but their neighbor's, and look upon their neighbor like a mother looked upon her child. Because what did a mother do? "First she gives it milk, then gruel, then eggs and soft food, whereas if she turned about and gave it solid food, the child would never thrive" (1 Corinthians 3; Hebrews 5). So they should also deal with their "brother, have patience with him for a time, have patience with his weakness and help him bear it (1 Peter 2; Romans 14 and 15), as was done with us, until he, too, grows strong, and thus we do not travel heavenward alone, but bring our brethren, who are not now our friends, with us."

Yes, that was good. "Let us act with fear and humility, cast ourselves at one another's feet, join hands with each other, and help one another. I will do my part, which is no more than my duty, for I love you even as I love my own soul. For here we battle not against pope or bishop, but against the Devil (Ephesians 6), and do you imagine he is asleep? He sleeps not, but sees the true light rising, and to keep it from shining into his eyes he would like to make a flank attack—and he will succeed, if we are not on our guard. . . . Therefore all those have erred who have helped and consented to abolish the Mass; not that it was not a good thing, but that it was not done in an orderly way. You say it was right according to the Scriptures. I agree, but what becomes of order? For it was done in wantonness, with no regard for proper order and with offense to your neighbor."

The next morning, the first Sunday of Lent, did he eat breakfast before Mass, and his sermon, including even some meat? He wasn't terribly concerned about fasting anymore, and you didn't have to fast on Sundays during Lent anyway. Still, the strict Brother Martin still might have, because it was hard to break old habits.

He made his way to church, freshly tonsured and barbered. When it was time for the sermon, he went to the left front of the church that he knew so well, then started climbing the few steps up the pulpit, presumably in his new black habit, ready to start reshaping the world that his labors over these past four years had done so much to break apart.

Luther Preaching.

A Word After

JUST AS THE TOWN COUNCIL had hoped, Dr. Martin's eight days of sermons restored order to Wittenberg. By March 20 the old-style Mass was back, with candles, vestments, Latin, and communion in one kind only. The only thing that changed for the moment about worship was that private masses ended, and the Mass was no longer called a sacrifice.

Karlstadt was banned from preaching, and made to feel so generally uncomfortable that in 1523 he renounced his academic titles, left town, and started a more evangelical congregation in another part of Saxony. He and Dr. Martin kept arguing at a distance, and one day even up close, at the old Black Bear Inn in Jena. A month later, Prince Frederick and Duke George both banned Karlstadt from all of Saxony.

Brother Martin announced in spring 1523 that the time for change had come at last in Wittenberg: communion would be offered in both kinds, for those who wanted it. But he let images stay, and candles, and vestments, and Latin, because they were all trivial externals, he said. In 1526, he finally published a wholly German Mass. He also started preaching against All Saints Day, and from 1524 it was no longer celebrated in town. Prince Frederick even stopped showing his relics, which were taken in secret to his castle at Torgau and put to other uses by his tailor and goldsmith (Dr. Martin got a drinking glass that had supposedly belonged to St. Elisabeth). Dr. Martin also stopped wearing his habit in October 1524, so he really wasn't "Brother Martin" any longer. Most daringly of all, he got married in 1525.

But not even changes like these were enough for thoroughly zealous reformers around Saxony, like Thomas Müntzer, and who was even more thoroughly zealous than Karlstadt, and who had 2,000 people flocking to his sermons, and who called Luther "Dr. Pussyfoot," "Brother Fattened-Swine," and "Brother

Soft-Life," among other things. Müntzer was also one of the leaders of the Peasants' War that began in October 1524, that tried to bring about the entire overhaul of society in the name of Christ, and that grieved Dr. Martin to his joints—not just because of the destruction the war brought to hundreds of convents and castles and thousands of human lives, but especially because so many rebels (who were hardly all peasants) claimed to find their inspiration in his teachings, to the point that they wrote up their demands in the form of theses and then demanded to be shown from scripture how they were wrong! He denounced this violence, just like he'd always denounced violence, but the only remedy he saw to it now was an even bigger dose of violence: kill all the rebels, he urged nobles, in his *On the Murderous and Thieving Hordes of Peasants*. The noble armies tried their best, crushing the rebels and killing some 100,000 people, including Müntzer, by the time the fighting was over in 1525.

The Peasants' War didn't help Dr. Martin's popularity among princes, who were only confirmed in their belief that heresy led to revolution. And his angry pamphlet against "murderous peasants" didn't help his popularity among the remnants of the (mostly) peasant army either. Still, maybe diluting his reputation most of all was the arguing he did with other reformers who had emerged around the empire, over the direction that reform ought to go. The top reformers came together in 1529 in Marburg to try to unify themselves, and they agreed on 14 of 15 points—everything except the Lord's Supper. The two most stubborn participants were Dr. Martin, who insisted that Christ was present in the elements, and Ulrich Zwingli of Zurich, who insisted that the ceremony was purely symbolic. When neither would budge, it not only caused hard feelings but kept the reformers from finding the unity they'd been hoping for: if they couldn't agree on something as crucial as the most basic way that Christians showed community, then how could they possibly agree on a religious and political alliance? Dr. Martin's influence in the south of the empire faded some, although it was still spreading east, and north to Scandinavia too.

His old orthodox rivals attacked and blamed him more than ever in the 1520s and 1530s, and new ones joined in against him. Henry VIII in England had already written against Luther's view of the sacraments, and Thomas More now dismissed Luther too, putting all of his writing down to the usual motives it was always easy to see in your religious enemies: ambition, pride, vanity, wanting to lead people astray, and a hope for worldly immortality "which he presumes is going to last several thousand years after this present time." Others blamed Luther for all the empty Augustinian friaries, never pausing to think that maybe he wasn't preaching things that were entirely new to his brothers but instead just things they'd been primed to hear. The very first martyrs of Luther's teachings were Augustinians, burned in 1523 in Antwerp, where it was easier than in German lands for Charles to get a friar to the stake. Another martyr soon followed, the Augustinian Jean Vallière of Paris, where Staupitz had once urged Dr. Martin to flee, thinking it would be safe.

Staupitz of course had also left the Augustinians but to become a monk, not to enter the world. He and Dr. Martin stayed in infrequent but affectionate contact, with Staupitz even writing in April 1524 that his faith in Christ and the gospel was the same as ever, and his love for Dr. Martin unbroken. But just as Dr. Martin thought certain Wittenbergers were changing things too fast, so Staupitz thought the same of Dr. Martin: "you seem to me to condemn many external things which do not affect justification. Why is the cowl a stench in your nostrils when many in it have lived holy lives?" Still, Staupitz closed this

Luther Depicted as an Animal.

final letter he would ever write to Dr. Martin by calling himself the forerunner of the blessed evangelical teaching that Martin had proclaimed. Staupitz died in December.

As sure as he was about how things ought to go in the church, Dr. Martin was always pained when they went otherwise, especially as Christianity, and even the reformers themselves, seemed to be dividing into numerous rival groups. And since Christianity wasn't just about religion but everything else too, that division ran deeper than just along the metaphorical floors of the church, and had future consequences he couldn't have possibly imagined or liked. But even in his own lifetime, Dr. Martin had plenty to regret about the dividing: the fears that maybe he really was to blame for the Peasants' War, just like his enemies said, and that he really had sent tens of thousands of souls to hell, had plenty to do with the bad health and *Anfechtungen* that kept on plaguing him.

He survived a serious kidney stone in 1526, but in early 1527 he thought the end had come, as he felt a tightness in his chest and a "rush of blood to the heart" and heard buzzing in his ears. His priestly friends Justus Jonas and Johannes Bugenhagen heard his final confession and gave him absolution and the Lord's Supper and wrote down his last words, two days in a row. His biggest regret, he told them, was that he hadn't been found worthy to shed his blood for Christ, as he'd always expected he would. And his biggest worries were the usual: had he been wrong? And was God really good, specifically to him? Augustine Schurff finally came by and wrapped the ice-cold Dr. Martin in hot towels, and he survived. But his doubts survived too, at least sometimes. He wrote Melanchthon on August 2 that he was still trying to find the merciful God, and that his sickness hadn't just been physical. "I was close to the gates of death and hell," and trembling "in all my members. Christ was wholly lost. I was shaken by desperation and blasphemy of God," that was how afraid he was that he wouldn't be saved.

His low spirits of 1527 probably had something to do as well with the dismal results of the first official visitations made around Saxony that year, to see how well preachers and people were understanding the gospel he had taught them. "Merciful God, what misery I have seen," he said about the visits. "The common people know nothing at all of Christian doctrine . . . and unfortunately many pastors are well-nigh unskilled and incapable of teaching." He couldn't just blame other pastors, though, because his own flock in Wittenberg wasn't exactly a shining beacon to the world. He was soon complaining to them in his sermons about their sinful and ungrateful ways, despite all his preaching. Yes, they were sinners, and no, good works couldn't save them, but if they really had faith it would show in their good works! "We are not saved by works; but if there be no works, there must be something amiss with faith." It would be the classic anxiety among reform-minded people from that time on. Dr. Martin even threatened to stop preaching if they didn't improve. No wonder that when he and his friends celebrated the tenth anniversary of his 95 theses, on All Saints Day in 1527, they also consoled each other over their failures. And in 1530 he was again telling Wittenbergers that he would rather preach to raving dogs than their ungrateful selves.

Yet for all his troubles and sorrows, Dr. Martin could still marvel (and sometimes lament) that he was at least alive to have them, and it was surely because of God, and Prince Frederick. As soon as news spread in March 1522 that Martin Luther was back in Wittenberg, Duke George had started whipping up the Diet at Nuremberg and the imperial council to push Frederick to arrest him. But most at the Diet said that with the emperor Charles away, it wasn't time to act, and left Frederick alone. In 1524, even though Charles was still away, the next Diet reissued the Edict of Worms, led by Joachim of Brandenburg and Bavarian princes and Charles's brother Ferdinand, but Frederick kept ignoring it. In 1526, the Diet of Speyer then suspended the Edict of Worms, deciding to allow each German territory to manage the religious question in a way their leaders felt they could justify before God (and the emperor), and proclaiming the idea that one day would be law in the empire: whatever the prince's religion was also his territory's religion, *cuius regio eius religio*. This kept Dr. Martin safe enough for the moment, as long as he stayed in Saxony (which he did, the rest of his life).

And of course Frederick did more than any other human to keep him safe. How glad Dr. Martin was that he'd stayed with his wise prince, instead of following the steel-toed protection of Sickingen or Hutten, who had both offered their services, but who both died miserably in 1523. Where would he be if he'd followed them? Yet Frederick seemed glad to protect him, and to be influenced by him as well. Their possible meeting at Worms, after Dr. Martin's speech, was likely the only one they ever had, but they wrote occasionally directly and frequently indirectly through George Spalatin. That Frederick stopped showing his relics had a lot to do with Dr. Martin, and it couldn't have been easy for him to stop either, psychologically or financially, because they brought in piles of money for the castle church and university, and because he'd invested so much in them. Frederick also endured more nasty letters from the pope, who marveled that the Wettins had once been such staunch defenders of the church: "Who has bewitched you?" wondered the pope, using all the imagery he could think of. "Who has invaded the vineyard of the Lord? Who but a wild boar? We have you to thank that the churches are without people, the people without priests, the priests without honor, and Christians without Christ. The veil of the temple is rent. . . . Separate yourself from Martin Luther and put a muzzle on his blasphemous tongue." But Frederick stayed his stubborn protector to the end.

That end came sooner than Frederick might have wanted, and even then Dr. Martin's influence was apparent. On Palm Sunday 1525, Frederick heard the Gospels read in German for the first time; days later he heard the Eucharistic prayers in German for the first time; and days after that, just after midnight on May 5, he took the holy sacrament in both kinds for the first time. He also asked for no extreme unction before he died that morning between 4 and 5, and his final will made no mention of the usual pious offerings to monasteries, or of masses for the dead. The evangelical trend continued with his two funerals: the first, at Lochau in his beloved hunting lodge, was very old-faith, but when his coffin was carried to the castle church at Wittenberg for burial, people sang evangelical songs the whole way, and Brother Martin preached twice at the service. Sometime before 1600 Frederick finally got his nickname: the Wise. Some said it was because of how well he understood protocol, but others said it was because of how he'd handled the Luther affair. He was succeeded by his brother Johann, who died in 1532, and who was in turn succeeded, just as planned, by his son Johann Frederick, both of whom were Dr. Martin's very ardent supporters.

Thanks to his protectors, and so much popular support still too, Dr. Martin did more than merely stay alive. Despite his worries and chronically bad health and tireless critics, he carried on his labors for years.

He stopped being the official city preacher in 1523, because he was so busy with other things, but he kept preaching when he could, so often that he said he'd worn out not only his shoes walking back and forth to St. Mary's but his feet too. Over the course of his preaching life, he gave at least 4,000 sermons (2,300 of which survived), more than 100 per year.

He kept reaching thousands with his writings too: 1523 was his biggest year ever, with 400 editions printed, and even though that number declined severely after the Peasants' War, to around 50 a year, it was still a lot more than anybody else was putting out. Over the course of his publishing life, he averaged 1,800 pages of new writing a year, and unlike in other reforming traditions that would divide up publishing tasks, he did the Bible, catechism, liturgy, and hymnbook all by himself. He wasn't proud of everything he wrote: when he heard in 1536 that his books were in the library of Prince Johann Frederick, he was embarrassed by some of them. Still, he kept on being the best friend of printers everywhere, especially in Wittenberg, where there were an astonishing six by 1543. It was thanks almost entirely to him that this little town became the most important printing center in all German lands during the sixteenth century. By the end of his life alone, his works

Luther Translates the Bible with Melanchthon.

would number some 600 titles, 2,551 editions, and 3.1 million copies.

This wasn't even counting his New Testament, which he finished soon after returning from the Wartburg, with Melanchthon and Spalatin. The first edition of 3,000 came out in September 1522 and quickly sold out, even though it wasn't cheap: a half gulden—the same price as the cheapest St. Peter's indulgence had been. He started working on the Old Testament right away, and it came out in three parts, to keep prices down, in 1523 and 1524. The two Testaments were published together starting in 1534, and one shop alone in Wittenberg sold 100,000 copies; by 1545, 500,000 copies had been sold in shops everywhere, including in Ducal Saxony, even though George had forbidden it. By Dr. Martin's death, 443 editions of his Bible had been printed.

In 1524, he also started lecturing at the university again. He held off until then supposedly because he was so busy translating, but also because he and Frederick had worried about his being excessively public, given the delicacy of his

Das Neue Testament.

presence in town. He started with Deuteronomy, and he considered the lectures one of the best things he'd ever done. He also fittingly helped to revive the practice of disputation, which had declined during the troubles.

Dr. Martin also started something entirely new for him: being a husband and father. His future wife Katharina von Bora had fled to Wittenberg in 1523 with eight other nuns, and Dr. Martin found husbands for all of them except her. She finally declared that she would only marry either Dr. Martin or Nicholas von Amsdorf, and Dr. Martin decided he would give it a try himself, saying very unromantically that he did it to make his father happy, to spite the pope and the Devil, and to practice what he preached before he was martyred, which was sure to happen very soon. The ceremony took place in June 1525, in the former Augustinian friary, which became the couple's home. At last Brother Martin had some women in his life, which his enemies now claimed was actually what he'd always wanted; even his friends worried that marrying would hurt his reputation, since it was still so daring for a clergyman to do so, especially since he married during the horrors of the Peasants' War. But he and Katharina went ahead, and started adding children to their life (six in total, two of whom died young). He was terrified about the first pregnancy, because some said a two-headed monster was bound to emerge from a marriage between a former friar and former nun, but the boy came out just fine in June 1526, and Dr. Martin urged him, "Kick, little fellow. That is what the pope did to me, but I got loose." The couple added six more children when Dr. Martin's widowed sister moved into the big friary with her family in 1529. He and Katharina supported them all with his 100-gulden salary as a professor (up to 400 by 1540), her market garden and (later) farm, fees from student lodgers, and gifts from the prince, but it wasn't always easy to make ends meet, especially because of Dr. Martin's habitual generosity, maybe left over from his vow of poverty, and his refusal to take any money for his books. It helped in 1532 when Prince Johann gave the title of the friary to Dr. Martin, plus 100 gulden to renovate it. The city was also renovating and strengthening its surrounding walls at the same time, including the part of the wall that ran by the friary, which made Dr. Martin fear that his precious tower, from where he had "stormed the papacy," would be torn down. He made a new study for himself deeper inside the building, and the tower did indeed come down a little later.

The reform movement itself carried on too, even though Dr. Martin and other reform leaders hadn't been able to agree on a common confession. They all got the common (and derogatory) name "Protestants" at the 1529 Diet of Speyer, because princes and cities and nobles inclined to reform formally leveled a *protestatio* against assorted recent imperial decisions, including the revival of the Edict of Worms and the insistence that traditional Catholicism be reinstated everywhere. Then at the 1530 Diet of Augsburg, Charles V, back in German lands for the first time since Worms, asked the reformers to present their beliefs; those inclined to follow Dr. Martin (led by Melanchthon) drew up a set that became known as the Augsburg Confession and that became the foundation for "Lutheranism." The confession was an important statement, but it might have been more important still if it (or some other confession) had been the only one to come from Protestants: instead, Zwingli presented one too, and four southern German towns presented theirs. Charles didn't like any of them, and he gave all Protestants until April 1531 to submit to the church or he would raise his formidable sword against them. Fortunately for them, Charles again soon left the empire, and was back only one more time before 1543. Dr. Martin's survival, and Protestantism's, had a lot to do with Prince Frederick, but it also had a lot to do with the long, long absences of the exceedingly propertied Charles V.

Protestant princes showed some unity by forming a military alliance in 1531, called the Schmalkaldic League, led by Philip of Hesse (cities that still disagreed with Luther's view of the Lord's Supper didn't join). Dr. Martin never liked the idea of a military anything, but finally he went along with the idea of a defensive alliance. The League was full of confidence in the 1530s, as every Protestant prince in the empire seemed to join it, and the kings of France and England supported it, and all of Scandinavia became officially Lutheran by 1537. And in 1539, miracle of miracles, wicked Duke George of Ducal Saxony died and his successor and brother, Henry, went over to Lutheranism. So did Henry's son Maurice, when he succeeded in 1541: all of Saxony was now Lutheran! Dr. Martin and Melanchthon rode together to Leipzig in May 1539, just like they had in 1519, except this time they sang songs the whole way because they were going to introduce a new religious order instead of to dispute.

But as Dr. Martin had always warned, it was dangerous to rely on the sword. The Schmalkaldic League fell apart in the early 1540s, mostly over the scandal of Philip of Hesse's bigamy (which it turned out Brother Martin had secretly recommended, to everyone's alarm). Then when Protestant leaders in the empire refused Charles's invitation to join in a general church council called by the pope, the emperor had had enough. Seeing the weakness of the League, he decided now was the time to finally take up arms. He rounded up his soldiers and marched north toward Hesse and Saxony, where what remained of the League was centered, under the leadership of Philip of Hesse and Johann Frederick of Saxony, who was much less inclined to diplomacy than his old Uncle Frederick had been, and who was maybe still fuming that Charles had long ago backed out of his promise to marry his sister to Johann Frederick. On the way north, Charles isolated the League even further by luring Johann Frederick's Protestant cousin, Maurice of Ducal Saxony, to the imperial side: if Maurice fought with him and they defeated Johann Frederick, promised Charles, then Maurice would get the electoral title, and thus Wittenberg. It was just what Frederick had always feared: conquest by the Ducal cousins. Maurice couldn't resist: he joined with Charles in 1546 and helped conquer most of Electoral Saxony, including Wittenberg in May 1547. At least Charles didn't plunder the place, because it was Maurice's new electoral seat after all. And Charles left a few lands in Ernestine Saxony for Johann Frederick's sons, because Charles didn't want Maurice getting *too* powerful. But Catholic services were restored in Wittenberg, and Maurice could have closed the university in favor of Leipzig's, and completely undone Martin Luther's legacy in his own town.

That situation didn't last long, though. In fact as soon as the cathedral bells of Meissen rang to signal Charles's greatest victory of the Schmalkaldic War, at Mühlberg, the steeples at Meissen were struck by lightning and burned down, which Luther's followers everywhere took as God's judgment. German Protestant princes, alarmed by Charles's aggression, started making new alliances against him. In 1551 they even got the support of the new king of France, Henri II, and in 1552 sneaky Duke Maurice decided to change sides again and fight against Charles now (although he didn't give back Wittenberg or the electoral title to his cousin). Soon the emperor was retreating to his family lands in Innsbruck, and was forced into a treaty at the Diet of Augsburg in 1555, which put grudgingly into law the principle agreed on at Speyer three decades before: each prince in the empire would determine the religion of his state. Charles hated the thought so much he decided to abdicate as emperor right during the Diet. His goal had always been peace and prosperity and unity, including of course in religion, but by the end there was more war than ever, more taxes and debt, and a divided church.

Dr. Martin wasn't around to see the horrors of a conquered Wittenberg, or the official division of German Christendom, or the even more splintery division of European Christendom that happened once the new Reformed religion of Geneva's John Calvin began seriously to spread, including in the empire, because Dr. Martin died in early 1546. And to his deep disappointment, he never did die for his faith, but just from his ever-worsening health. Through the 1530s and '40s, he often had gout, insomnia, excessive mucus, hemorrhoids, constipation, stones (one almost killed him in 1537), numb legs, dizziness, ringing in his ears, headaches, swollen joints, ear infections, and heart problems. Katharina was skilled with herbs, poultices, massages, and more (their son Paul would become a renowned doctor, but not yet), but it still wasn't enough.

At least he outlived his parents. Hans Luther died in May 1530, while Dr. Martin was in Coburg. Two nights before he heard the news, Dr. Martin had a dream that he'd lost a big tooth, which he took as an omen of something bad, and sure enough, the bad news followed. When it came, he "took his psalter, went to his room, and wept so that he couldn't think clearly for two days, but he has been all right since," he wrote his secretary. Dr. Martin then wrote his mother to comfort her, then she died too in June 1531.

Dr. Martin outlived George Spalatin as well. After Frederick died, Spalatin left the court and moved to Altenburg, where he was a canon, and pushed his brother canons to reform themselves. He married there, and became one of the official visitors of churches and schools in Saxony charged with bringing about Dr. Martin's reforms. He died in January 1545.

Dr. Martin outlived many of his rivals too, including Andreas Karlstadt, who ended up a professor of Hebrew at the University of Basel, where he died of the plague in 1541, but not before becoming an inspiration for more radical versions of reform than Martin Luther's.

Luther in 1545.

He also outlived (the original) Johann Eck, who fought for the papal cause to the end. A tribute to him read, "Pope, emperor, king, and the undoubtedly larger part of Christianity praises him." His critics, though, including Dr. Martin, kept repeating rumors about his arrogance, drunkenness, gluttony, greed, and lust. In fact, upon hearing a rumor of Eck's death in 1542, Dr. Martin said, "I wonder how he was able to live so long, for he was a man of insatiable lust and inexhaustible addiction to drink." He probably said the same thing the next year when the news about Eck's death turned out to be true.

The ailing Dr. Martin even outlived the younger Archbishop Albrecht, who died in 1545. Albrecht kept growing his relic collection while Frederick was reducing his, and eventually he had 21,484 pieces, which were also worth a lot more time off from purgatory than Frederick's collection ever offered. But Albrecht's debts were so serious that he had to start selling relics in 1530. In 1539, his favorite town of Halle accepted the Lutheran Reformation, and he had to move his relics to Aschaffenburg. He always had an odd relationship with Dr. Martin, sometimes stopping in Wittenberg to talk with him about theology, and sending Katharina 20 gulden for their wedding, and toward the end even calling Dr. Martin the "dear prophet" and "father in Christ."

Dr. Martin outlived by far Pope Leo X, who died in December 1521, only 45 years old. The report said he died from a cold he caught at La Magliana, surely while out hunting, but some said it was poison. His successor was the sober reformer Adrian VI, former tutor of Charles V, but not even this reformer impressed Brother Martin, and the feeling was mutual. Adrian lasted even shorter than Leo, dying in 1523 amid more whispers of poison.

Dr. Martin outlived Cajetan and Aleandro too, who both continued to be diplomats and men of letters. Cajetan was, surprisingly, eventually even in favor of making certain concessions to "Lutherans," including allowing the clergy to marry and giving laypeople the Eucharist in both kinds. Before dying in 1534, he also wrote the decree that denied Henry VIII of England his divorce. Aleandro died in 1542, after serving for many more years as the pope's ambassador on various missions, especially in the empire, most of which, like the Luther affair, didn't end as the popes wanted.

Despite outliving those many friends and foes, life got harder for Dr. Martin in the 1540s, as he was sicker and crankier than ever. He turned a very old 60 in 1543, and even began to dislike Wittenberg. "My heart has grown cold, and I don't like it there anymore," he told Katharina. It wasn't just the weather, but the neverending stiffneckedness of his flock: "If you do nothing but mumble and grumble, then go join the cattle and swine! You can commune with them and leave the church in peace," he said one Sunday, and the next he stormed out in the middle of the service.

He'd always had an up-and-down temperament, and had always been feisty in his writings, but he seemed to get even angrier toward the end, especially toward his old enemy the pope, and now toward Jews too. He told his flock that the oil of the papacy "had penetrated to the very marrow" of his bones, and he still couldn't completely rid himself of that poisonous influence. He took out his resentment in a 1545 tract that was more scathing than anything he'd ever written about the pope, *Against the Papacy at Rome, Founded by the Devil*. He also resented that the general council beginning that very year, in Trent, ended up condemning just about everything he'd stood for, starting with justification by faith alone. Members of the new religious order called the Jesuits, who were in charge of justification at the council, certainly recognized how important his teachings on that subject were: and they decided that even if those teachings were connected to some tradition within the church, they should be condemned anyway if they sounded too Protestant. After that, Luther's views on the once perfectly disputable subject of justification couldn't be called Catholic anymore. The council went on to denounce every other crucial teaching of his too and to affirm current Catholic ones, like that there were indeed seven sacraments, and that the sacraments worked because of authority conferred by

God on priests (through the pope) rather than by faith, and that *sola scriptura* was just plain wrong, and that the Latin Vulgate had come straight from God and was therefore infallible. The council also urged finally putting together the list of prohibited books that had been necessary ever since people like Dr. Martin started exploiting the printing press: in 1559 that list appeared, and all of Brother Martin's writings were prominently on it, along with those of 550 or so other authors too. And it wouldn't have made him any less grumpy about the pope to know that the basilica of St. Peter's, which in a way started his troubles, would finally be completed only in 1666.

In 1543 he was scathing against Jews too, in a book called *On the Jews and Their Lies.* In 1523 he'd written a gentler tract called *That Jesus Christ was Born a Jew,* to urge Catholics to stop condemning Jews so much, mostly because he was so optimistic that now that the true gospel was here Jews would surely convert. But they didn't, and in 1538 he heard rumors they were even trying to convert Christians. Now he couldn't condemn them enough: their worship blasphemed God, he said, which would bring down God's wrath on everyone. They should be deported to the Holy Land, be forced to stop their usurious moneylending, be banished to farms, have their scriptures confiscated and their synagogues burned. He wasn't the only one denouncing Jews: they'd already been expelled from England, France, Spain, and Saxony, including by Frederick in the early 1490s, and for good measure Johann Frederick kicked them out again in 1536. But Dr. Martin went after them more heatedly than most. His very last sermon was about how Jews defamed Christ, and called Mary a whore, and would gladly "kill all of us!" He didn't advocate killing them, in fact he advocated instead that "We want to practice Christian love toward them and pray that they convert." But in the end, Christians needed to beware.

By January 1546 Dr. Martin described himself as "old, decrepit, sluggish, weary, worn out, and now one-eyed . . . I am dead—as I seem to myself," but also as busy as ever. Even though he'd given up teaching at the university, people still sought his help. In February, he was asked to settle a dispute involving the always squabbling Count of Mansfeld, and so he traveled from Wittenberg to his hometown of Mansfeld in February. One hundred knights rode with him, but "such a cold wind blew from behind through the cap on my head that it was like to turn my brain to ice." He also fainted during the trip, and had shortness of breath, and palpitations of his heart so heavy that he sweated through his shirt, and his left arm became stiff. He survived for the moment, and helped bring about the reconciliation the count had hoped for, and also convinced the count to expel any Jews from his lands. But Dr. Martin felt sick again on February 16, the day before he left Mansfeld, and suspected the end was near: "If I make it home to Wittenberg, I will lay myself in my coffin to let maggots feast on the stout Doctor." He left Mansfeld on February 17, then got worse while passing through his birth town of Eisleben, and was taken to a bed in the house of a physician. Friends gathered around Dr. Martin at 2 in the morning on February 18, including the Count of Mansfeld, and Dr. Martin's own teenaged sons, and Justus Jonas, who was always with him it seemed. They gave him medicines, and rubbed him with warm towels, and aqua vitae, and lavender water, and rose vinegar, which stirred him enough that he could pray and make his last confession of faith. There was no ceremony, and no priest, no cross placed on his chest, no extreme unction, but just a prayer to "take my little soul to you." Three times he said Jesus's words, "Into your hands I commend my spirit." And then he was gone.

His death was a shock to Protestant Europe, which wanted to hear the details. One hour after the death, Jonas wrote a report, to assure all that he'd died in the faith, that he hadn't given in to his great *Anfechtung* not to believe. Enemies wanted to hear details too, to see whether they could detect any sign of the Devil. But Jonas and others affirmed that when he was asked if he would remain steadfast and intended to die in Christ and the teaching he had preached, he had said *Ja.* It was his last word. His last written word suited him even better: a sheet of paper next to his bed contained a few sentences that ended, "We are beggars. That is true." The artist Lucas Furtenagel came the next day and drew his death-portrait.

The news of his death reached Wittenberg on February 19, when a messenger sent by Jonas burst into the classroom where Melanchthon was lecturing on Romans. Melanchthon trembled and quoted the words that Elisha had used when Elijah went up to heaven: "The charioteer of Israel has fallen."

Dr. Martin's body started its long two-day procession back to Wittenberg, as church bells rang and guards rode alongside. People came from all over to the funeral on February 22, in the castle church, where he'd disputed and preached and posted theses so many times. Prince Johann Frederick declared that he should be buried in that church too, and in an honored place. At the interment, Melanchthon said "we are very much like orphans deprived of a fine and faithful father."

Dr. Martin's final resting place was only 50 feet away from his protector, Prince Frederick. Down there in the ground, he really was maggot-fodder now, just like he'd always said.

SOURCES AND FURTHER READING

More has supposedly been written about Martin Luther than anyone except Jesus himself, and even if that can't be proved, I'm inclined to believe it after trying to manage the mountain of materials available. Since this book is meant for general readers, I don't include detailed footnotes or an exhaustive bibliography, but instead mention things I found most helpful and that may interest those searching for more detailed things to read.

SOURCES AND STUDIES USEFUL THROUGHOUT THE BOOK

Primary Sources: Parts of Luther's writings and letters began to be published first in the early sixteenth century, but many more have appeared in the last couple of centuries, with the most basic being the monumental G. Ebeling and R. Hermann et al., *Martin Luthers Werke: Kritische Gesamtausgabe*, 120 vols. (Weimar: Verlag Hermann Böhlaus Nachfolger, 1883–2009); especially helpful were *Briefe/Briefwechsel*, vols. 1–2, and *Schriften/Werke*, vols. 1–9, and 55–57. The American edition of Luther's writings is H. Lehman, ed., *Luther's Works,* 78 vols. (Philadelphia: Fortress Press, 1955–), which draws heavily on the Weimar edition but is much shorter: for example it contains only 119 letters from Luther up to March 17, 1522, while the Weimar edition has 458 before the same date; especially helpful in the American edition were vols. 10, 11, 13, 14, 21, 25, 26, 27, 29, 31, 32, 35, 36, 39, 42–45, 48–51, and 54. Preserved Smith, *The Life and Letters of Martin Luther* (Boston and New York: Houghton Mifflin, 1911), is technically a secondary source, but it contains many summaries of letters not only to and from Luther but those around him as well.

Some other helpful but smaller collections of sources were L. D. Reed and E. H. Jacobs, eds., *Works of Martin Luther,* 6 vols. (Philadelphia: A. J. Holman Company, 1915); H. J. Hillerbrand, ed., *The Protestant Reformation* (London: Harper & Row, 1964); E. Lund, ed., *Documents from the History of Lutheranism* (Minneapolis: Fortress Press, 2002); K. I. Stjerna, ed., *The Annotated Luther,* vol. 2: *Word and Faith* (Minneapolis: Fortress Press, 2015); T. J. Wengert, ed., *The Roots of Reform,* vol. 1 (Minneapolis: Fortress Press, 2015); D. O. Scheel, *Register und Nachträge zu den Dokumenten zu Luthers Entwicklung* (Tübingen: Verlag J. C. B. Mohr, 1917); T. G. Tappert, *Luther: Letters of Spiritual Counsel* (Philadelphia: Westminster Press, 1955), and the helpful chronology by D. G. Buchwald, *Luther-Kalendarium,* bound with D. G. Kawerau, *Verzeichnis von Luthers Schriften* (Leipzig: M. Heinsius Nachfolger Eger & Sievers, 1929). Much is available online, such as at http://www.famous-trials.com/luther/297-narratives, or the website www.projectwittenberg.org. Like most books written for general audiences, this one too is based mostly on secondary sources, but I read as widely in these primary sources as possible to try to get a sense of the voices and minds of Luther's world.

Secondary Sources: Helpful general studies of the Reformation were especially C. Eire, *Reformations: The Early Modern World* (New Haven, CT: Yale University Press, 2016); D. MacCulloch, *The Reformation* (New York: Penguin, 2003); B. Gregory, *The Unintended Reformation* (Cambridge, MA: Belknap Press of Harvard University Press, 2012) and his forthcoming *A Rebel in the Ranks: Martin Luther, the Reformation, and Why They Still Matter* (San Francisco: HarperOne, 2017) (which I read in draft form); C. Lindberg, *The European Reformations* (Cambridge, MA: Blackwell Publishers, 1996); E. Cameron, *The European Reformation,* 2d ed. (Oxford: Oxford University Press, 2012), and more such surveys, plus group studies such as K. Aland, *Four Reformers: Luther, Melanchthon, Calvin, Zwingli* (Minneapolis: Augsburg Publishing House, 1979), or P. G. Bietenholz and T. B. Deutscher, eds., *Contemporaries of Erasmus: A Biographical Register of the Renaissance and Reformation* (Toronto: University of Toronto Press, 2003). Severely outdated but fun anyway was J. H. Merle d'Aubigné, *History of the Reformation of the Sixteenth Century* (London: Oliver & Boyd, 1846). A reliable reference was *The Oxford Encyclopedia of the Reformation,* 4 vols., ed. H. J. Hillerbrand (New York: Oxford University Press, 1996). Useful studies of the general theology of the Reformation included A. E. McGrath, *Reformation Thought* (Cambridge, MA: Blackwell Publishers, 1988); and H. Oberman, *Forerunners of the Reformation: The Shape of Late Medieval Thought Illustrated by Key Documents* (Philadelphia: Fortress Press, 1981).

Studies of Luther himself are overwhelming in number, and those commemorating the 500th anniversary of his theses started appearing well before 2017. Exceedingly useful to me were numerous articles in the reference works: *The Cambridge Companion to Martin Luther,* ed. D. K. McKim (Cambridge: Cambridge University Press, 2003); *Das Luther-Lexikon,* eds. V. Leppin and G. Schneider-Ludorff (Regensburg: Bückle & Böhm, 2014); and especially the blow-by-blow biography by M. Brecht, *Martin Luther: His Road to Reformation, 1483–1521* (Minneapolis: Fortress Press, 1985), which continues in two more volumes: *Martin Luther: Shaping and Defining the Reformation, 1521–1532* (Minneapolis: Fortress Press, 1990), and *Martin Luther: The Preservation of the Church*

(Minneapolis: Fortress Press, 1999). Also important were H. Oberman, *Luther: Man between God and the Devil* (New Haven, CT: Yale University Press, 1990); F. Posset, *The Real Luther: A Friar at Erfurt and Wittenberg* (St. Louis: Concordia Publishing, 2011); R. Bainton's famous *Here I Stand: A Life of Martin Luther* (Nashville: Abingdon Press, 1950); and A. Pettegree's *Brand Luther* (New York: Penguin, 2015). I also benefited from H. Boehmer, *Martin Luther: Road to Reformation* (New York: Meridian Books, 1957); H. Bornkamm, *Luther in Mid-Career* (Philadelphia: Fortress Press, 1983); R. H. Fife, *The Revolt of Martin Luther* (New York: Columbia University Press, 1957); E. W. Gritsch, *Martin—God's Court Jester: Luther in Retrospect* (Philadelphia: Fortress Press, 1983); H. G. Haile, *Luther: An Experiment in Biography* (Princeton, NJ: Princeton University Press, 1980); S. Hendrix, *Luther* (Nashville: Abingdon Press, 2009), *Luther and the Papacy* (Philadelphia: Fortress Press, 1981), *Martin Luther: A Very Short Introduction* (New York: Oxford University Press, 2010), and his more recent *Martin Luther: Visionary Reformer* (New Haven, CT: Yale University Press, 2015); H. Jungbans, *Martin Luther: Exploring His Life and Times* (Minneapolis: Fortress Press, 1998) (CD format); J. M. Kittelson, *Luther the Reformer: The Story of the Man and His Career* (Minneapolis: Augsburg Publishing House, 1986); V. Leppin, *Martin Luther* (Darmstadt: WBG Verlag, 2006), and *Martin Luther: Vom Mönch zum Feind des Papstes* (Darmstadt: Wissenschaftliche Buchgesellschaft, 2013); P. Manns (text), H. Loose (photography), and J. Pelikan (introduction), *Martin Luther: An Illustrated Biography* (New York: Crossroad Publishing Company, 1982); M. Marty, *Martin Luther* (New York: Penguin Group, 2004); M. A. Mullett, *Martin Luther* (New York: Routledge, 2004); G. Ritter, *Luther: His Life and Work* (New York: Harper & Row, 1963); G. Rupp, *Luther's Progress to the Diet of Worms* (Greenwich, CT: Leabury Press, 1951); H. Schilling, *Martin Luther: Rebell in einer Zeit des Umbruchs* (Munich: C. H. Beck, 2012); E. Schwiebert, *Luther and His Times: The Reformation from a New Perspective* (St. Louis: Concordia Publishing, 1950); D. Steinmetz, *Luther in Context* (Bloomington: Indiana University Press, 1986); G. Tomlin, *Luther and His World* (Downers Grove, IL: InterVarsity Press, 2002). Examples of brand-new and surely insightful books that appeared too late for me to consult include L. Roper, *Martin Luther: Renegade and Prophet* (New York: Random House, 2016), and D. MacCulloch, *All Things Made New: The Reformation and Its Legacy* (Oxford: Oxford University Press, 2016).

Especially useful studies of Luther's theology were R. Kolb, I. Dingel, and L. Batka, eds., *The Oxford Handbook of Martin Luther's Theology* (Oxford: Oxford University Press, 2014); D. V. N. Bagchi, *Luther's Earliest Opponents* (Minneapolis: Fortress Press, 1991); B. Hamm, *The Early Luther: Stages in a Reformation Reorientation* (Grand Rapids, MI: Eerdmans Publishers, 2014), and *The Reformation of Faith in the Context of Late Medieval Theology and Piety* (Boston and Leiden: Brill Publishers, 2004); R. Kolb, *Martin Luther as Prophet, Teacher, and Hero* (Grand Rapids, MI: Baker Books, 1999), and *Martin Luther: Confessor of the Faith* (Oxford: Oxford University Press, 2009); B. Lohse, *Martin Luther: An Introduction to His Life and Work* (Minneapolis: Augsburg Fortress Publishers, 2000) and *Martin Luther's Theology* (Minneapolis: Fortress Press, 2011); A. McGrath, *Luther's Theology of the Cross,* 2nd ed. (Oxford: Wiley-Blackwell, 1991). I also learned from P. Althaus, *The Theology of Martin Luther* (Minneapolis: Fortress Press, 1966), and from such specialized studies as K. Hagen, *A Theology of Testament in the Young Luther: The Lectures on Hebrews* (Leiden: E. J. Brill, 1974), and J. G. Kiecker, "Luther's Preface to His First Lectures on the Psalms (1513): The Historical Background to Luther's Biblical Hermeneutic," *Wisconsin Lutheran Quarterly* 85 (Fall 1988): 287–95.

The German and European setting of the Reformation are explained especially well in T. Brady, *German Histories in the Age of Reformations, 1400–1650* (Cambridge: Cambridge University Press, 2009); and T. Brady, H. Oberman, and J. Tracy, eds., *Handbook of European History, 1400–1600*, 2 vols. (Grand Rapids, MI: William B. Eerdmans Publishing Company, 1994).

ADDITIONAL SPECIALIZED STUDIES, BY TOPIC, IN ROUGHLY THE ORDER
THE TOPICS APPEAR

Justification: J. Pereira, *Augustine of Hippo and Martin Luther on Original Sin and Justification of the Sinner* (Helsinki: Unigrafi, 2012).

Johann von Staupitz: the highly enlightening F. Posset, *Frontrunner of the Catholic Reformation* (Aldershot: Ashgate Publishing Limited, 2003), and D. Steinmetz, *Luther and Staupitz* (Durham, NC: Duke University Press, 1980).

Disputation, the Disputation Against Scholastic Theology, and Scholasticism: K. Aland, "Die theologischen Anfaenge Martin Luthers," *Internationale Katholische Zeitschrift* (1983): 556–66; A. J. Novikoff, *The Medieval Culture of Disputation* (Philadelphia: University of Pennsylvania Press, 2013), and his "Toward a Cultural History of Scholastic Disputation," *American Historical Review* 117/2 (2012): 331–64; E. Rummel, *The Humanist-Scholastic Debate in the Renaissance and Reformation* (Cambridge, MA: Harvard University Press, 1995); W. A. Wallace, "Scholasticism in Europe, 1450 to 1789," in *Encyclopedia of the Early Modern World* (The Gale Group Inc., 2004), at http://www.encyclopedia.com/philosophy-and-religion/philosophy/philosophy-terms-and-concepts/scholasticism.

Rhetoric: P. Matheson, *The Rhetoric of the Reformation* (Edinburgh: T&T Clark, 1998); J. J. Murphy, *Rhetoric in the Middle Ages: A History of Rhetorical Theory from Saint Augustine to the Renaissance* (Berkeley: University of California Press, 1974).

Universities: especially good was H. de Ridder-Symoens, ed., *A History of the University in Europe*, vol. 2: *Universities in Early Modern Europe* (Cambridge: Cambridge University Press, 1996).

Indulgences: primary sources include "Archbishop Albert's Instructions to the Sub-Commissioners," *Translations and Reprints from the Original Sources of European History*, 2/6 (Philadelphia: University of Pennsylvania, 1899); J. Tetzel, "The Text of a Sermon on Indulgences," trans. W. Köhler, *Dokumente zum Ablassstreit*, http://biblelight.net/tetzel.htm; C. Woodward, trans., "A Sermon on Indulgences and Grace" (manuscript), from the Weimar edition of Luther's works, vol. 1; D. Kramer, ed., *Johann Tetzel's Rebuttal against Luther's Sermon on Indulgences and Grace* (Atlanta: Pitts Theology Library, 2012). Also J. Wicks, "Martin Luther's Treatise on Indulgences," *Theological Studies* 28 (September 1967): 481–518; and R. Kiermayr, "How Much Money was Actually in the Indulgence Chest?" *Sixteenth Century Journal* 17/3 (Autumn 1986): 303–18.

Archbishop Albrecht: D. Eichberger, "A Renaissance Reliquary Collection in Halle, and its Illustrated Inventories," *Art Journal* 37 (1996): 19–36, at http://www.ngv.vic.gov.au/essay/a-renaissance-reliquary-collection-in-halle-and-its-illustrated-inventories/; *Staatliche Galerie Moritzburg Halle: Geschichte Und Sammlungen* (Halle: Staatliche Galerie Moritzburg, 1994); H. Reber and B. Roland, *Albrecht von Brandenburg* (Mainz: Verlag Philipp von Zabern, 1990); R. Anderson, *Cardinal Albrecht of Brandenburg as Saint Jerome by Lucas Cranach the Elder,* http://ringlingdocents.org/albrecht.htm; W. Hubatsch, *Albrecht von Brandenburg-Ansbach* (Heidelberg: Quelle & Meyer, 1960); Albrecht's fantastic prayer book is at http://www.getty.edu/art/collection/objects/1402/simon-bening-prayer-book-of-cardinal-albrecht-of-brandenburg-flemish-about-1525-1530/.

Wittenberg, including the Friary, Castle, and City Church: E. C. Reinke, ed., "The Dialogues of Andreas Meinhardi: A Utopian Description of Wittenberg and its University, 1508" (Valparaiso University: University Microfilms International, 1976); M. Treu, *Martin Luther in Wittenberg* (Wittenberg: Luther Memorial Foundation of Saxony-Anhalt, 2013); M. Treu, *Archäologie am Lutherhaus: Neue Funde und Ergebnisse* (Wittenberg: Stiftung Luthergedenkstätten in Sachsen-Anhalt, 2005); F. Bellman, M. Harksen, and R. Werner, *Die Denkmale der Lutherstadt Wittenberg* (Weimar: Herrman Böhlaus Nachfolger, 1979); J. Haussleiter, *Die Universität Wittenberg vor dem Eintritt Luthers* (Deichert, 1903); W. Hoffmann, *Luther: Travel Guide* (Calbe: Schmidt-Buch-Verlag, 1995); G. Krüger, "How Did the Town of Wittenberg Look at the Time of Luther?" at http://thewittenbergproject.org/about/how-did-the-town-of-wittenberg-look-at-the-time-of-luther/, originally in *Luther: Vierteljahresschrift der Luthergesellschaft* 15 (1933): 13–32; "Lutherstadt Wittenberg: A Guide to the Famous Sights of Lutherstadt Wittenberg" (Wittenberg: Drei Kastanien Verlag, 2015); A. Neser, *Luthers Wohnhaus in Wittenberg* (Leipzig: Evangelische Verlagsanstalt, 2005); A. Neugebauer, *Das Ernestinische Wittenberg: Stadt und Bewohner Textband,* H. Lück and E. Brünz et al., eds. (Petersberg: Michael Imhof Verlag, n.d.); and such local guide books as A. Steinwachs, *St. Mary's: The Protestant Parish Church in Lutherstadt Wittenberg* (Edition Akanthus, n.d.); "Experience Luther," at http://www.luther2017.de/en/erleben; E. Strauchenbruch, *Luthers Wittenberg* (Leipzig: Evangelische Verlagsanstalt, n.d.); *Schaustelle Reformation Wittenberg* (Wittenberg: Lutherstadt Wittenberg Marketing GmbH, n.d.).

Maximilian: G. Benecke, *Maximilian I (1459–1519): An Analytical Biography* (London: Routledge & Kegan Paul, 1982).

Frederick the Wise: featured in M. Grossmann, *Humanism in Wittenberg, 1485–1517* (Nieuwkoop: De Graaf, 1975), but see especially I. Ludolphy, *Friedrich der Weise: Kurfürst von Sachsen, 1463–1525* (Göttingen: Vandenhoeck & Ruprecht, 1984), and S. Wellman, *Frederick the Wise: Seen and Unseen Lives of Martin Luther's Protector* (St. Louis: Concordia Publishing House, 2015); additional information at Wellman's helpful website at http://www.frederickthewise.com/. Also P. M. Bacon, "Art Patronage and Piety in Electoral Saxony: Frederick the Wise Promotes the Veneration of His Patron, St. Bartholomew," *Sixteenth Century Journal* 39/4 (Winter 2008): 973–1001.

George Spalatin: I. Höss, *Georg Spalatin* (Weimar: Hermann Böhlaus Nachfolger, 1989).

Cardinal Cajetan: J. Wicks, *Cajetan Responds: A Reader in Reformation Controversy* (Washington, DC: Catholic University of America Press, 1978).

Altenburg: H. J. Kessler and J. Penndorf, *Spalatin in Altenburg: Eine Stadt plant ihre Ausstellung* (Halle: Mitteldeutscher Verlag GmbH, 2012); G. Hesekiel, "Aus dem Leben des Schlosses zu Altenburg," in *Altenburg Schloss,* ed. G. Keil and U. Kunzl (Kleine Kunstfuhrer, n.d.); *Schloss Altenburg* (Regensburg: Verlag Schnell & Steiner GmbH, 2014).

Johann Eck: E. Iserloh, *Johannes Eck (1486–1543): Scholastiker, Humanist, Kontroverstheolog* (Münster Westfalen: Verlag Aschendorff, 1981); M. Ziegelbauer, *Johannes Eck: Mann der Kirche im Zeitalter der Glaubensspaltung* (Sankt Ottilien: EOS-Verlag, 1987).

Andreas Karlstadt: R. J. Sider, *Andreas Bodenstein von Karlstadt* (Leiden: E. J. Brill, 1974); C. A. Pater, *Karlstadt as the Father of the Baptist Movements: The Emergence of Lay Protestantism* (Toronto: University of Toronto Press, 1984); especially interesting, and highly sympathetic to Karlstadt, was J. S. Preus, *Carlstadt's "Ordinaciones" and Luther's Liberty: A Study of the Wittenberg Movement, 1521–22* (Cambridge, MA: Harvard University Press, 1974); A. Zorzin, "Andreas Bodenstein von Karlstadt (1486–1541)," in *The Reformation Theologians: An Introduction to Theology in the Early Modern Period,* ed. C. Lindberg (Oxford: Blackwell Publishers/Wiley, 2002), 327–37.

Leipzig Disputation: Interesting but odd, W. H. Dau, *The Leipzig Debate in 1519: Leaves from the Story of Luther's Life* (St. Louis: Concordia Publishing House, 1919), at https://archive .org/details/cu31924029232372.

Fools: S. Lipscomb, "All the King's Fools," *History Today* 61/8 (2011); and especially H. C. E. Midelfort, *A History of Madness in Sixteenth-Century Germany* (Stanford, CA: Stanford University Press, 1999); also J. Doran, *The History of Court Fools* (New York: Haskell House, 1966).

Philip Melanchthon: M. Rogness, *Philip Melanchthon: Reformer without Honor* (Minneapolis, MN: Augsburg Publishing House, 1969); T. J. Wengert, *Philip Melanchthon, Speaker of the Reformation: Wittenberg's Other Reformer* (Cornwall, UK: Variorum Collected Studies Series, 2010).

Leo X and His Hunting Lodge: "Castello Della Magliana," at http://www.lifeinitaly.com/ tourism/lazio/castello-magliana; C. Kidwell, *Pietro Bembo: Lover, Linguist, Cardinal* (Montreal: McGill-Queen's University Press, 2004); J. Klaczko and J. Dennie, *Rome and the Renaissance: The Pontificate of Julius II* (New York: G.P. Putnam's Sons, 1903); M. Marshall, L. Carroll, and K. McIver, *Sexualities, Textualities, Art and Music in Early Modern Italy* (Aldershot: Ashgate Publishers, 2014); I. Verstegen, ed., *Patronage and Dynasty: The Rise of the Della Rovere in Renaissance Italy* (Kirksville, MO: Truman State University Press, 2007); R. A. Lanciani, *The Golden Days of the Renaissance in Rome, from the Pontificate of Julius II to that of Paul III* (Boston: Houghton, Mifflin, 1906); H. Vaughan, *The Medici Popes (Leo X and Clement VII)* (Port Washington, NY: Kennikat Press, 1908).

The Coronation of Charles V at Aachen: R. M. Woolley, *Coronation Rites* (Cambridge: Cambridge University Press, 1915); *Römischer Küniglicher Maies: Krönung zu Ach geschehe[n]* (Augsburg: S. Grim, M. Wirsung, 1520), available at https://www.bl.uk/ treasures/festivalbooks/BookDetails.aspx?strFest=0078; on the Aztec treasures, see C. L.

Johnson, *Cultural Hierarchy in Sixteenth-Century Europe: The Ottomans and Mexicans* (Cambridge: Cambridge University Press, 2014); for more, see Charles V below.

Luther and Printing: Especially helpful were M. Edwards, *Printing, Propaganda, and Martin Luther* (Berkeley: University of California Press, 1994); A. Pettegree, *Brand Luther* (London: Penguin, 2015); R. Scribner, *For the Sake of Simple Folk: Popular Propaganda for the German Reformation* (Cambridge: Cambridge University Press, 1981).

Luther and Cranach: G. Schuchardt, *Cranach, Luther und die Bildnisse* (Regensburg: Verlag Schnell & Steiner GmbH, 2015).

Worms: one translation of the Edict of Worms is at http://www.crivoice.org/creededictworms .html. Also D. L. Jensen, *Confrontation at Worms* (Provo, UT: Brigham Young University Press, 1973).

Charles V: W. Blockmans, *Emperor Charles V 1500–1558* (London: Hodder Headline Group, 2002); K. Brandi, *Charles V: The Growth and Destiny of a Man and of a World Empire* (London: Thirty Bedford Square, 1960); H. Kleinschmidt, *Charles V: The World Emperor* (Stroud, UK: Sutton Publishing Limited, 2004); C. R. Kemp, "The Hapsburg and the Heretics: An Examination of Charles V's Failure to Act Militarily Against the Protestant Threat" (master's thesis, Brigham Young University, 2011).

Ulrich von Hutten: C. Gräter, *Ulrich von Hutten: Ein Lebensbild* (Stuttgart: Konrad Theiss Verlag, 1988); H. Holborn, *Ulrich von Hutten and the German Reformation* (New Haven, CT: Yale University Press, 1937).

The Wartburg: J. Morris, *Luther at Wartburg Castle: A Reformation Story of 1521* (Philadelphia: Lutheran Publication Society, 1882); J. Reston, *Luther's Fortress* (New York: Basic Books, 2015); *Wartburg Jahrbuch* (Regensburg: Schnell & Steiner, 2011).

Justification by Faith, at Trent: N. Phair, "Jesuit Influence on the Tridentine Decree on Justification" (honors thesis, Brigham Young University, 2016).

MUSEUMS

Excellent museums about Luther abound in Germany and are a great way to be introduced to him. Particularly informative and helpful to me, for Luther's early years, were the various sites that are part of the Stiftung Luthergedenkstätten in Sachsen-Anhalt, including the Luthers Elternhaus (the home of Luther's parents) in Mansfeld (along with the guide *Mansfeld* [Regensburg: Verlag Schnell & Steiner GmbH, 2005]), the Luthers Geburtshaus (Luther's birth house) and Luthers Sterbehaus (death house) in Eisleben, the Melanchthonhaus in Wittenberg, and most especially the Lutherhaus in Wittenberg, which is situated in the former Augustinian friary where Luther lived and is overflowing with images and information. Also helpful were the display in the Nikolaikirche in Jüterbog on Tetzel and indulgences, with its accompanying *Kirche St. Nikolai Jüterbog: Ein Kirchenführer* (Gemeindebriefdruckerei Groß Oesingen, Evangelische Kirchengemeinde St. Nikolai Jüterbog, n.d.); the Evangelischen Augustinerkloster zu Erfurt, where Luther entered the religious life and lived for many years; the Lutherhaus in Eisenach, along with *Eisenach Erleben: Enjoy Eisenach* (Eisenach: Eisenach-Wartburgregion Touristik GmbH, n.d.); the monumental museum of the Wartburg; the Schloss Altenburg; and the Wettins's castle in Torgau. The churches in all of these towns where Luther lived or worked are worth visiting too, with guides such as V. Friedrich, *The Cathedral of St Mary in Erfurt* (Passau: Kunstverlag Peda, 2010). There are many other churches where Luther simply preached, which seem to be almost as numerous as beds where Napoleon slept. A helpful guide to all was C. Dömer, *Traveling with Martin Luther* (St. Louis: Concordia Publishing House, 2010).

ILLUSTRATION CREDITS

Entire books have been written about the many ways Luther has been depicted over the centuries, in art and film, such as E. P. Wipfler, *Martin Luther in Motion Pictures: History of a Metamorphosis* (Göttingen: Vandenhoeck & Ruprecht, 2011). I won't elaborate on the subject here, except to say that images were chosen not because they were necessarily precise representations but because of how they helped illustrate the text.

FRONTISPIECE

The Miriam and Ira D. Wallach Division of Art, Prints and Photographs: Print Collection, The New York Public Library. "Martin Luther," *The New York Public Library Digital Collections*. 1521. http://digitalcollections.nypl.org/items/147f7020-2f1d-0133-2318-58d385a7b928.

MAPS

The Holy Roman Empire around 1520. Kathryn Richey. viii
Wittenberg in Luther's Time. Kathryn Richey, adapted from *Luther and His Times* © 1950, 1978 Concordia Publishing House. Used with permission. www.cph. ix

ILLUSTRATIONS

Curtain Up

Chapter 1

Chapter 2

Chapter 3

Chapter 4

Chapter 5

GRATIA

In addition to the long list of scholars, museums, and libraries, mentioned under "Sources and Further Reading" and "Illustration Credits," I am indebted to still others, starting with Theo Calderara at Oxford University Press, who first approached me with the idea for this book, then offered helpful advice throughout the entire process of its production.

A grant from the College of Family, Home, and Social Sciences at Brigham Young University enabled me to travel to Germany for research there, while a Public Scholar Fellowship from the National Endowment for the Humanities (long may it live) allowed me to work full-time on the project for an entire year. My department chairman, Don Harreld, and dean, Ben Ogles, arranged for that year of leave from teaching, without which I wouldn't have finished this book in time, at least in any state of decent health.

Fellow historians Ron Rittgers and Robert Christman offered expert advice about sources, while Carlos Eire, Brad Gregory, Robert Kolb, Diarmaid MacCulloch, and Eddy Put read the manuscript and offered crucial suggestions and support. My research assistant extraordinaire, Claire Woodward, was truly that, from summarizing sources and taking notes to being utterly dependable and making all the complicated arrangements for the book's many illustrations. Jenna Barton assisted with the illustrations as well. Cameron Donahue,

Marcela Maxfield, Rob Wilkinson, Jeremy Toynbee, and Mary Sutherland were all professional and helpful in the production process. Courtney Lees Cook compiled the index. My sister Kathryn Richey created the lovely maps, and my wife, Paula, read the manuscript with her usual critical eye, and offered her usual reliable support.

My profound thanks to all.

INDEX